Speed It Up!

A NON-TECHNICAL GUIDE *for* SPEEDING UP SLOW COMPUTERS

Michael Miller

800 East 96th Street,
Indianapolis, Indiana 46240

621.
391
6
MI

Speed It Up! A Non-Technical Guide for Speeding Up Slow Computers

Copyright © 2009 by Pearson Education, Inc.

ISBN-13: 978-0-789-73947-6
ISBN-10: 0-7897-3947-X

Library of Congress Cataloging-in-Publication Data
Miller, Michael, 1958-
  Speed it up! : a non-technical guide for speeding up slow computers / Michael Miller. -- 1st ed.
       p. cm.
  ISBN 978-0-7897-3947-6
  1. Microcomputers--Maintenance and repair. 2. Microcomputers--Upgrading. I. Title.
  TK7887.M5534 2009
  621.39'16--dc22
                              2009003466

Printed in the United States of America

First Printing: March 2009

Trademarks

All terms mentioned in this book that are known to be trademarks or service marks have been appropriately capitalized. Que Publishing cannot attest to the accuracy of this information. Use of a term in this book should not be regarded as affecting the validity of any trademark or service mark.

Warning and Disclaimer

Every effort has been made to make this book as complete and as accurate as possible, but no warranty or fitness is implied. The information provided is on an "as is" basis. The author and the publisher shall have neither liability nor responsibility to any person or entity with respect to any loss or damages arising from the information contained in this book.

Bulk Sales

Que Publishing offers excellent discounts on this book when ordered in quantity for bulk purchases or special sales. For more information, please contact:

  U.S. Corporate and Government Sales
  1-800-382-3419
  corpsales@pearsontechgroup.com

For sales outside the U.S., please contact:

  International Sales
  international@pearsoned.com

This Book Is Safari Enabled

The Safari® Enabled icon on the cover of your favorite technology book means the book is available through Safari Bookshelf. When you buy this book, you get free access to the online edition for 45 days.

Safari Bookshelf is an electronic reference library that lets you easily search thousands of technical books, find code samples, download chapters, and access technical information whenever and wherever you need it.

To gain 45-day Safari Enabled access to this book:

- Go to www.quepublishing.com/safarienabled.
- Complete the brief registration form.
- Enter the coupon code.

If you have difficulty registering on Safari Bookshelf or accessing the online edition, please email customer-service@safaribooksonline.com.

Associate Publisher
Greg Wiegand

Acquisitions Editor
Rick Kughen

Development Editor
Rick Kughen

Managing Editor
Patrick Kanouse

Project Editor
Seth Kerney

Copy Editor
Keith Cline

Indexer
Tim Wright

Proofreader
Elizabeth Scott

Technical Editors
Terri Stratton
Andy Walker
Aaron Ricadela
Sean Carruthers

Publishing Coordinator
Cindy Teeters

Book Designer
Anne Jones

Contents at a Glance

Table of Contents

About the Author

Michael Miller has written more than 80 non-fiction how-to books over the past two decades, including Que's *Absolute Beginner's Guide to Computer Basics, Easy Computer Basics, Your First Notebook PC, Wireless Networking with Microsoft Windows Vista*, and *How Microsoft Windows Vista Works.*

Mr. Miller has established a reputation for clearly explaining technical topics to non-technical readers and for offering useful real-world advice about complicated topics. More information can be found at the author's website, located at www.molehillgroup.com.

Dedication

To Sherry—slow is also good sometimes.

Acknowledgments

Thanks to the usual suspects at Que, including but not limited to Greg Wiegand, Rick Kughen, Terri Stratton, Seth Kerney, and Keith Cline.

We Want to Hear from You!

As the reader of this book, *you* are our most important critic and commentator. We value your opinion and want to know what we're doing right, what we could do better, what areas you'd like to see us publish in, and any other words of wisdom you're willing to pass our way.

As an associate publisher for Que Publishing, I welcome your comments. You can email or write me directly to let me know what you did or didn't like about this book—as well as what we can do to make our books better.

Please note that I cannot help you with technical problems related to the topic of this book. We do have a User Services group, however, where I will forward specific technical questions related to the book.

When you write, please be sure to include this book's title and author, as well as your name, email address, and phone number. I will carefully review your comments and share them with the author and editors who worked on the book.

Email: feedback@quepublishing.com

Mail: Greg Wiegand
         Associate Publisher
         Que Publishing
         800 East 96th Street
         Indianapolis, IN 46240 USA

Reader Services

Visit our website and register this book at www.quepublishing.com/register for convenient access to any updates, downloads, or errata that might be available for this book.

Introduction

"Can you help me out? My computer is running really slow."

I can't tell you how many times I've heard this complaint over the past several months. First it was my stepdaughter with a slow PC, then a friend, then another friend, then my wife, and it kept on coming. It seems that just about everyone I know is coming to the conclusion that their computers are running too slow. It's an epidemic!

Of course, it's possible that not all these PCs are actually running slow; it's likely that some of this slowness is perceived rather than real. But even perceived sluggishness is still annoying when you're trying to get something done and are forced to wait… and wait… and wait for your PC to respond.

The point is, we all get frustrated when our computers take too long to do what we want them to do. Whether that slowness is caused by insufficient memory or power, whether it's caused by viruses or spyware, whether it's caused by a sluggish Internet or network connection, or whether it's simply a matter of trying to make an old computer do new things it's not capable of doing, you want to give that pokey PC a kick in the electronic pants so that it runs just a *little* faster, if it can.

The bad news is, even a fast PC can slow down over time, for a number of different reasons. The good news is, there are things you can do to speed up even the slowest of computers. These are the things I talk about in this book.

Speed It Up! A Non-Technical Guide for Speeding Up Slow Computers is, as the title implies, a guide that anyone can use to make their computers a little less sluggish. You don't have to be a tech geek to speed up a slow computer; anyone can make these simple changes to put a little more "oomph" behind their day-to-day computing.

Want to speed up your computer's startup process? I show you how to do it. Need to clean up unnecessary programs or remove a virus or spyware program? I show you how to do it. Want to power up your computer when you're editing digital photos or videos? I show you how to do it. Need more memory to run your favorite applications? I show you how to do it. Want to upgrade your computer so that you can run the latest PC games? I show you how to do it. Want to turn a listless Internet connection into a lively one? I show you how to do that, too. Heck, I even show you what type of new PC to buy if your old computer can't be speeded up enough. (That is sometimes the best solution, unfortunately.)

That said, this book isn't a highly technical guide for tweakers and speed freaks; if you want to turn your PC into a customized high-tech hot rod, you'll have to turn elsewhere. This book is more like a guide to tuning up your family sedan, or the computer equivalent of it. The instructions are easy to follow and don't require you to get your hands too dirty.

So if you think your computer is running a little slow, you've turned to the right place for some quick and easy solutions. Spend a few hours reading this book and I guarantee you'll learn more than a few ways to de-pokify even the most sluggish of machines.

What's in This Book

As promised, this book shows you how to speed up your Windows-based computer. The book presents software-based speedups, hardware-based speedups, and Internet- and network-related speedups—a little something for everyone.

This book contains 18 chapters, divided into 6 major parts. Each part walks you through a different aspect of the speedup process, from initial diagnosis to various types of solutions:

- **Part I: Quick Diagnosis for Sluggish PCs** is the place to start if you think your computer is slower than it used to be (or than you want it to be). You'll learn how to troubleshoot what might be slowing down your computer, as well as how to back up your data before you start implementing potential solutions.

- **Part II: Simple Speedups Anyone Can Do** walks you through some of the easiest-to-achieve performance improvements for your PC. You'll learn how to identify and remove harmful computer viruses and spyware, clean out unnecessary programs from your computer's memory and hard disk, optimize your PC's hard disk, and make Windows start up and run faster.

- **Part III: Power Speedups for Power Users** is for the more adventurous user. These speedups require a bit more effort than the previous solutions but can result in significant performance improvements. This is where you learn how to clean up and tweak the Windows Registry, as well as perform a "clean install" of Windows—which lets you reinstall Windows from scratch and create a like-new machine.

- **Part IV: Upgrading Your PC for Speed** presents hardware-based solutions for sluggish systems. You'll learn how to prepare for a computer upgrade and then how to add more memory and hard disk space, install a faster video card, and even upgrade your PC's CPU (central processing unit).

- **Part V: Internet and Network Speedups** recognizes that it's not always your computer that's slow; sometimes it's your Internet or network connection. You'll learn how to make your web browser go faster, how to reconfigure a sluggish Internet connection, and how to wring the most speed out of your home network.

- **Part VI: The Ultimate Speedup: Buying a New PC** is for those users who just can't get their old PCs to go fast enough, no matter what they try. (It happens.) You'll learn when to throw in the towel, what types of applications require newer and faster PCs, and how to tell what type of new PC you need.

I'm guessing that you probably won't read all of this book or perform all the speedups suggested—because you probably won't need to. I've presented the easiest and most effective speedups first, both in the book and in each individual chapter. So work your way through the various suggestions and feel free to stop when you've achieved the performance you're looking for.

Who Can Use This Book

You don't have to be a technical expert to use this book; many of the solutions offered require nothing more than a few clicks of the mouse. It helps if you know your way around the Windows desktop, of course, and there are a few more advanced solutions that require some simple hardware upgrades. But in general, just about anybody can perform most of the solutions presented here.

One thing, though: The solutions in this book are for computers running the Microsoft Windows operating system, either the newer Windows Vista or the older Windows XP. If you have an Apple Mac, that's a whole other world of problems and solutions that I'm not equipped to address, sorry.

How to Use This Book

I hope that this book is easy enough to read that you don't need instructions. That said, a few elements bear explaining.

First, this book contains several special elements, presented in what we in the publishing business call "margin notes." There are different types of margin notes for different types of information, as you see here.

 Note
This is a note that presents information of interest, even if it isn't wholly relevant to the discussion in the main text.

 Tip
This is a tip that might prove useful for whatever it is you're in the process of doing.

 Caution
This is a caution that something you accidentally do might have undesirable results.

Because many of the solutions presented in this book involve third-party software utilities or new hardware devices, lots of web page addresses in the text accompany the mentions of these products. When you see one of these addresses (also known as a URL), you can go to that web page by entering the URL into the address box in your web browser. I've made every effort to ensure the accuracy of the web addresses presented here, but given the ever-changing nature of the Web, don't be surprised if you run across an address or two that's changed. For that matter, some of the products and prices presented here are likely to change by the time you read this text. I apologize in advance, but that's the way the world works.

There's More Online...

When you need a break from reading, feel free to go online and check out my personal website, located at www.molehillgroup.com. Here you'll find more information about this book and other books I've written. And if you have any questions or comments, feel free to email me directly at speed@molehill-group.com. I can't guarantee to respond to every email, but I do guarantee I'll read them all.

Speed It Up!

With all these preliminaries out of the way, it's now time to get started. Put on your reading glasses, fire up your mouse, and get ready to *Speed It Up!*

Quick Diagnosis for Sluggish PCs

What's Slowing Down Your Computer?

So you think your computer is getting sluggish. Is it really slowing down, or is it more of a perceived problem—that is, does it feel slower because you need to do faster stuff? And if it is slowing down, why?

Speeding up slow computers is what this book is all about, of course, and this chapter is the place to get started. Read on to learn more about what kinds of things can slow down your personal computer—and how to troubleshoot a sluggish PC.

Signs That Your Computer Is Getting Slower

The longer you have your computer, the slower it seems to get. Now, some of that is perception; that slight wait while a folder opens seems longer the more times you have to sit through it. But there is some truth to the notion that computers get slower over time. In fact, some computers can get really sluggish really fast.

How can you tell whether your computer is really getting slower? Let's examine some of the more common situations.

It Takes Longer for Your PC to Start

Not everyone reboots their computer every day. (Fortunately!) Most of us leave our PCs on for days at a time, and only turn it off when we're gone for an extended period of time—or reboot it when we're forced to by some new program installation or unexpected program crash or freeze.

But when you do reboot your computer, it takes a long time to turn back on. This is true even with a fast new PC; the boot-up process is time consuming. Still, if you have to wait more than a few minutes for your computer to get up and running, something may be wrong—especially if it used to boot up much faster.

Let's examine why it takes so long for a typical computer to turn itself on. Not that you need to understand any of this to make your PC work, but it's nice to know what's going on as you wait for your computer to boot up.

It all starts when you press your computer's "on" button. At this point power is sent through the PC's power supply to the motherboard (which holds all the important pieces and parts of your system), and your system reads instructions stored in your computer's *basic input/output system* (BIOS), which is stored in *read-only memory* (ROM). These instructions tell your computer to perform a *power-on self test* (POST), which checks and verifies the status of all the low-level hardware in your system—*random access memory* (RAM), controllers, and so on.

After the self-test, your computer looks for the first bootable drive on your PC. This is probably your hard drive (C:), although it could also be a disk drive (on an older computer) or CD/DVD drive with a bootable disc inserted. A bootable disc contains, in a sector called the Master Boot Record (MBR), those important system files necessary for your system to operate—files that are normally hidden from view, and not displayed in a normal folder listing. When your computer accesses a bootable

 Note

Don't confuse read-only memory (ROM) with random access memory (RAM). ROM is a small amount of static memory, housed on your PC's motherboard, used to permanently store firmware instructions on how to start up your system. RAM is a much larger amount of memory, housed on removable memory chips, that can be written to and read from over and over again (and so is used to temporarily store programs and data that are open on your system).

drive (normally the C: hard drive), it reads into RAM the contents of the disk's *boot sector*, which contains certain files that tell your system how to load the Windows operating system.

The first file found on and run from the hard disk is the Windows Boot Manager (sometimes called the *bootstrap loader*). Its purpose is simple: It tells your system to launch other Windows preboot applications—utilities that Windows needs to get started. Next, the Boot Manager reads from hard disk a *Boot Configuration Data* (BCD) file. This file is essentially a "data store," in that it functions as a container for all the files and processes used in the boot sequence. The Boot Manager also loads into memory a few other items, including the Windows kernel and the contents of the Windows Registry.

Note

The Windows Registry is a database of configuration settings for the operating system and for all Windows applications. Learn more about the Registry in Chapter 7, "Cleaning Up the Windows Registry."

Next, the Boot Manager scans the Registry to determine which behind-the-scenes processes, applications, and device drivers to launch during the startup process—in most cases, items that Windows needs loaded to perform essential operations. For example, Windows might load a device driver to enable your printer to print, or maybe launch a process that speeds up the launching of the Adobe Reader program. These drivers, processes, and applications remain in memory, where they can quickly be called into action when needed. (Loading a process or program from hard disk takes a lot longer than it does to access that same process or program in memory.)

When all these files and drivers have been loaded, Windows now displays the welcome screen and prompts you to select a user account (if the PC has multiple users). Once you log on as a specific user, Windows loads all the configuration and policy settings for that user from the Windows Registry. Windows then displays the XP or Vista desktop for that user—and the computer is now ready to use.

Note

Not all startup programs are launched from the Windows Registry. To determine which programs to load on startup, Windows looks both in the Registry and in a special Startup folder that you can access through the Windows Start menu.

And here's where we get into one of the most common causes of a slow PC. The more processes and applications launched at startup, the more memory used—and the slower your system will start up and run. Not only do more programs take longer to load, one after another, but a system with overtaxed memory itself runs slower. So if your computer is taking longer to start up, even if it's just a few seconds longer, it's probably because you have too many programs or utilities loading automatically at launch—and why a simple speedup solution is to keep some of those programs from loading.

Note

If your PC runs Windows Vista, the startup process may seem to be faster than on an older Windows XP machine. That's because Vista incorporates a new Fast Boot and Resume function that helps to get your computer up and running in less time. With Fast Boot and Resume, not all processes are loaded before the Windows desktop appears. Some processes are loaded in the background after the initial startup (and so you can see the desktop and start working faster than you could before).

Why would your computer have more programs or utilities loading at startup? It's simple: Just about every software program you install these days thinks that it's so important that it must load whenever your computer starts. These programs typically install some sort of startup utility or process that loads into your system's memory whenever Windows launches. You can view some of these utilities as icons in the Windows system tray, like the one shown in Figure 1.1.

FIGURE 1.1

A typical Windows Vista system tray; every icon represents a program or utility running in the background.

For example, if you install Adobe Photoshop or Photoshop Elements, it installs a Photo Loader utility that loads automatically when Windows launches. It stays in the background, taking up a piece of system memory, waiting for you to connect a digital camera to your computer. When a camera is connected, the Photo Loader utility senses the camera and automatically downloads pictures from the camera to your hard drive. It seems useful enough, except that it's just one more program slowing down your computer's startup process and taking up system memory.

Multiply that one instance by all the different programs you have installed on your computer, and you see the issue. The more programs you have installed, the more processes that load automatically at startup, and the longer it takes for the startup process to complete. This is one of the prime reasons why a computer tends to get slower over time; you install more programs, and each program you install takes up more system resources.

So if you think your computer is taking longer to start up, you're probably right— and now you know why.

 Note

Not all programs, of course, automatically load processes into memory during the startup process. And of those that do, not all of these processes are necessary. Many of these autoloading programs can be safely deleted or configured not to load on startup, as you'll learn in Chapter 4, "Cleaning Out Unnecessary Programs."

It Takes Longer to Do Familiar Tasks

Here's another good sign that your computer is really slowing down: A task that used to take 30 seconds to complete now takes a minute or more.

The nice thing about this type of slowdown is that it's easy enough to measure. Assuming you know the approximate amount of time it took to perform a particular task in the past, you can time the task today to see if it takes longer.

Suppose, for example, that you want to copy a large file from one folder to another on your hard drive. In the past, your computer took less than 20 seconds to copy the entire file, but today it takes 30 seconds or longer. That's a definite slowdown (50% slower, in this instance).

And it could be anything. The slowdown could be in how long it takes to open a particular program, load a specific file, activate a given tool within a program (such as an editing tool in Photoshop), copy a file, delete a file, you name it. It's especially noticeable when it's an operation you perform often; you'll know when something you do everyday takes longer to do.

So, yes, your computer is slowing down. But the question is, why?

The two most probable culprits in this instance are memory and hard disk space. Your computer uses both to run applications and perform basic operations. The less you have of either, the longer said operations will take to perform.

Let's put it more directly: When your memory or hard disk space gets low, your computer slows down. If not enough free memory or hard disk space is available, it will take longer to open new applications, pull down menus, copy files, and the like.

Note

Learn more about upgrading system memory in Chapter 10, "Adding More Memory." Learn more about upgrading hard disk storage in Chapter 11, "Adding More Disk Space."

But why would your computer get less memory or hard disk space over time? The hard disk space issue is easy enough to comprehend: The more you use your PC, the more software programs you install and files you create, both of which take up hard disk space. And the less hard disk space you have, the less space programs can use to temporarily store data while you're using them, causing your computer to slow down.

As to memory, this also has to do with the number of new programs you install. As you recall from the previous section on startup behavior, many programs automatically load utilities into memory when Windows launches. The more programs you install, the more memory that gets eaten up by these autoloading programs.

So if your computer's sluggishness is caused by insufficient memory or hard disk space, the solution is simple—even if the execution is less so. The more and newer programs you install on your system, the more memory and hard disk space you need. This requires you to upgrade your computer's memory or add more hard disk space. For the non-technical user, this might appear daunting, but it's not as difficult as it sounds—and it may be necessary to get your computer back up to speed.

Know, however, that insufficient memory or hard disk space isn't the only thing that can slow down your system in this manner. You may also have a fragmented or damaged hard disk, have too many programs running simultaneously, or have too many background processes automatically loaded into system memory, as discussed in the previous section. Unload some of those programs and processes, and you'll be surprised at how speedy your computer now appears.

The bottom line is that when common tasks take longer to complete, your computer is slowing down. There might be a number of reasons for this, but the problem is real.

Your Computer Gets Sluggish When You Have Two or More Windows Open at a Time

Here's a related situation. Your computer runs fast enough when you have a single program open on your desktop, but when you open a second (or third or fourth) program, your computer gets very sluggish.

Some wags might respond to this issue by telling you that if your computer slows down when you open multiple windows, don't open multiple windows. (Duh!) That's fine and dandy in theory, but in the real world you sometimes need to run more than one application simultaneously; if this slows down your PC, you have a real problem.

The likely cause of this problem is similar to the most likely cause of the previous problem: You need more memory and/or disk space. That's because every program, when launched, loads a portion of its program code into your computer's memory. With two programs running, that's twice as much memory space used.

Similarly, your computer uses space on your hard disk as "virtual" memory that augments the normal random access memory that it uses to run these programs. The less free space you have on your hard disk, the less virtual memory you have—and the slower your programs will run.

The interesting thing about insufficient memory or hard disk issues is that they can appear quite suddenly. For example, you may be able to open three windows or programs with no problem, but when you open the fourth your computer slows to a crawl. It's kind of an all-or-nothing situation; you may have just enough memory for three programs, but there isn't any to spare for that fourth one. It's not a gradual slowdown, it's an immediate one.

Your Computer Pauses for Long Stretches at a Time—or Freezes Up

Even worse than your computer slowing down is when it seems to stop what it's doing for long seconds or even minutes—or, even worse, completely freezes up. This can happen with no warning, or after a period of increasing sluggishness.

Most so-called freeze ups really don't represent a frozen computer, but rather one that is taking excessively long to perform a specific task. That is, your computer isn't frozen, it's just "thinking" about what it's supposed to be doing. If you wait long enough, the computer gets moving again and any pending tasks are eventually executed.

Not that you won't occasionally get a frozen computer. It's just your computer is more likely to crash (resulting in an onscreen error message or forced reboot) than it is to actually freeze. Of course, a really long pause looks and feels just like a freeze, so there may be no practical difference from your end. In fact, in many instances it's quicker to reboot a paused computer than it is to wait for the slow process to finally be completed.

Why would your PC slow down to such a degree that you think it's frozen? Again, there are multiple possible culprits, although low memory is always a favorite. If you get a lot of these frozen situations, try running fewer applications at the same time—or just bite the bullet and increase your system memory.

Whatever the cause, a frozen computer is a definite sign that something is slowing down your system—and should be addressed.

Signs That Your Computer Really Isn't Getting Slower—Even if You Think it Is

Not every computer that seems slow has actually slowed down. Sometimes the computer only seems slow; other times the computer is fast enough, but it's something else in your system (such as your Internet or network connection) that is sluggish.

As an example, just this week I went into my wife's office to look up some files she had stored on her laptop. Said laptop is about four years old (it's one of my old machines that got handed down), and it took *forever* to do some simple file finding and opening. I couldn't believe how slow it was, and immediately went to work trying some of the simple speedups I discuss later in this book. But I didn't find anything wrong with the PC (and my wife said she didn't think that the computer's performance was any different from what it had been in the past).

What I had experienced, then, was a perceived sluggishness. That older computer seemed (and in fact was) slow in comparison to my own newer and faster computer. My wife's computer hadn't slowed down at all, but merely seemed slow compared to what I was used to. No real problem there.

A few days later I fielded a complaint from my stepdaughter about her computer acting slow. Her complaint was real, but she had misidentified the culprit. When I examined her PC, I found nothing that would compromise system performance. I did discover, however, that when she sensed her PC was running slow, what she was doing at the time was watching video over the

Internet, and that video was stuttering and stopping at frequent intervals. A quick perusal led to the conclusion that her computer hadn't slowed down, but her Internet connection had. The next day the cable company was out front repairing a bad cable, which had led to connection slowdowns for all the houses on our little cul de sac. When the repairs were completed, our Internet connection was back up to speed and nobody was complaining about anything being slow.

All this is just to illustrate that your computer can seem slow but not have any issues of its own. In other words, you can't always blame your computer for what's slowing down! Instead, look for outside causes that you may or may not be able to fix. At the very least, you need to learn how to deal with them intelligently.

That said, let's take a look at some of the most common situations that you may think signal a slow computer but in fact have external causes.

New Programs Run Slowly

Let's say you purchased your computer two or three years ago, and it ran fine with the programs you had installed at the time—typically Microsoft Office, Quicken or Microsoft Money, and your web browser and email program. But three years down the road you've supplemented these initial programs with some newer applications, and your computer doesn't run these new programs as snappily as it does your older ones. What's the deal?

As much as you might want to believe otherwise, this situation does not indicate that your computer is slowing down. What's happening is that you're asking an old PC to run newer, more-demanding programs—and these programs don't run all that fast on your older computer. Your computer is fast enough for your three-year-old programs, but not near fast enough for these newer programs.

Many newer applications are simply more power hungry than your older applications. First off, some types of applications are quite demanding of system resources; examples include photo-editing programs (such as Adobe Photoshop) and video-editing programs (such as Adobe Premier). An older computer might not have the juice, in terms of memory and processing power, required to efficiently run these challenging applications. The result is that your system seems sluggish when these applications are running.

In addition, newer versions of older applications often require more system resources than previous versions did. It's not untypical to upgrade from an older version of a program to a newer version and then find that the newer version runs slower than the older one. So if you've recently upgraded from Office XP to Office 2007, for example, and find that your system all of a sudden seems slower, it's the upgrade that's the problem. Your system is just as fast as it ever was, but the upgraded application requires more memory and system resources than the older version did.

Bottom line: Your computer doesn't slow down when you install new programs or upgrade to new versions. It just seems that way because these new and upgraded apps require additional system resources.

Your Computer Has Trouble Running the Latest Games

Similarly, the latest greatest computer games can make even a recent PC seem sluggish. That's because today's state-of-the-art computer games are the most demanding applications out there. They need lots of memory, processing power, and graphics power to display those detailed, fast-moving onscreen graphics. An older PC—or even a newer one that doesn't have an adequate CPU or graphics card—can seem terribly slow when running one of these demanding games.

Again, trying to run a demanding PC game doesn't make your computer any slower than it was before. It's just that the game itself requires more power than your computer is capable of providing.

You Upgrade to Windows Vista and Your PC Gets Sluggish

Here's another upgrade that can make your computer feel like it's slowing down. Upgrading your operating system from Windows XP to Windows Vista can display the sluggish side of any older system.

Windows Vista is a great upgrade. I like it and recommend it—*if* your system has enough oomph to make it work. Not all older systems do. In particular, Vista is quite demanding in terms of graphics capabilities; a PC with an older or lesser-powered graphics card can appear quite sluggish running Vista's new Aero interface.

Right now you may be asking just how different Windows Vista really is compared to Windows XP. Windows is Windows, after all; it's an operating system that you use to run programs and control your computer. To that end, Vista does pretty much the same things that Windows XP or the even older Windows 2000 did.

On closer inspection, however, there's a world of difference between Vista and all older versions of Windows. Even the most jaded user can see that Vista looks different. Sure, there's still a taskbar and Start menu at the bottom of the screen, but these items look cooler in Vista. That's due to Vista's new Aero user interface, which displays true 3D elements with a see-through, glass-like look. And everything else in Vista looks a bit different, too. Folder and file icons now show thumbnails of their contents, as do the program buttons on the Windows taskbar. The Start menu is a lot more streamlined, especially if you have a lot of programs installed. When you go to switch between open applications, the windows twist and turn to display in a three-dimensional stack. And the windows themselves are smoother and rounder and translucent, heightening the sense of depth when you view multiple windows onscreen.

These nifty graphic elements require more graphics horsepower to display. In fact, not all older computers can be easily upgraded to Vista. Processor- and memory-wise, most mid- to high-end PCs sold in the past few years will probably do the job. But unless your PC has a high-end 3D video card, it might not be able to display the new Aero glass interface and all those fancy visual elements. If your video card isn't up to snuff, you'll be limited to the Windows Vista Basic interface—which looks a little better than Windows XP does, but doesn't offer all the neat translucent 3D effects.

So what are the system requirements for running Windows Vista? Let's take a quick look, system component by system component:

- **Microprocessor:** To run Windows Vista, Microsoft says that your PC must have a "modern CPU." (CPU is short for *central processing unit*, which is another word for microprocessor—the brains of your computer.) For the Home Basic edition, that translates into a 32-bit or 64-bit microprocessor running at a minimum of 800MHz. For all other editions, you need at least a 1GHz microprocessor.

- **Memory:** The more memory your PC has, the better. To run the Home Basic edition, you need at least 512MB RAM. For all other editions, Microsoft says you should go with a minimum of 1GB of memory—although 2GB will make things run *much* faster.

- **Hard disk:** You need at least a 20GB hard drive with 15GB of free space to run Windows Vista Home Basic. For all other editions, Microsoft recommends a minimum 40GB hard drive. In reality, you need a much larger hard disk—100GB or more—if you want to install additional applications and store a fair number of files.

- **Graphics:** Here's the tough one. To display the Windows Vista Basic interface, you need a 3D video card that's compatible with DirectX 9.

To display the snazzier Aero interface, your PC's video card must support DirectX 9 with Pixel Shader 2, have a minimum of 64MB graphics memory and 1280 x 1024 resolution, and offer 32 bits per pixel, Windows Display Driver Model (WDDM) support. And not all older computers (especially older or lower-priced notebooks) have this type of graphics processing power.

So compare these specs with those of your PC. If you come up short in any instance, your system will run slower with Vista than it did with XP. Again, it's not that your computer is any slower; it's that the new operating system is more demanding.

Internet Sites Take Forever to Load

Here's a common situation. You think your computer is running slow because the Internet is running slow. In reality, it doesn't take a lot of PC power to browse the Internet or download email; web surfing is one of the least demanding activities you can do with your computer. So if your surfing is getting sluggish, it's probably not your computer.

When your surfing slows down, look instead to your Internet connection. Image-intensive web pages present a lot of data that need to be downloaded to your computer, as do web videos. If you have a slow Internet connection, even the simplest of Internet-based activities can take a painfully long time.

The solution here, of course, is to upgrade to a faster Internet connection. If you're unfortunate enough to still have a dial-up connection, ditch it in favor of a faster broadband cable or Digital Subscriber Line (DSL) connection, either of which can be 5 or 10 times faster than what you're used to. In fact, if you're still on dial-up, I recommend *against* watching web videos or anything similarly taxing; it's just too painful.

But what if your connection used to be fast enough but appears to have slowed down in recent days or weeks? This very well could be the case; Internet connections can get slower, due to any number of factors. Whatever the cause, however, it's not normal. If you think that your connection has gotten slower, contact your Internet service provider and have them check your lines. When you're paying for a fast broadband connection, you want the speed that was promised.

 Note

Learn more about sluggish Internet connections in Chapter 15, "Reconfiguring Your Internet Connection."

Just remember, that in most instances, an Internet slowdown is not the fault of your computer; it's your connection that's slow, not your PC.

Note

Learn more about dealing with slow network connections in Chapter 16, "Speeding Up Your Home Network."

It Takes a Long Time to Copy Files Across Your Network

If your PC is connected to a home network, a slow network connection can make it seem as if your computer is getting sluggish. This is particularly so on a wireless network, where maintaining a fast connection is sometimes problematic.

When your network connection is slow, everything you do on the network is similarly slow. Copying files from one PC to another may take forever, playing online games may be next-to-impossible due to excessive latency, and your connection to the Internet may be sluggish.

Again, a slow network connection has nothing to do with a slow PC. Even the fastest PC can't work to its full potential if the data stream coming to it over the network is compromised. And, as you might suspect, a previously healthy network connection can slow down at times, due to a variety of factors.

So if your computer is on a network and network-related tasks appear sluggish (while local operations, such as opening a word processing or spreadsheet document, are still zippy), you have a network problem, not a computer problem.

Quick Fix: Five Quick Steps to Improve Your PC's Performance

Yes, this entire book is about how to speed up a slow PC. But if you don't want to read the whole book or simply want the fastest and biggest bang for your buck, here are five quick steps you can take to improve your PC's performance. (Don't forget to read the rest of the book, however; there are lots of effective speedups you can do!)

Quick Step 1: Reboot Your Computer

When you open and close programs on your PC, doing so sometimes results in little bits of system memory not being freed up for future use, especially on machines running Windows XP. (Windows Vista is less prone to this type of problem.) The less memory available, the slower your system runs. The only way to free up these bits of lost memory is to shut down and then restart your computer—which is something you should do once a day. Leave your PC running for weeks at a time and you'll notice a definite slowdown!

Quick Step 2: Delete Unnecessary Files

As noted earlier in this chapter, your computer uses space on your hard disk as "virtual" memory that augments your system's normal random access memory. If you don't have enough free space on your hard drive, there isn't enough virtual memory for your programs to run properly. This is why you should periodically go through and delete all unnecessary files to free up hard disk space. You can do this automatically with Windows' Disk Cleanup utility. Just click the Start menu and select All Programs, Accessories, System Tools, Disk Cleanup. The more files you delete, the more disk space you free up—and the faster your computer will run.

Quick Step 3: Remove Unused Programs

Along the same lines, removing unused programs from your system will free up lots of hard disk space. You use the Windows Add/Remove Programs utility (found in the Control Panel) to uninstall old programs. This utility will remove all traces of the old program—and even remove it from the Windows Start menu.

You can also stop unnecessary and unwanted programs from loading automatically when your computer launches. Many of these utilities and programs are launched from a special Startup menu. Examine the contents of this menu by clicking the Start button and selecting All Programs, Startup. Right-click and delete any unwanted programs from this menu, and they won't launch the next time you reboot your PC.

Quick Step 4: Defragment Your Hard Disk

File fragmentation is like taking the pieces of a jigsaw puzzle and storing them in different boxes along with pieces from other puzzles; the more dispersed the pieces are, the longer it takes to put the puzzle

Note

Additional startup programs can be found in the Windows Registry, and thus have to be deleted via the Registry Editor utility. Still more startup programs can be deleted by using options present in the Microsoft Windows Defender antispyware program. Learn more about these options in Chapter 4.

together. You fix the problem when you put all the pieces of the puzzle back in the right boxes. Your computer's hard drive can get fragmented every time you run a program or open or close a file, and can therefore cause your system to slow down over time. For that reason, you should defrag-

Note

Learn more about disk defrag-menting in Chapter 5, "Optimiz-ing Your Hard Disk."

ment your hard disk at least once a month. This is accomplished with the Windows Disk Defragmenter utility. Just click the Start menu and select All Programs, Accessories, System Tools, Disk Defragmenter.

Quick Step 5: Add More Memory with ReadyBoost

Many computer slowdowns are caused by insufficient system memory. Normally you solve this problem by physically adding more memory, in the form of new or additional memory chips, which can be a little daunting for the less technically inclined among us. But if your computer is running Windows Vista, you can add more memory without opening up the case; all you have to do is insert a low-cost USB memory drive.

You see, Windows Vista includes an instant memory-enhancing technology dubbed ReadyBoost. With ReadyBoost, you can use a USB flash memory device to temporarily increase the amount of RAM on your per-sonal computer. Insert one of these devices into the appropriate slot on your PC, and your system's memory is automatically increased—and your system's performance is automatically improved.

Note

ReadyBoost works with USB flash memory devices, as well as Com-pactFlash (CF) and Secure Digital (SD) memory cards. Unfortu-nately, ReadyBoost technology is not available in Windows XP or older Microsoft operating systems.

When you insert an external memory device into your Vista computer, you are prompted as to how you want to use that device. Select Speed Up My System, and your PC will automatically access avail-able memory on the device. The result? An instant speed boost, just when you need it!

Note

Learn more about using ReadyBoost in Chapter 10.

The Bottom Line

So what's happening if you think your computer is slowing down? Here's the bottom line:

- If your computer takes longer to do the same tasks it used to do quicker, it's slowing down.

- If your computer is slow running new or upgraded software, it's not slowing down—although it may not have enough power or memory to efficiently run the newer software.

- If your computer is slow while browsing the Internet but fast enough when performing other tasks, it's not slowing down. Blame your problems on a slow Internet connection.

- If your computer is slow while accessing programs or files over a network, but is fast enough running its own programs, it's not slowing down. You have a network problem, instead.

- A number of things can cause your computer to slow down, including insufficient system memory, insufficient hard disk space, a fragmented or damaged hard disk, and too many unnecessary programs loaded into memory.

- When you need a quick fix for a slow computer, consider these options: Reboot your computer, delete unnecessary files from your hard drive, remove unused programs from your system, defragment your hard disk, and—if you're running Windows Vista—add more memory via a USB memory stick and the new ReadyBoost feature.

Before You Start: Protect Your Data

Before we get into speeding up your computer, some preliminary activities are in order. Because some of these speedups involve editing critical system files or installing new pieces of hardware, you need to protect your programs and files in case something goes wrong.

That's right, if you make a big enough mistake trying to speed up your computer, you could lose all your data!

I know that sounds frightening and might scare off some of you from performing some necessary speedups. So I want to soften the scary language and assure you that most speedups are completely harmless; they'll either speed up your system or they won't, and won't cause any new problems either way. But there are some things you can do that could cause your system to stop working, and you need to take precautions just in case something bad does happen.

Potential Problems: What Can Go Wrong When Speeding Up Your PC

Okay, so what can you do to speed up your PC that will cause your system to crash or lose data?

Don't get all freaked out about this, but a few speedups you can perform on your PC can potentially have undesirable side effects. Fortunately, the side effects are rare (especially if you follow directions well) and can be protected against.

The Wrong Programs Are Uninstalled

One way to speed up your system is to delete unwanted or unnecessary programs from your computer's hard disk, to free up more valuable hard disk space. If you delete truly unused programs, this poses no problems. However, if you accidentally delete a program that a favorite application or even Microsoft Windows needs to operate, you might find that application no long runs—or that Windows no longer starts. This is not a good situation.

 Note

Learn more about deleting files and programs in Chapter 4, "Cleaning Out Unnecessary Programs."

Similarly, you can often speed up a computer by making sure that unnecessary programs or utilities aren't automatically launched when your system starts up. Again, if you remove truly unnecessary utilities from the startup process, no harm ensues. But if you keep a key process from loading automatically, you might find that Windows or a key application has trouble running.

Valuable Data Gets Deleted

Along the same lines, one way to free up valuable hard disk space is by deleting files that you no longer use. No problem there, unless you get carried away and accidentally delete data files that you still need—or might need in the future.

The way it works, when you delete a file it's gone—you can't get it back. This may not be a big deal if you delete a Christmas card list from 1997, but it's a much bigger deal if you erase all the digital photos from your last family vacation.

Note

Not to confuse the issue, but most files when deleted go into the Windows Recycle Bin, which temporarily holds "deleted" files until it fills up. (This enables you to recover some deleted files, if absolutely necessary.) It's at that point that the files are permanently wiped from your hard drive. The point remains that when a file is deleted from your hard drive, it's gone.

A Registry Edit Goes Bad

Another way to speed up your computer's operation is to edit some of the configuration settings found in the Windows Registry. The Windows Registry holds all the configuration settings for your PC; it

Note
Learn more about the Windows Registry in Chapter 7, "Cleaning Up the Windows Registry."

tells your computer which devices and processes to load, where important files are located, and how to configure your system.

If you edit the wrong setting in the Registry or enter an incorrect value for a particular setting, you have no idea as to what effect that mistake may have. Some Registry errors can cause your entire system to crash or shut down; it's that big a deal. Being able to recover from a misedited Registry is paramount.

You Have to Reformat Your Hard Drive (and Reinstall Windows)

This is kind of a last-chance speedup: You wipe your hard drive clean and reinstall the Windows operating system and all your software programs. As you can probably figure out on your own, wiping your hard drive clean means deleting everything stored on it, including all your valuable data files, digital photos, downloaded music, and the like.

While this is often an effective way to speed up your system, it's the computer equivalent of setting off a nuclear bomb. Everything on your hard disk is nuked, and you get start over on fresh terrain. But before you nuke your hard drive, you need to back up all your data files so that you can later restore them to the newly reformatted hard drive. If you don't back up your data, it's gone forever.

Note
Learn more about the nuclear option in Chapter 8, "When All Else Fails: Reinstalling Windows from Scratch."

Hard Disk Maintenance Fails

Some speed can be restored to your system by working with your PC's hard disk, where all your programs and data (and the Windows operating system) are stored. A fragmented or damaged hard drive can cause a system to run sluggishly. Defragmenting or repairing the hard disk can restore your system to previous performance levels.

That said, not all hard disk maintenance goes the way it should. It's possible—although not very likely, admittedly—for a disk to end up more fragmented than before, or for a repair to shut off access to hard disk sectors on which critical system files are stored, or for a repair to go horribly wrong if power is lost mid-procedure. It doesn't happen often, but when hard disk maintenance goes bad, it's not a pretty sight.

Note

Learn more about hard disks in Chapter 5, "Optimizing Your Hard Disk."

A Hardware Upgrade Doesn't Take

Finally, you may have to revert to hardware-oriented solutions to your computer's speed problem. That might mean adding more memory to your system, upgrading to a larger hard drive, or even replacing your system's graphics board. Any time

Note

Learn more about hardware upgrades in Chapter 9, "Preparing for a Computer Upgrade."

you muck about inside your computer, there's the chance that your computer won't recognize the new component, or that you damage something else in the process. I don't mean to scare off anyone from performing these types of speedups, but the potential downsides need to be presented, in the interest of full disclosure.

Backing Up and Restoring Your Valuable Data

Okay, let's assume that you've taken my warnings to heart and resigned yourself to the fact that you need to back up your data before you attempt any of the riskier speedups we discuss later in this book. Just how do you make backup copies of everything that's important to you—including your work documents, music files, digital photos, and the like?

Caution

For many users, the most important data files stored on your PC are your digital photographs and music. If you don't have backups of these important files, you could lose several years' worth of photos and music if a speedup procedure goes south.

Choosing a Backup Device

The first thing to consider when planning data backup is to choose a backup device. That is, where should you store the backup copies of all your data files?

I won't pretend to present all the possible backup options, because there's one primary method I recommend. Put simply, the easiest way to back up your data files is to use an external hard disk. These days a fairly large external hard drive can be had for as little as $100. (For example, as I write this book in October 2008, Best Buy is selling a 250GB Western Digital drive, like the one in Figure 2.1, for just $95; obviously, larger drives are a tad more expensive.) At these prices, it's foolish not to purchase a hard drive for backup purposes.

FIGURE 2.1

An affordable Western Digital external hard drive.

How big a backup drive do you need? Obviously, you should have an external hard disk that's big enough to hold all your digital data files—Word documents, Excel spreadsheets, PowerPoint presentations, downloaded or ripped music tracks, digital photos, home videos, and the like. The easy way to do this is to get an external drive that's about the same size as the hard disk on your PC. For example, if you have a 200GB hard drive on your PC, get a 200GB external hard disk.

Most external hard drives connect to your PC via USB. Some bigger disks use the faster FireWire connection. Either type of connection is fine, and both are easy enough to connect and install.

Once the external hard drive is connected, you need to run a software program that automates the backup process. Most external hard drives come with their own proprietary backup programs. These are typically easy to use, and get the job done. You can also use one of the many third-party backup programs sold at your local computer or electronics store, such as Acronis

True Image Home (www.acronis.com/homecomputing/products/trueimage/) or CMS Bounceback Express (www.cmsproducts.com/product_bounceback_profes-sional.htm). You'll typically pay less than $50 for one of these programs.

Backing Up in Windows Vista

You may not have to purchase a backup program, however. If your PC is running Windows Vista, you have a backup program built in to the operating system. Windows Backup (included with all but the Vista Home Basic edition) enables you to schedule automatic backups of your key data. You launch Windows Backup by clicking the Start button and then selecting All Programs, Accessories, System Tools, Backup Status and Configuration.

When the window shown in Figure 2.2 appears, click the Back Up Files button (in the left panel), and then click the Set Up Automatic Backup option. Windows will now scan your system for a backup device

Tip

In addition to standard Windows Backup utility, the Business, Enterprise, and Ultimate versions of Vista come with an enhanced type of backup, dubbed CompletePC, that creates an exact image of all the files on your system—including program and system files. Most backups only copy data files; a system image backup copies every single file on your hard drive. When you recover from a system failure, CompletePC lets you restore your complete system exactly the way it was before the crash.

(typically an external hard disk) and ask you to select that device for your backup.

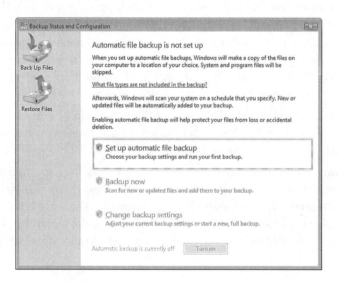

FIGURE 2.2

Use Windows Backup (in Windows Vista) to back up your valuable data files.

The next screen, shown in Figure 2.3, asks you what types of files you want to back up. You can choose from picture, music, video, email, and other common types of files.

FIGURE 2.3

Select which types of files you want to back up.

Click Next and you now get to select how often (and when) you want to back up your files. As you can see in Figure 2.4, you can choose to back up daily, weekly, or monthly. The more often you back up, the better. When have finished, click the Save Settings and Start Backup button, and Vista starts your first disk backup.

Caution

Windows Backup, like most backup programs, only backs up data files—*not* program or operating system files. If your hard disk is damaged or reformatted, you need to first reinstall the Windows operating system, and then reinstall all the software programs previously installed. (This argues for keeping the original installation discs for all the software programs you purchase.) Then you can restore your data files from their backup copies.

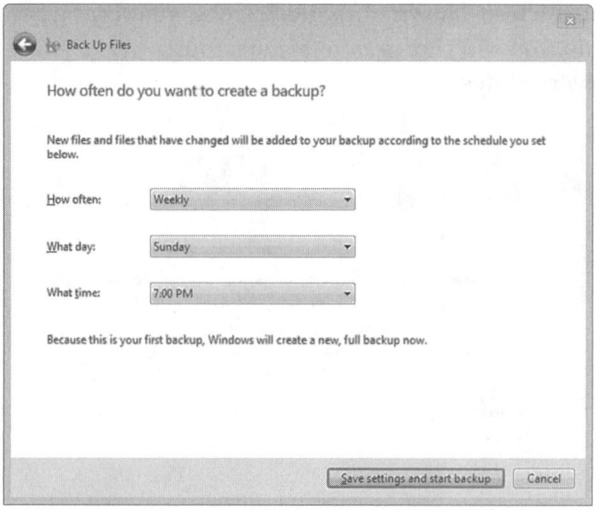

FIGURE 2.4

Setting your backup schedule.

Restoring in Windows Vista

Okay, you've been diligent and created regular backup copies of all your important data. How do you restore those backup copies if you lose the originals from your hard drive?

In Windows Vista, it's a matter of starting up Windows Backup (after you've reinstalled or repaired Windows itself, of course) and using that program's Restore Files function. From the main Windows Backup window, click the Restore Files button (in the left panel), and then select the Restore Files option.

You're now asked what files you want to restore—files from your latest backup or files from an older backup. Let's assume that your most recent backup includes the most recent copies of your files, as it should, and select the first option.

Windows now presents you with a list of folders and files included in the most recent backup. Click the Select All button to select all of these files, and then click the Next button. In the next window, choose to restore these files to their original locations, and then click the Start Restore button. Your backup files will now be restored to your hard drive, in their original locations.

Backing Up and Restoring in Windows XP

As you can see, Windows Vista makes it easy to back up and restore files from and to your hard drive. But what do you do if you're running the older Windows XP operating system?

The sad reality is that Windows XP Home Edition does not automatically install a backup utility. Windows XP Professional does include the Microsoft Backup program, shown in Figure 2.5, but it's not really that good a program; it's old and outdated and not that well suited to today's extra-large hard drives. (Plus it's very, very slow compared to third-party backup programs.) It's certainly not as easy to use as Vista's Windows Backup utility.

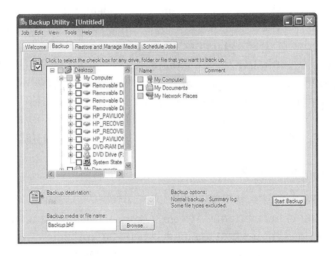

FIGURE 2.5

Windows XP's Microsoft Backup utility.

So if you're running Windows XP (Home Edition or Professional), I recommend that you use the backup program that came with your external hard disk drive—or invest in a third-party program like the ones I discussed previously.

Protecting Your System with System Restore

If you try to perform a speedup procedure that results in a system crash, all is not lost. That's because both Windows XP and Windows Vista include Microsoft's System Restore utility. This utility can automatically restore your system to the state it was in before the crash occurred—and save you the trouble of reinstalling any damaged software programs.

System Restore is probably the most useful utility for users who screw up their systems or otherwise experience major system problems. (I'm almost ashamed to admit how many times I've used it to restore my system after botching some upgrade or another.) Prior to System Restore, it wasn't uncommon to run into problems that required you to reinstall your entire operating system. With System Restore, reinstallations are a thing of the past—because it can automatically restore your system to a prior working state.

Caution

Because System Restore monitors only system files and Registry settings, you can't use it to restore damaged or deleted data files. For complete protection, you still need to back up your important data files manually.

You should think of System Restore as a safety net for your essential system files. It isn't a backup program per se, because it doesn't make copies of your personal files. (You still need a separate backup program—and external hard drive—for that.) It simply keeps track of all the system-level changes that are made to your computer, and (when activated) reverses those changes.

Setting System Restore Points

How does System Restore work?

It's quite simple, actually. System Restore actively monitors your system and notes any changes that are made when you install new applications. Each time it notes a change, it automatically creates what it calls a restore point. A *restore point* is a "snapshot" of the Windows Registry and selected system files just before the new application is installed.

Just to be safe, System Restore also creates a new restore point after every 10 hours of system use. You can also choose to manually create a new restore point at any moment in time. It's a good idea to do this whenever you make any major change to your system, such as installing a new piece of hardware or editing the Windows Registry.

Setting a Manual Restore Point in Windows XP

To set a manual restore point in Windows XP, follow these steps:

1. Click the Start button and select All Programs, Accessories, System Tools, System Restore.

2. When the System Restore window opens, select Create a Restore Point and click Next.

3. When the Create a Restore point screen appears, as shown in Figure 2.6, enter a name for the restore point, and then click the Create button.

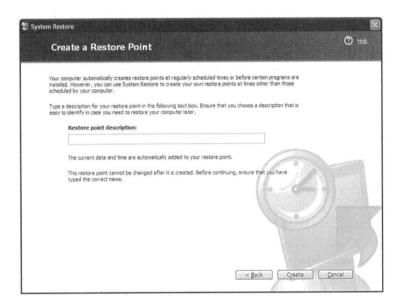

FIGURE 2.6
Creating a restore point in Windows XP.

Setting a Manual Restore Point in Windows Vista

To set a manual restore point in Windows Vista, the process is subtly different:

1. Click the Start button and select All Programs, Accessories, System Tools, System Restore.

2. When the System Restore window opens, click the Open System Protection link.

3. When the System Properties dialog box appears, make sure the System Protection tab is selected, and then click the Create button.

4. When the Create a Restore Point window appears, as shown in Figure 2.7, enter a description for the restore point, and then click the Create button.

FIGURE 2.7

Creating a restore point in Windows Vista.

And that's all you have to do. Windows notes the appropriate system settings and stores them in its System Restore database.

Restoring Your System

If something in your system goes bad when you're trying to speed up your PC, you can run System Restore to set things right. Pick a restore point before the problem occurred (such as right before a new hardware upgrade or Registry edit), and System Restore will then undo any changes made to monitored files since the restore point was created. This restores your system to its pre-problem condition.

To restore your system from a restore point in Windows XP, follow these steps:

1. Click the Start button and select All Programs, Accessories, System Tools, System Restore.

2. When the System Restore window opens, check the Restore My Computer to an Earlier Time option, and then click Next.

3. When the Select a Restore Point screen appears, as shown in Figure 2.8, you'll see a calendar showing the current month. (You can move backward and forward through the months by clicking the left and right arrows.) Any date highlighted in bold contains a restore point. Select a restore point, and then click the Next button.

4. When the confirmation screen appears, click Next.

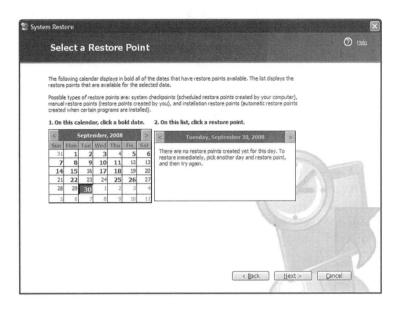

FIGURE 2.8
Selecting a restore point in Windows XP.

To restore your system in Windows Vista, follow these steps:

1. Click the Start button and select All Programs, Accessories, System Tools, System Restore.

2. When the System Restore window appears, click Next.

3. When the Choose a Restore Point window appears, as shown in Figure 2.9, select a restore point from the list. (To display older restore points, check the Show Restore Points Older Than 5 Days option.) Make your choice and click Next.

4. When the confirmation screen appears, click the Finish button.

Windows now starts to restore your system. Because Windows will need to be restarted during this process, you should make sure that all open programs are closed.

When the process is complete, your system should be back in tip-top shape. Note, however, that it might take half an hour or more to complete a system restore—so you'll have time to order a pizza and eat dinner before the operation is done!

Caution

Make sure you pick a restore point well before you started experiencing problems. If you pick a more recent restore point that reflects the status of your system with a problem or virus infection, you'll just restore the problem or virus.

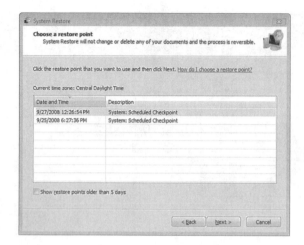

FIGURE 2.9

Selecting a restore point in Windows Vista.

The Bottom Line

How do you protect your valuable data files if you screw something up while trying to speed up your PC? Here's the bottom line:

- You should back up all your data files—including digital photos and music—before attempting any major speedup procedure.

- The easiest way to back up your data is to purchase and install an external hard disk drive. Most external hard disks come with their own backup software. If not, you can purchase third-party backup programs for less than $50.

- If you're running Windows Vista, you have the Windows Backup program included free of charge. If you're running Windows XP, go with a third-party backup program, instead.

- The backup process only backs up your data files, not your program or operating system files. To protect these files, use the System Restore utility, which can restore your system files to their condition prior to whatever it was that you did to screw them up.

Simple Speedups Anyone Can Do

Removing Spyware and Viruses

Many things that can slow down your computer—insufficient memory, a fragmented or damaged hard disk, too many unwanted programs taking up too many system resources, you name it. (And we'll talk about all of these items in due course throughout the balance of this book, don't worry.) But one of the more common causes of a sudden onslaught of sluggishness is the introduction of external factors into your system, in the form of harmful computer viruses and spyware.

When someone tells me their computer has suddenly (not gradually) slowed down, the first thing I look for is a virus or spyware program. These nasty critters can wreak all manner of havoc on your system, slowing things down to a crawl if not freezing them completely. Viruses and spyware are computer files designed to do deliberate damage to an infected PC. If you have a virus or spyware infection, slow performance may be the least of your problems.

Dealing with Computer Viruses

Let's start with the most dangerous type of malicious software (malware), the computer virus. A computer virus can delete or damage system or data files on your PC, eat up valuable system resources, or even take over your PC to launch "zombie" attacks on other systems. If your system is infected, you'll notice all sorts of strange behavior, often including a sudden and dramatic slowdown in performance.

How Computer Viruses Slow Down Your System

So what does a computer virus do that slows down your computer? To answer that question, you need to know a little bit about how a computer virus works.

As the name implies, a computer virus is similar to the types of biological viruses that attack human bodies. Contrary to what you might think, a biological virus isn't truly a living entity; as biologists will tell you, a virus is nothing more than a fragment of DNA sheathed in a protective jacket. It reproduces by injecting its DNA into a host cell. The DNA then uses the host cell's normal mechanisms to reproduce itself.

How is a computer virus like a biological virus? First, it's not alive (duh!). Second, and most important, it must piggyback on a host (another program or document) in order to propagate.

You see, many computer viruses are hidden in the code of legitimate software programs—programs that have been infected, that is. These viruses are called *file infector viruses*, and when the host program is launched, the code for the virus is executed and the virus loads itself into your computer's memory. From there, the virus code searches for other programs on your system that it can infect. If it finds one, it adds its code to the new program, which, now infected, can be used to infect other computers. And all those infected programs loaded into memory can really slow down your computer.

But that's not all a virus can do. Most viruses also perform other operations—many of which are wholly destructive. A virus might, for example, delete certain files on your computer. It might overwrite the boot sector of your hard disk, making the disk inaccessible. It might write messages on your screen, or cause your system to emit rude noises. It might also hijack your email program and use the program to send itself to all your friends and colleagues, thus replicating itself to a large number of PCs.

And if you want to talk about slowing things down, consider those viruses that replicate themselves via email or over a computer network. These fast-replicating viruses—called *worms*—cause the subsidiary problem of increasing the amount of Internet and network traffic and can completely overload a company's network, shutting down servers and forcing tens of thousands of users offline.

Note

Some viruses open a back door to your system that can then be exploited by the virus writer. These types of backdoor viruses turn your machine into a so-called *zombie computer*, which the hacker operates via remote control to perform all manner of nefarious tasks. Hijacked computers of this sort are responsible for a large number of computer attacks and spam campaigns.

How to Catch a Virus

Let's say your computer has suddenly become quite sluggish, and you suspect the cause may be a computer virus. Just how did your computer become infected?

Here's the simple fact: Viruses are spread by direct contact with other computers, or by contact with data copied from other computers. So whenever you share data with another computer or computer user, you risk exposing your computer to potential viruses.

There are many ways you can share data and many ways a virus can be transmitted:

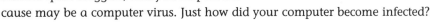

- Opening an infected file attached to an email message or instant message
- Launching an infected program file downloaded from the Internet
- Sharing a data CD, USB memory drive, or floppy disk that contains an infected file
- Sharing over a network a computer file that contains an infected file

Of all these methods, the most likely way your system can become infected today is via email—with instant messaging close behind. Whenever you open a file attached to an email message or instant message, you stand a good chance of infecting your computer system with a virus—even if the file was sent by someone you know and trust. That's because many viruses "spoof" the sender's name, thus making you think the file is from a friend or colleague. The bottom line is that no email or instant message attachment is safe unless you were expressly expecting it.

Almost as risky is the act of downloading files from so-called file-sharing sites or peer-to-peer (P2P) networks. This is the type of infection I see most often when troubleshooting sluggish PCs used by teenagers. The teen downloads what he thinks are music files from a file-sharing site, and in the process infects his com-

 Note

P2P file downloading networks also harbor lots of harmful spyware, as you'll learn in the "Dealing with Spyware" section, later in this chapter.

puter with one or more viruses. As a result, the computer slows way down almost immediately. It's an extremely common occurrence.

How Do You Know If a Virus Is Slowing Down Your System?

If your system has become sluggish, how do you know if a virus is the cause?

First, look for other odd things happening. For example, you might see strange messages or graphics displayed on your computer screen or find that normally well-behaved programs are acting erratically. You might discover that certain files have gone missing from your hard disk or that your system is suddenly crashing or freezing or failing to start at all. You might even find that your friends are receiving emails from you that you never sent, or that you're getting returned emails from people you've never heard of (a sure sign that your computer has been hijacked to send out reams of spam messages).

In other words, if your computer is slowing down *plus* exhibiting other unusual behavior, the sluggishness (and the other behavior) is probably caused by a virus.

Also look to just *when* your computer started to slow down. If the sluggishness and other odd behavior started after you downloaded a file from the Internet or opened a suspicious email message, it's likely that the file or email contained a virus, and your computer is probably infected.

Preventing Virus Attacks with Safe Computing

If you want to keep a computer virus from slowing down your system, you need to keep your computer from getting infected. Fortunately, this is relatively easy to do.

The easiest way to prevent your computer from catching a computer virus is to avoid files that are known to harbor viruses. That means taking the following precautions:

- **Don't open email attachments.** Most virus infections today are spread via email. The virus is typically encased in a file attached to an email

message. When you click to view or
open the file, you launch the
virus—and your computer is automatically infected. With this in
mind, the best way to reduce your
risk of virus infection is to never
open email attachments. Never.
Especially from people you don't
know, but even from people you *do* know—especially if you aren't
expecting them. (That's because some viruses can hijack the address
book on an infected PC, thus sending out infected email that the owner
isn't even aware of.) If you know you're getting an attachment, it's
probably okay, but steer clear of any unexpected ones!

Caution

If you remember nothing else
from this chapter, remember this:
*Never open an unexpected file
attachment.* Period!

- **Don't click links in email messages**. Another way to infect your system is to let you do it yourself. This happens when you get an email
message (typically very official-look-
ing) that encourages you to click a
link to do something; you click the
link and you're taken to a website
that automatically downloads a
virus onto your system. Even if the
text accompanying the link *looks*
legitimate, the underlying URL may
be spoofed into something completely different. Bottom line, don't
click any email links!

Tip

If you feel you must go to a website referenced in the email, enter
it by hand instead. This elimi-
nates the danger of spoofed
URLs—ones that look like one
address but take you to another
address instead.

- **Don't open files sent via instant messaging**. The previous advice
about opening email files goes for any files sent to you via instant messaging, as well. IM is a growing source of virus infection, if only
because users (especially younger ones) are naturally trusting of other
users. The takeaway is that you shouldn't accept any files sent to you
via instant messaging, even if they appear to come from people on
your buddies or friends list. If a trusted friend really wants to send you
a file, ask him to email it to you—and then use normal caution before
opening it.

- **Don't click IM or chat links.** While we're on the subject of instant
messaging, here's another bit of common sense that can greatly reduce
your risk of virus infection. If a someone you don't know sends you a
link to another site while you're instant messaging or in a chat room,

don't click it! Nine times out of ten, this link either directly downloads a virus file to your PC, or takes you to a website that has plenty of infected files to download. In any case, ignore the unsolicited links and you'll be a lot safer.

■ **Don't run files found in newsgroups or message boards.** Email and instant messaging aren't the only channels for downloading virus infected files. You can find plenty of infected files in web message boards, blogs, and Usenet newsgroups. For this reason, resist download-ing programs you find in these channels; while many are safe, some are not.

■ **Don't download files from suspect websites.** Lots of websites out there hold infected files. The owners of these sites are just waiting for naïve users to download the files, so that their PCs can become infected. For this reason, avoid downloading files from sites with which you're not familiar. Instead, download files only from reliable file archive web-sites, such as Download.com (www.download.com) and Tucows (www.tucows.com). These sites scan all their files for viruses before they're available for downloading. It's the only safe way to download files from the Internet.

■ **Don't visit file-sharing sites.** Yeah, I know you like to download free music and videos from these sites, even if the practice is legally ques-tionable. I'll reserve judgment on the legality and voice my opposition as a purely practical one. Many of the files on these sites are infected with viruses and spyware. The easiest way to protect yourself is to avoid P2P file sharing, period.

■ **Limit your sharing of removable media.** The logic is simple. Any file you receive via removable media can potentially carry a computer virus. It doesn't matter what that file looks like (its filename and exten-sion) or who gave it to you, the bottom line is that you don't know where that file came from. If you run that file on your system—either from the storage device or after you've saved it to your computer's hard disk—any malicious code contained within can infect and potentially trash your system. To that end, you should share disks, memory sticks, and files only with users you know and trust. Or, to be completely safe, don't accept *any* files given to you on any portable storage medium.

■ **Beware of risky file types.** Certain types of files can carry virus infec-tions; certain types of files can't. Potentially *unsafe* file types have the following extensions: BAT, COM, DOC, DOT, EXE, INF, JS, REG, SCR,

SYS, VB, VBE, VBS, XLS, and XLW. Avoid opening files with these extensions unless you're sure they come from a safe source. (For that matter, also avoid ZIP files, because they can contain compressed files of any type—including executable files.)

■ **Don't let anyone else use your computer.** It only takes a minute for another user to compromise your system. I know this from experience; my stepson has a habit of downloading suspicious software whenever he "borrows" my wife's laptop, which inevitably leads to performance problems. You don't have to be nice to friends and family—protect your data by keeping your computer out of others' hands.

> **Caution**
>
> One of the more common Trojan activities is to disguise a bad file type as a safe file type. This is typically accomplished by adding a seemingly safe .JPG or .TXT to the first part of the filename, before the real extension. You end up with a name like **thisfile.jpg.exe**, which, if you're not fully alert, might appear to be a safe file—but isn't. (Windows hides file extensions by default; to display file extensions, open the Control Panel, click Folder Options, select the View tab, and uncheck the Hide Extensions for Known File-types option.)

All this advice should be heeded, but know that the only surefire way to shield your system from computer viruses is to completely cut off all contact with other computers. That means no Internet connection, no sharing files via CD or USB memory drive, no connecting to a home or office network. In today's connected world, however, none of these things is practical. So, minimizing your exposure to potentially infected files is the best approach.

Protecting Your System with Antivirus Software

Previous advice noted, you should supplement your safe computing practices by installing an antivirus software program on your computer. Antivirus programs vigilantly guard your system for any viruses that might arrive via file download or email attachment, scan all the files on your system for hint of infection, and either clean or delete any files that have been found to be infected.

For this reason, if your computer is connected to any network or the Internet, or if you share files with any other users, you should install an antivirus program on your system. To not do so is to expose your computer to an unacceptable level of risk.

Most antivirus programs detect both known viruses and protect your system against new, unknown viruses. These programs check your system for viruses each time your system is booted and can be configured to check any programs you download from the Internet. They're also used to disinfect your system if it becomes infected with a virus.

The most popular antivirus programs for the home and small business include the following:

- avast! antivirus (www.avast.com)
- AVG Anti-Virus (www.grisoft.com)
- CA Anti-Virus (www.ca.com)
- ESET NOD32 Antivirus (www.eset.com)
- F-PROT Antivirus (www.f-prot.com)
- F-Secure Anti-Virus (www.f-secure.com)
- Kaspersky Anti-Virus (www.kaspersky.com)
- McAfee VirusScan Plus (www.mcafee.com)
- Norman Antivirus & Antispyware (www.norman.com)
- Norton AntiVirus (www.symantec.com)
- Panda Antivirus (www.pandasecurity.com)
- Trend Micro Antivirus plus AntiSpyware (www.trendmicro.com)
- Vexira Antivirus (www.centralcommand.com)
- Windows Live OneCare (onecare.live.com)

All of these programs do a good job—although their prices vary somewhat. Some programs are sold for a one-time price but require additional subscriptions (beyond the first year) to receive updated definitions. Others are sold on a yearly subscription basis. For example, AVG Anti-Virus is available in a Free Edition (free.grisoft.com) that offers basic protection that's perfect for most home users. Norton AntiVirus offers more functionality but costs $39.99 for a one-year subscription, and Windows Live OneCare costs $49.95 per year—although you can use it on up to three different PCs, which makes it a real bargain for multiple-PC households.

 Note

Some of these programs combine virus and spyware protection. Other options to consider are the full-blown "security suites" offered by many of the same companies, which combine virus protection with other forms of Internet security.

Using an antivirus program is simplicity itself. When you install the program, you typically configure it to run automatically, in the background, whenever your computer is turned on. (Figure 3.1 shows the configuration screen for Windows Live OneCare, one of my preferred antivirus programs.)

Note

Microsoft intends to discontinue its Live OneCare product in the second half of 2009, replacing it with a free anti-virus product at that time.

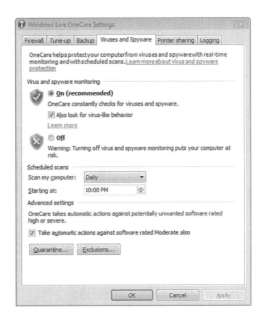

FIGURE 3.1

Configuring Windows Live OneCare for automatic operation.

Running in this fashion, the program will scan any file you try to copy or download to your hard disk; any USB memory drives, floppy disks, or data CDs you insert in your system; and any files attached to email messages, instant messages, and the like. If a virus is found, the file won't be copied or downloaded, and you'll be alerted to the problem.

Caution

Some antivirus programs can cause more harm than good, slowing down or even crippling your system while they perform their checks. (I've had particular bad luck with Symantec's Norton products, while others say the same about McAfee.) Learn more in Chapter 4, "Cleaning Out Unnecessary Programs."

In addition to this automatic background scanning, all antivirus programs include full scans of files currently on your hard disk. This type of all-system scan will find any bad files that got through the first line of defense, and alert you to the problem. You can perform this type of scan manually, or schedule scans on a regular basis. I recommend running automatic scans at least weekly, if not daily.

Tip

Schedule automatic scans during the overnight hours, when you're not otherwise using your PC, to minimize the drain on system resources. Otherwise, you'll notice a slowdown in system performance while the virus scan is running—an ironic side effect when trying to speed up a slow computer!

You also want to configure your antivirus program to scan all incoming email messages and instant messages for infected attachments. If you have your antivirus software scanning your attachments, it becomes safer to open those attachments that pass muster (although still not recommended, in general). If an attachment is found to contain a virus, your antivirus program will block the download of the file, and alert you of the infected message. The infected file never makes it to your hard disk, and your system remains safe.

Finally, know that every antivirus program includes a built-in database of virus definitions. You need to configure your program to periodically go online and download the latest virus definitions. Downloading once a week is a good idea. Wait much longer than that, and you're likely to miss the definition for any "hot" virus circulating that week.

Speeding Up Your System After a Virus Infection

What do you do if you discover that your sluggish PC has been infected with some sort of computer virus? First, you shouldn't panic. Most virus infections can be successfully recovered from, with minimal effort on your part. You don't, as a friend of mine once thought, have to throw away your PC and buy a new one. With today's antivirus tools, you can remove the virus from your system and recover most infected files, with relative ease.

If your computer is still up and running—albeit slowly, of course—you're in relatively good shape. In this situation, all you have to do is use your antivirus program to manually scan your system to see if it really is infected, and then (if the news is bad) disinfect or delete the infected files.

How you perform a scan depends on your specific antivirus program. For example, Windows Live OneCare presents you with an option for both a Quick Scan (scans only most likely infected files) and a Complete Scan (scans all files), as shown in Figure 3.2. In the event of a suspected virus infection, you should choose the Complete Scan option to scan every possible place a virus could hide.

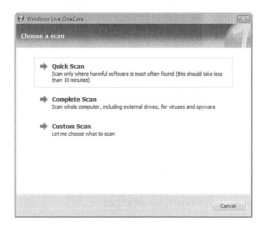

FIGURE 3.2
Performing a manual scan with Windows Live OneCare.

Once the scan is underway, any infected files will be identified. Some antivirus programs automatically repair or delete any infected files found. Others ask what you want to do with them. If you're asked, try repairing them first. If the fix doesn't take, you can quarantine or delete the infected files.

And that's it. Most virus infections—those that don't crash your system, that is—can be simply and easily dealt with by your antivirus software. Just run the software and follow all instructions. After the infected files are appropriately dealt with, you should notice a marked increase in your system's speed.

Note

If a virus causes your computer to lock up or not start, you have bigger problems. You'll need to get your system up and running again first, and then go through the necessary virus removal techniques. You'll also need to restore any files damaged during the infection. If Windows system files were damaged, you may need to reformat your hard disk and reinstall Windows. Learn more in Chapter 8, "When All Else Fails: Reinstalling Windows from Scratch."

Dealing with Spyware

If your computer has suddenly slowed down, it might not be a virus problem. Instead, your computer might be infected by *spyware*—which is similar to but technically different from a computer virus.

Like a virus, spyware is a type of program that installs itself on your computer, typically without your knowledge or consent. Unlike a virus, however, most spyware doesn't do deliberate harm to your PC. Instead, it surreptitiously sends information about the way you use your PC to some interested third party.

That said, spyware can and often does affect your computer's performance. This happens because spyware programs (almost always multiple programs) use up valuable system resources; the programs load into your computer's memory, taking up space that is needed by your regular programs and processes. The more spyware on your system, the slower your system runs.

And that's not all. Some spyware programs do more than just slow down your system; they hijack your computer and launch pop-up windows and advertisements when you visit certain web pages. Other spyware programs literally spy on you, tracking the keystrokes you type, the websites you visit, and the passwords you enter. Unless you really like the idea of a third party spying on your computer sessions, spyware is not something you want installed on your system.

Note

Unfortunately, most antivirus programs won't catch spyware because spyware isn't a virus. To track down and uninstall these programs, therefore, you need to run a separate antispyware utility.

How Spyware Slows Down Your System

A spyware program is a stealth program. It runs in the background, hidden from view, and monitors your computer and Internet usage. That could mean recording the addresses of each web page you visit, the recipient and sender addresses and content of each email you send or receive, the contents of all your instant messages and chat room conversations, or even each keystroke you type with your computer keyboard—including usernames, passwords, and other personal information. It's a little scary.

The information recorded by the spyware is typically saved to a log file. That log file, at a predetermined time, is transmitted (via the Internet) to a central source. That source can then aggregate your information for marketing purposes, use the information to target personalized communications or advertisements, or steal any confidential data for illegal purposes.

And here's the thing. To perform these surreptitious activities, the spyware has to stay loaded in your computer's memory. That means less memory for your normal programs and processes, which means that your system will run noticeably slower when doing common tasks. The problem gets worse the more spyware you have on your system. Unfortunately, if you've left your system open for one spyware infestation, you've probably left it open for additional infestations, as well.

How to Become Infected with Spyware

Spyware gets installed on your system in many of the same ways that viruses infect your PC. Typical means of transmission include email attachments, misleading links on websites, and files downloaded from the Internet.

 Note

Some advertisers use a special type of spyware, called *adware*, to gain access to your system. Like other types of spyware, adware is typically placed on your PC when you install some other legitimate software, piggybacking on the main installation. Once installed, the adware works like spyware, monitoring your various activities and reporting back to the host advertiser or marketing firm. The host firm can then use the collected data in a marketing-related fashion—totally unaware to you, of course.

From my experience, some of the biggest sources of spyware are peer-to-peer music-trading networks. I'm not talking legitimate online music stores, such as Apple's iTunes Store, which are almost totally free of viruses and spyware. Instead, it's the rogue file-trading networks, such as Blubster, iMesh, Kazaa, LimeWire, and Morpheus that are risky. In many instances, spyware is actually attached to the file-trading software you have to download to use the network; when you install the software, the spyware is also installed. (And, believe it or not, you can't remove the spyware without also removing the host software—which causes some users to keep the spyware!)

Here's the thing that's tricky. Many spyware authors present their malicious programs as helpful utilities. For example, you may be prompted to download what is advertised as a web accelerator utility, only to find that you're downloading spyware instead. In this regard, spyware is a bit like a Trojan horse, but using social engineering as the way into your system.

It's easy to get tricked into installing spyware on your system. For example, you may go to a website, perhaps one mentioned in a spam email message, and click a link there. What you see next looks like a standard Windows dialog box, asking you whether you want to scan your system for spyware, or optimize your Internet browsing, or something similar. In reality, the "dialog box" is just a pop-up window designed to look like the real deal, and when you click the Yes button, you're authorizing the installation of spyware on your system. In some instances, clicking No also installs the software, so you're damned if you do and damned if you don't.

In addition, some spyware is installed through known security holes in the Internet Explorer browser. When you navigate to a web page controlled by the software author (again, typically from a link in a spam email message), the page contains hidden code that exploits the browser weakness and automatically downloads the spyware.

It's a sure sign that spyware is slowing down your system if you've engaged in any of the aforementioned activities and then experienced sudden system sluggishness. So, for example, if you download music or video from a P2P site and then find your system slowing down, you probably downloaded some spyware, too.

Note

This behind-the-scenes installation of spyware on a specially coded website is called a *drive-by download*.

Caution

There's a new breed of spyware program, called *rogue software*, which poses as an antispyware program. Most of these programs are installed via fake Windows dialog boxes or pop-up advertisements or warnings. You're warned that spyware has been detected on your system and encouraged to download this free program to help get rid of it. Woe be you if you agree; all you get is yet another piece of spyware gunking up the works.

Is Spyware Slowing Down Your PC?

Before we discuss how to avoid and get rid of spyware, let's take a moment to see if you already have spyware installed on your system. It's certainly possible, especially if you frequent file-swapping websites.

Most spyware infections are recognizable by how they affect the performance of your system. Put simply, spyware tends to slow down operations on most computers—and sometimes worse. Some spyware programs can cause Internet Explorer to freeze or not work properly. Others may actually cause your computer to crash. So if you're computer is suddenly acting slowly or suspiciously, the usual suspect is some sort of spyware infection.

In particular, take notice if your computer exhibits any or all of the following behaviors—all symptomatic of a spyware infection:

- **Your computer runs slow.** Spyware is just another software program, and the more programs you have running at one time, the slower your computer will run. Spyware can be especially draining, making its presence known via sluggish system performance.

- **Your system freezes or crashes.** These situations are often caused by spyware programs behaving badly around other legitimate programs.

- **Your computer has a mind of its own.** Spyware doesn't just run in the background; it also performs a variety of operations that make it look as if your computer is being remote controlled. If your computer sends emails to people in your address book without your knowledge or permission, or shows a lot of hard disk activity or Internet access when you're not actively using it, all that activity could be a symptom of the spyware doing its thing in the background.

- **Your computer's hard disk / network activities lights constantly blink or stay lit.** This indicates a lot of hard drive activity or Internet access. Unless you yourself are causing this activity, it's likely do to spyware doing what it does best—reporting back to the mothership, without your explicit approval.

Note

Some spyware programs don't control your email program per se, but instead "borrow" your address book to send spam from another computer to users in your address book.

- **You get a lot of returned or bounced back emails.** Many spyware programs take control of your email program and use it to mail out loads of spam—without your knowledge or permission. A raft of returned emails that you don't remember sending could be the aftereffect of a spyware-induced spam attack.

- **Your web browser's home page has been changed to another site, without your approval.** This is a common trick of many spyware programs, to force you to view a particular website.

- **You see a strange new toolbar in your web browser.** Many spyware programs install such toolbars for their "sponsor" sites.

- **When you perform a web search, you end up at some strange site.** Again, a favorite trick of spyware developers, to send you to a site of their choosing whenever you perform a search.

- **You see a new error page in your web browser.** If you try to go to a website that doesn't exist, instead of seeing the browser's typical "404 error" page, you see the page for a previously unknown website.

- **Your antivirus and firewall programs have been turned off.** This is how spyware programs try to stay "alive" on your PC, by deactivating your normal means of protection—without your knowledge or approval.

■ **You see a lot of unexpected pop-up windows onscreen.** Spyware likes to open pop-up windows; so if you see a lot of the things, you know the cause. (For example, some adware display pop-up advertisements every few minutes, like clockwork.)

■ **Windows displays strange icons in your taskbar or new shortcuts on your desktop.** These are signs that a new spyware program has been installed on your computer.

■ **You see one or more strange new sites in the Favorites section of your web browser.** These favorites are typically put there when a spyware program has been installed on your PC.

■ **You find new programs in the Add or Remove Software utility in the Windows Control Panel.** Almost all programs installed on your computer should be able to be uninstalled via this utility, so new programs listed there are most certainly spyware.

■ **When you try to run an antispyware program, it won't launch.** That's because many spyware programs block access to their nemesis antispyware programs.

■ **You receive frequent alerts from your firewall program about some unknown program or process trying to access the Internet.** This one's easy; the offending program is the spyware program.

■ **The Java console appears in the Windows taskbar even though you haven't recently run any Java software.** Obviously, the spyware program is the one that ran Java.

■ **You become a victim of identity theft.** Spyware, by definition, is software that collects your personal data and then sends it back to the spyware companies or their surrogates for use in identity theft and other such crimes. If you're checking your credit card regularly and find some irregularities, it's possible that those irregularities were caused by the data breach resulting from the data purloined by the spyware program.

 Note

A single spyware program on your computer may not noticeably affect system performance. Unfortunately, however, the most at-risk computers tend to be infected with multiple spyware programs. It's the combination of all these programs running at the same time that can make your computer slow to a crawl.

As you can see, many of these symptoms are similar to what you might expect from a computer virus infection. Other symptoms are wholly unique to the world of spyware. In any instance, if your computer exhibits one or more of these symptoms, it's time to run an antispyware program—which we discuss later in this chapter.

Avoiding Spyware-Infested Websites and Programs

The best way to avoid the sluggish performance resulting from a spyware infestation is to defeat the spyware at the source—by not installing it in the first place. If you know where you're likely to find spyware programs, you can avoid those sites, and thus avoid installing spyware on your system.

That said, you should know that you may inadvertently agree to install some spyware or adware programs. That's because the installation of these programs is often optional when you install the host program that the spyware is bundled with. If you look closely, you'll see that you're given the option *not* to install these so-called companion programs when you install the host program. Check (or uncheck) the proper box on the installation screen, and you avoid installing the spyware.

Other spyware programs, however, are *not* optional components; they install automatically when you install the host program. If you know that a particular program includes piggyback spyware, and you don't have the option not to install the adware, you can always opt not to install the main software itself. Why, in the end, do you want to deal with a company that allows other companies to secretly exploit its users?

Of course, most spyware is installed entirely without your knowledge or approval. In most instances, you're tricked into clicking a link in an email or on a website that automatically installs the spyware. And some of these links are trickier than others.

Particularly annoying are those sites that display a window that looks like a standard Windows dialog box. When you click

Tip

Some of the biggest offending sites for piggyback spyware are file-sharing and illegal music download sites, such as Kazaa and LimeWire. In many instances, spyware is piggybacked onto the official file sharing software you have to download to use the site; you may or may not have the option of declining the installation of the spyware. Because these noncommercial music sharing networks are so rife with spyware, I advise all my friends to block their teenage sons and daughters from using these file-trading networks. The legality of file sharing aside, it's tiring to keep removing the same spyware from the same computers used by the same teenagers.

Tip

You can safely close any window by clicking the "X" button in the top right corner.

the Cancel button to close the dialog box, you instead install a spyware program.

Also effective are sites that display what appears to be a pop-up window advertising an antispyware program. The ad says something along the lines of "your system may be infected—click here to remove all spyware from your system." Instead of removing spyware, the program you install is itself a spyware program, and your system is newly infected.

The takeaway here is to be careful what links you click and what sites you download from. The only truly safe download sites are reputable sites such as Tucows.com and Download.com. Most other sites offering free downloads also feature piggyback adware and spyware as part of the package. And when you do download a file, read the user agreement first—you may be able to opt out of installing piggyback spyware.

In other words—look before you click!

Speeding Up Your PC with Antispyware Programs

Even if you take precautions going forward, you may have already installed some spyware on your computer. And even the most diligent user can sometimes be tricked into installing unwanted spyware. What do you do about any spyware programs you find installed on your PC?

Fortunately, several companies offer antispyware programs that scan your system for known spyware. These programs work much the same way that antivirus programs detect and remove computer viruses. Antispyware programs are designed to identify any and all spyware programs lurking on your computer, and will also uninstall the offending programs and remove their entries from the Windows Registry.

Know, however, that spyware is different enough from a computer virus that most antivirus programs won't detect spyware—and vice versa. While there are some exceptions (many of the major antivirus programs have added antispyware components), you'll probably need to install an antispyware program *in addition to* an antivirus program.

The most popular of these antispyware programs include the following:

- Ad-Aware (www.lavasoftusa.com)
- CounterSpy (www.sunbelt-software.com)
- ParetoLogic Anti-Spyware (www.paretologic.com/products/paretologicas/)

- Spybot Search & Destroy (www.safer-networking.org)
- Spyware Doctor (www.pctools.com/ spyware-doctor/)
- Webroot Spy Sweeper (www.webroot.com)
- Windows Defender (www.microsoft.com/windows/products/winfamily/defender/)
- ZoneAlarm Anti-Spyware (www.zonelabs.com)

Note

Windows Defender is included free with Windows Vista and available as a free download for Windows XP users.

Most of these are low-cost (under-$30) programs, and many of them are free. In addition to these standalone programs, some of the major Internet security suites, such as Norton Internet Security and the McAfee Internet Security Suite, include antispyware modules.

To determine whether a program is spyware, an antispyware program checks to see if a program performs some or all of the following activities:

Tip

There is so much spyware circulating today that I find that no single one of these programs will catch it all. To that end, I recommend you use at least *two* antispyware programs, one after another. This approach, although somewhat duplicative, does a much better job of rooting all the offending spyware on my system.

- Runs processes on your computer without notifying you
- Collects or communicates your personal information and behavior without your consent
- Attempts to circumvent the security features on your computer
- Undermines your computer's performance

In addition, most antispyware programs check for all programs listed in the company's database of malicious software. So if a program is recognized as spyware, it is flagged by the antispyware program.

Like an antivirus program, an antispyware program can be configured to either manually or periodically scan your system for infection. (Figure 3.3 shows Windows Defender in the middle of such a scan.) If a spyware program is found, it is automatically quarantined or uninstalled from your system.

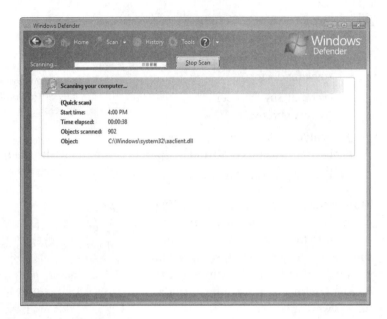

FIGURE 3.3
Scanning for spyware with Windows Defender.

In addition, several of these programs provide real-time protection against the download and installation of new spyware programs. This works much like the similar function in antivirus programs; all new files and incoming network/Internet traffic is scanned for spyware signatures, with all offending programs blocked from being installed.

And here's the good news. When your antispyware program finds and deletes spyware on your system, you should notice an immediate and appreciable increase in your computer's speed. Remove the spyware, speed up your PC—that's the way it works!

 Tip

Because most antispyware programs in part depend on a database of known spyware programs, it's important to keep this database of spyware definitions up-to-date. You'll need to configure your program to update its list of definitions on a regular basis—weekly at the least, daily if possible.

Removing Stubborn Spyware Programs

An antispyware program should do a decent job of finding and deleting most spyware programs, and thus speeding up your PC. Some spyware, however, is more stubborn, resisting the antispyware programs' simple removal techniques.

Some savvy spyware authors devise their programs to work in pairs—that is, to either run two instances of the program, or to launch two similar (but differently named) executable files. When an antispyware program terminates or removes one running process, the other one remains running and then re-creates and reinstalls the killed program.

Note

Safe mode is a special mode of operation, typically used for troubleshooting startup problems, that loads Windows in a minimal configuration. This minimal configuration runs Windows as cleanly as possible, with a low-resolution display and without any unnecessary device drivers or software.

Similarly, some spyware detects any attempt to remove its key in the Windows Registry, immediately adding the deleted keys. This keeps the program on your system, even if you think you've deleted it.

Most of these stubborn spyware programs can be more effectively deleted by booting your system into Safe mode. When running in Safe mode, your antispyware program stands a better chance of avoiding the reinfestation techniques and deleting all remnants of the offending program.

So if you think you've deleted a spyware program only to see it crop back up almost immediately, you need to reboot your computer and enter Safe Mode on the restart. To do this, restart your computer and wait for the text-based startup screen to display, just before the Windows welcome screen appears. When this text-based screen appears, press the F8 key on your keyboard, and then select Safe mode from the resulting startup menu. Then, when you're running in Safe mode, launch your antispyware program and try again to delete the offending program; you should have more success.

The Bottom Line

How do you keep computer viruses and spyware from slowing down your PC? Here's the bottom line:

- If you experience a sudden system slowdown, perhaps accompanied by other unusual system activity, your computer may be infected with a computer virus or infested with unwanted spyware.

- Viruses and spyware both use up valuable system resources (memory, especially), which can slow down your PC's performance.

■ Computer viruses and spyware are often introduced to your system by visiting file-sharing websites, downloading files obtained from untrust-worthy sources, and opening unexpected email or IM attachments.

■ You protect against computer viruses by practicing safe computing and by running an antivirus program. If you think you've been infected by a virus, have your antivirus program run a manual scan of your system to detect, repair, and if necessary delete any infected files from your system.

■ You protect against spyware by practicing safe computing and by running an antispyware program. If you think you have spyware installed on your system, use your antispyware program to run a manual scan and delete the offending programs.

■ When you remove viruses and spyware, you should experience an immediate improvement in system performance.

3

4

Cleaning Out Unnecessary Programs

One cause of a gradual slowdown in PC speed is creeping bloat. By that I mean the tendency for users to have more and more "stuff" on their machines over time—more programs installed on the system, more utilities launched at startup, more files created and stored on the hard disk. The more "stuff" you have on your system, the slower your system will run, for a number of different reasons.

In this chapter, we examine why a leaner system runs faster, and how to make your system less cluttered. In other words, you'll learn how to get rid of all the "stuff" you don't need—and speed up your PC!

Removing Unwanted Programs and Files from Your Hard Disk

Let's start with all the "stuff" on your computer's hard disk. When you purchased your PC, lo those many years ago, the hard disk was relatively clean— that is, there weren't that many programs installed yet (save for the free programs installed by the manufacturer—which we discuss in a moment), nor had you created many (if any) data files. In this minimalist state, your new PC ran pretty darn fast.

But time changes everything. As the weeks and the months and the years went by, you installed lots of new programs and created tons of data files—letters, memos, email messages, digital photographs, music tracks, you name it. And the more things you installed and created, the slower your computer got. Oh, the sluggishness came gradually, maybe you didn't even notice it for the first year or so, but every new item taking up space on your hard disk worked to eventually slow down your system to the point that the performance change was noticeable. There is a direct correlation between the amount of "stuff" on your hard disk and how fast your system performs.

But why is this? Why does installing more programs and creating more files slow down your computer? And what can you do about it, after the fact?

Why a Crowded Hard Disk Slows Down Your System

Here's the rule: The more unused hard disk space your computer has, the faster it will run. There are a number of reasons for this.

First, your computer sometimes uses your hard disk as a kind of backstop when system memory fills up. In this instance, your hard disk serves as *virtual memory*, temporarily storing programs and data just as your system's random access memory (RAM) normally does. This facilitates *file swapping*, where program and data files are swapped between random access memory (for immediate access) and virtual hard disk memory (for not-quite-immediate access).

If there's a lot of free hard disk space, that means there's lots of virtual memory available for this file swapping, which lets your system run quickly. If there's not a lot of free hard disk space, that means less data can be loaded into this virtual memory—and the less stuff loaded into memory, the slower your system runs. It's a simple equation: Free up hard disk space for virtual memory and speed up your system.

But memory, virtual or otherwise, isn't the only thing that affects your system's performance. Every time you open or save a program or document, that program or document file has to be read from or written to your computer's hard disk; that's basic computer operation. If you only have a few files on your hard disk, it's relatively easy for your computer to find the right file to read or write to, which makes for speedy operation. The more files you have on your hard disk, however, the more files your computer has to sort through to find the right one to read or write to, which slows down your computer's performance. In other words, the more things stored on your hard drive, the longer it takes to access any one thing.

How Much Free Space Do You Need?

So if you want to speed up your system, you need to delete all but the most essential programs and files, and leave plenty of spare hard disk space for potential use as virtual memory. But how much free hard disk space do you need?

I recommend keeping at least 20% of your hard disk free; this should leave plenty of room for virtual memory, file swapping, temporary file storage, and the like. For example, if you have a 200GB hard drive, you want to utilize no more than 80% of the available space, leaving at least 40GB of free disk space at any given time. Do the math to figure out how much free space you need on your particular hard drive.

Discovering All the Files Stored on Your Hard Drive

By this point in time, you're probably wondering what kinds of files you have stored on your hard drive—which ones are essential and which ones are expendable. While every user's hard drive is different, you can normally organize your files into one of the following categories:

- **System files:** These are files used by the Windows operating system, and should not be deleted. (If you do delete them, Windows will probably crash.) These include executable files (typically with a .DLL or .SYS extension), device drivers (.DRV extension), configuration files (.INI extension), and the like.
- **Program files:** These are the files used by the software programs installed on your system, typically with an .EXE file extension. Obviously, files for programs you don't use can be deleted from your hard disk; programs you do use should not be deleted.
- **Data files:** These are the documents, spreadsheets, presentations, music tracks, videos, digital photographs, and the like you create and run with your software programs, or download off the Internet. You

may find it better for system performance if you don't archive all your older data files on your main hard drive. Files you don't access frequently can be stored on external hard drives, CDs, or DVDs.

■ **Temporary files:** These are files stored in a special "cache" on your hard drive. These may be web pages downloaded by your web browser and cached for quick viewing, or data files opened and temporarily stored by the host application. Temporary files are typically created when data used by a program larger than the available memory space. Most temporary files are automatically deleted when the host application is closed, but sometimes, due to a program crash or ill-behaved application, they're not deleted—and continue to take up valuable hard disk space. Most temporary files have a .TMP extension, and can be safely deleted.

■ **Deleted files:** Here's one that might surprise you. Files that you delete from your hard drive actually aren't immediately deleted. Instead, they're moved to the Recycle Bin, a special folder that holds "deleted" files in case you want to *undelete* them in the immediate future. By default, Windows allocates to the Recycle Bin 10% of your hard disk space (in Windows XP) or 4GB plus 5% of your hard disk space (in Windows Vista). You can, however, change the amount of space allocated—and "empty" the Recycle Bin to free up hard disk space.

To summarize, system files should not be deleted (ever), program and data files can be deleted if you don't need them, and temporary and deleted files can always be deleted.

Understanding Bundleware

There's a special category of program files that should be addressed. I'm talking about *bundleware*, those programs that come preinstalled when you purchase a new PC. More often than not, these are not programs you want on your new PC, which is why some wits (including some Microsoft managers) describe these programs as crapware or craplets.

As you can tell by the nickname, most folks hate this stuff. Users hate having their brand-new desktops cluttered with this crap, and technicians hate having to clean it off users' sluggish PCs. It's just not popular.

About the only folks who like bundleware are the hardware manufacturers. That's because they get paid by each company to install their software in this fashion. Given the slim margins inherent in computer manufacturing, the pennies that various software companies pay per machine to preload their bundleware can be the difference between profit and loss for the hardware manufacturer.

What kind of programs are we talking about? It's all the stuff you find cluttering the desktop and Start menu of a new PC. This might include sign-up utilities for one or two Internet service providers, icons for a couple of online music services, a handful of instant messaging clients, some cheapo games, a web browser toolbar or two, an antivirus program that expires in 90 days or

so, maybe even trial versions of Microsoft Money or Quicken. Depending on the price of the PC, you might also get a functioning version of Microsoft Works or a 90-day trial version of Microsoft Office. All in all, expect at least 10% of your new PC's hard disk space to be taken up with these unwanted programs.

And here's the really annoying thing: Much of the bundleware isn't even fully functioning software. More often than not what you get is a "trial" version that only works for a set period of time (30 or 90 days), or one that is somehow crippled in functionality. If you want to use the full version of the program, you have to purchase it separately. The bundleware version is just a tease or advertisement.

Even more annoying is the fact that if you don't want the bundleware taking up valuable hard disk space (or, even worse, preloading itself into system memory), you have to manually uninstall the stuff. And, not surprisingly, some bundleware makes itself quite difficult to uninstall. It's unwanted stuff that's hard to get rid of—and it slows down your PC, to boot.

Tip

Some retailers, such as Best Buy, offer to remove all the bundleware from a new PC you purchase—for a price. Depending on the price, this may not be a bad thing, as some retailers also install any necessary operating system updates, drivers, and the like at the same time.

Tip

Because bundleware is so time-consuming and difficult to remove, the first thing many techie users do when they purchase a new PC is wipe off the hard disk (thus deleting all the bundleware) and reinstall Windows. This lets them start with a completely clean machine. (Although this doesn't work if you use the manufacturer's "restore" CD/DVD—which typically includes all the bundleware you're trying to get rid of!)

4

How to Free Up Valuable Hard Disk Space—and Speed Up Your PC

You're probably coming to the conclusion that whether you have an older PC or a newer one, you have a lot of stuff on your hard disk that you just don't need and is probably slowing down your system. How do you identify the stuff to get rid of—and how do you get rid of it?

Deleting Bundleware with PC Decrapifier

Let's start with the bundleware that comes with a new PC. You might think that all you have to do is drag the unwanted icons off your desktop into the Recycle Bin, but that only deletes the icons, not the programs themselves. You have to delete the programs separately, using one method or another.

One approach is to use a utility dedicated solely to identifying and deleted this so-called crapware. One such program is PC Decrapifier, which you can download for free from www.pcdecrapifier.com.

Figure 4.1 shows PC Decrapifier at work. When you start it up, it scans your system for potential crapware and lists them for you. Check those you want to delete and click the Next button. PC Decrapifier does the dirty work of uninstalling these nuisance programs so that you don't have to deal with them.

Tip

If you're not sure whether you want to use a program or not, don't let PC Decrapifier delete it. Wait a few days or weeks, then if you haven't used the program, you can rerun PC Decrapifier to delete it then.

FIGURE 4.1

Removing unwanted bundleware with PC Decrapifier.

Deleting Unwanted Files with the Disk Cleanup Utility

PC Decrapifier only deletes programs it identifies as bundleware or trial versions. As you're aware, you may also want to delete other types of files, which you can do with the Windows Disk Cleanup utility. You use Disk Cleanup to automatically free up extra hard disk space—and speed up your PC's performance.

To use Disk Cleanup, follow these steps:

1. Click the Start button, and then select All Programs, Accessories, System Tools, Disk Cleanup.

2. If prompted, select the drive or user files you want to clean up.

3. Disk Cleanup now analyzes the contents of your hard disk drive and presents its results in the Disk Cleanup dialog box, shown in Figure 4.2.

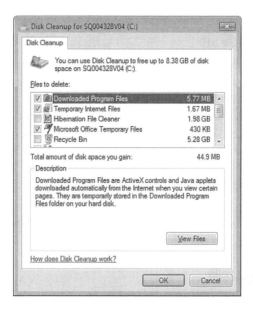

FIGURE 4.2

Use Disk Cleanup to delete unused files from your hard disk.

4. You now have the option of permanently deleting various types of files: downloaded program files, temporary Internet files, offline web pages, deleted files in the Recycle Bin, and so forth. Select which files you want to delete.

5. Click OK to begin deleting.

You can safely have Disk Cleanup delete all the listed files *except* for the setup log, content indexer, and Office setup files, which are often needed by the Windows operating system.

Deleting Files Manually

Of course, you can always delete unwanted files manually. You do this by opening the My Documents or Documents, navigating to the files you want to delete, and then pressing the Del key on your keyboard. This moves the selected files to the Recycle Bin, so don't forget to empty the Recycle Bin to formally free up that disk space—which we discuss next.

Caution

If you're using Windows Vista, the User Account Control (UAC) function may prompt you for permission if you try to delete key files or run some utilities; just click Continue to proceed with the operation. To disable UAC, see Chapter 6, "Making Windows Go Faster."

Emptying the Recycle Bin

As noted previously, Windows allocates 5% to 10% of your hard disk space to holding deleted files in the Recycle Bin. When you've deleted enough files to exceed this limit, the oldest files in the Recycle Bin are automatically and permanently deleted from your hard disk. That doesn't help you if you need an extra 10 to 20GB of free disk space, however. In this instance, you'll want to manually empty the Recycle Bin to thus free up some of that valuable hard disk space.

To empty the Recycle Bin, all you have to do is double-click the Recycle Bin icon on your desktop. Doing so opens the Recycle Bin folder, shown in Figure 4.3. Now click the Empty the Recycle Bin button. When the Delete Multiple Items dialog box appears, click Yes to completely erase the files.

Archiving Little-Used Files

To help speed up your PC, you may want to remove some of your data files from your main hard drive but not necessarily get rid of them forever. What we're talking about here is *archiving* old files on another medium—copying them to an external hard drive, USB flash drive, CD-ROM, or data DVD. This is something my wife does every year with her digital photos. Each January, she copies the previous year's photos to a series of data CDs, and then stores them in a secure location. The photos are there (on CD) if she needs to access them, but they're not taking up valuable hard disk space on her PC.

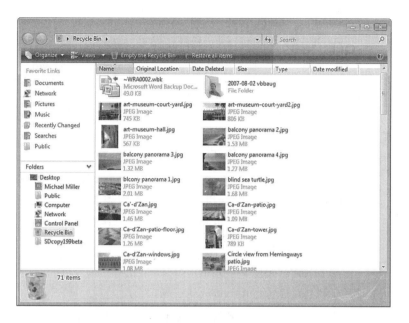

FIGURE 4.3

Empting the contents of the Recycle Bin in Windows Vista.

This process is as simple as inserting or attaching the backup device or medium, opening the My Documents or Documents folder, and then moving the selected files to the backup medium. This can be done using cut and paste, the Windows Move command, or by copying the files and then deleting them from their old locations. In any case, you end up with the selected files on the external device or disc, and lots of space freed up on your main hard disk.

Uninstalling Unwanted Programs

Finally, if you have one or more programs that you no longer want or use, you can free up valuable hard disk space by uninstalling those programs from your system. How you do this depends on whether you're using Windows XP or Windows Vista.

To remove a program from your PC in Windows XP, follow these steps:

1. Click the Start button and select Control Panel.

2. When the Control Panel opens, select Add or Remove Programs.

3. When the Add or Remove Programs dialog box appears, click the Change or Remove Programs button.

4. The next screen displays a list of all the currently installed programs on your PC. Select the program's name from the Currently Installed Programs list, and then click either the Change/Remove or Remove button.

5. If prompted, confirm that you want to continue to uninstall the application. Answer any other prompts that appear onscreen; then the uninstall process will start.

6. After the uninstall routine is complete, click the Close button to close the Add or Remove Programs utility.

 Note

Some programs might require you to insert the original installation disks or CD to perform the uninstall.

 Caution

In some instances, the add/remove utility may not be able to completely remove all aspects of a program. If you get an error message at the end of the uninstall process, you may need to manually delete any files remaining in the program folder on your hard drive.

To remove a program from your PC in Windows Vista, follow these steps:

1. Click the Start button and select Control Panel.

2. When the Control Panel opens, select Uninstall a Program (in the Programs section).

3. Windows displays a list of installed programs, as shown in Figure 4.4. Select the program you want to uninstall from this list.

4. Click the Uninstall button.

5. If prompted, confirm that you want to continue to uninstall the application. Answer any other prompts that appear onscreen; then the uninstall process will start.

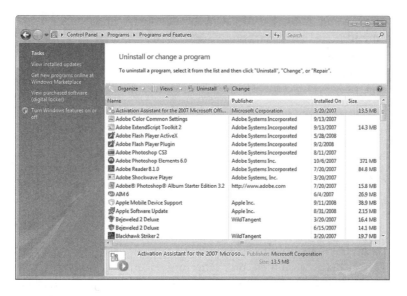

FIGURE 4.4

Deleting a program from your system in Windows Vista.

Removing Unwanted Programs and Processes from Your Computer's Memory

Now let's talk about the other way that too many software programs can slow down your system—by using up valuable and limited system memory. That's right, the more programs loaded into memory, the slower your system will run. The goal, therefore, is to remove all but the most essential programs from memory, thus speeding up your system's performance.

How Too Many Programs in Memory Slow Down Your PC

Your computer uses a form of chip-based electronic memory, called *random access memory* (RAM) to temporarily store program instructions, open files, and other data while it's being used. The more memory your computer has, the faster your applications will run—and the more applications (and larger files) you can have open at one time.

Depending on the age of your computer, it might have anywhere from 256MB to 4GB of memory. If you want to speed up your system's performance, you need as much memory installed in your system as it can accept—or that you can afford. I'd say that 512MB is the bare minimum necessary to run a Windows XP-based system, with 1GB the floor if you're running Windows Vista. Obviously, the more memory you have installed, the faster your system will run.

 Note

RAM is measured in terms of *bytes*. One byte is equal to approximately one character in a word processing document. A unit equaling approximately one thousand bytes (1,024, to be exact) is called a *kilobyte* (KB), and a unit of approximately one thousand (1,024) kilobytes is called a *megabyte* (MB). A thousand megabytes is a *gigabyte* (GB).

The more programs you have running (and the more documents you have open), the slower your computer will run. That's because all these programs and documents (and other system operating instructions) are stored in your system's RAM. Too many programs in not enough memory equals tepid performance.

You can easily demonstrate this yourself. Open a Word document, an Excel spreadsheet, a PowerPoint presentation, and a web page in Internet Explorer. Now open another Word document, another Excel spreadsheet, another PowerPoint presentation, and another web page. Now do this all again—and again. At some point you'll notice your system start slowing down; it will take longer to open the next window, longer for your screen to refresh, longer for a simple mouse click to have some affect. Open enough windows and your system will go beyond sluggish to frozen. That's what happens when you have too many programs loaded into your system's limited memory.

Discovering Programs That Load Automatically—Without Your Awareness

A simple way to speed up memory-related slowness is to not run so many programs at the same time. If you're web browsing, close your Word documents. If you're editing a digital photograph, close your web browser and email program. Only open those programs and documents that you're working on at this instant.

That said, there are probably some programs running on your computer that you're not aware of, and have little control over. These programs load automatically, without your explicit approval, whenever you turn on your computer and launch Windows. Once loaded, these programs stay in system memory—taking up valuable memory space and helping to slow down your system performance.

What kinds of programs are we talking about?

First, it's important to know that when Windows first launches, it has to load all the system files and processes necessary for the operating system to run. These include all the bits and pieces of the operating environment, as well as device drivers, background utilities, and the like. Dozens of these processes launch on startup, all are specified in the Windows Registry, and all are absolutely necessary for Windows to do its thing.

But here's the thing: Certain software programs are also loaded when Windows starts. To determine which programs to load on startup, Windows looks both in the Windows Registry and in the Startup folder.

Most users are surprised to find out just how much stuff is running in the background. You can view all the open processes on your system from the Windows Task Manager. Just right-click the Windows taskbar and select Task Manager. When the Task Manager opens, click the Processes tab.

As you can see in Figure 4.5, the Task Manager lists all the open processes along with how much memory is used for each process. As one example, my system has the Google Update program (GoogleUpdate.exe) running in the background; this is a minor utility that Google uses to check for updated versions of its software applications. This utility loads automatically without asking my permission and takes up 536KB of memory space, whether I ever use the program or not. This does not thrill me.

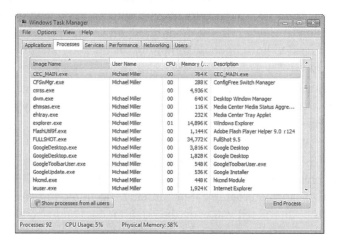

FIGURE 4.5

Viewing open processes with Windows Task Manager.

Most of these startup programs and processes are like Google Update, programs that think they need to be running all the time, *just in case* you ever decide to use them. On any given system, you're apt to find utilities of all shapes and sizes preloaded into system memory—utilities that check for program updates, help detect and download photos from attached drives and devices, preload bits of larger programs (to help those programs launch faster if you decide to run them), run sidebars and toolbars and widgets, you name it. You'll also find instant messaging programs preloaded into memory, along with utilities that manage various system operations.

Which Startup Programs Should You Delete?

Do you need all of these programs and utilities running the background every time you turn on your PC? Of course not. The more of this junk that's in memory—sitting there totally unused, in most instances—the less memory is available for running the programs you do use. It's an inefficient use of system resources, and one of the most common causes for sluggish PC performance.

The challenge, of course, is identifying which programs you can safely delete and which you need to load automatically. In general, you want to keep all programs associated with Windows itself, as well as those programs that you actually use and need to be running all the time. (For example, if you use Adobe Photoshop Elements to download photos from your camera to your hard disk and do so often, it's okay to automatically load the Adobe photo downloader utility.) On the other hand, any program that you don't use or don't need to have hanging around in the background can be removed from the startup list.

But when you look at a list of autoloading programs, what you typically see are obscure filenames. It's tough to figure out what exactly each filename means—what program it refers to, whether that program is good or bad or necessary or not, whether it's something you want to keep or not.

To help you determine what each of your startup files does, turn to one of several online databases of startup programs. These websites list tens of thousands of startup programs that you may encounter. Just enter the filename, and the site will tell you what the program does and whether it's likely to be a keeper or not.

Here are just a few of these startup program databases on the Web:

- AnswersThatWork Task List Programs (www.answersthatwork.com/Tasklist_pages/tasklist.htm)
- Application Database (www.greatis.com/appdata/)
- Bleepingcomputer.com Startup List (www.bleepingcomputer.com/startups/)
- Sysinfo.org Startup Applications List (www.sysinfo.org/startuplist.php)
- TechSpot Startup List (www.techspot.com/startup/)

How to Get Rid of Autoloading Programs

So now you know: Many software programs have the audacity to think that you want them to run whenever you start up your PC. So they configure themselves to launch whenever Windows launches—whether or not you want them to.

If you want to *stop* a program from launching automatically when Windows starts, you have to find out from *where* it is being launched. You see, some startup programs launch from the Windows Startup folder, others from the Windows Registry—both places that Windows works through when it first starts up.

Deleting Startup Programs from the Startup Folder

The first place to check for these autoloading programs is the Windows Startup folder. Click the Start button, and then select All Programs, Startup. Any program or utility listed here will launch when Windows starts. (Figure 4.6 shows the contents in a typical Startup folder.)

To delete a program from the Startup folder, just right-click it and select Delete from the pop-up menu.

 Note

Deleting a program from the Startup folder doesn't delete the program itself from your hard drive—it just removes it from the Startup folder and keeps it from loading automatically.

FIGURE 4.6
Viewing the contents of the Windows Startup folder.

Deleting Startup Programs from the Registry

If the offending program isn't in the Startup folder, it's probably being loaded via a setting in the Windows Registry. Several keys in the Registry can contain autoload instructions.

You can view and edit settings in the Registry using the Registry Editor, which we discuss in Chapter 7. You start the Registry Editor by accessing the Windows Run command and entering **regedit**. Once open, you navigate the Registry by *key*, each of which represents a particular setting.

The Registry keys most likely to contain autoload instructions include the following:

- HKEY_LOCAL_MACHINE\ SOFTWARE\Microsoft\Windows\ CurrentVersion\RUN
- HKEY_USERS\DEFAULT\ SOFTWARE\Microsoft\Windows\ CurrentVersion\RUN

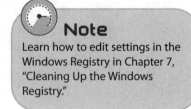

Note
Learn how to edit settings in the Windows Registry in Chapter 7, "Cleaning Up the Windows Registry."

- HKEY_CURRENT_USER\
SOFTWARE\Microsoft\Windows\
CurrentVersion\RUN

All programs you find listed in these keys, like those shown in Figure 4.7, are automatically loaded by Windows during the startup process. To delete a program, just highlight it and press the Del key. Once the program is deleted from the appropriate Registry key, it will no longer launch on startup.

Caution

Make sure you really want to delete an autoload program from the Registry before you press the Del key. Once the setting is deleted, it can't be recovered. Delete the wrong setting and you could do irreparable harm to your system!

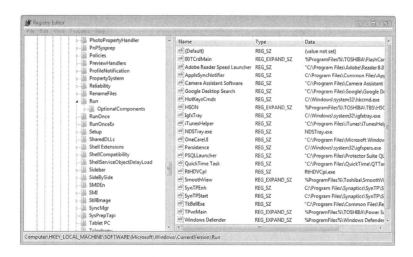

FIGURE 4.7
Viewing startup programs in the Windows Registry.

Deleting Startup Programs with the System Configuration Utility

Another way to lighten your system's load is to delete unwanted startup programs with the Windows System Configuration utility. This utility is typically used to troubleshoot your system by duplicating the procedures used by Microsoft's tech support staff when they try to diagnose system configuration problems. The System Configuration utility leads you through a series of steps that, one by one, disable various components of your system on startup, until you're able to isolate the item that's causing your specific problem. It can also be used to stop any number of programs and processes from loading at system startup.

To open the System Configuration utility, select Start, Accessories, Run. When the Run dialog box appears, enter **msconfig** and click OK. (In Windows Vista, you can more easily enter **msconfig** into the Start menu's search box.) When the System Configuration utility window appears, select the Startup tab.

As you can see in Figure 4.8, the Startup tab lists all those programs and processes that load when Windows launches, along with their location (Registry key or Startup folder). To stop a program or process from loading on startup, simply uncheck that item in the list. Click OK and your changes will be applied the next time you restart Windows.

Caution

Some spyware and virus programs may show up in the Startup tab with names that are very close to legitimate programs. Consult one of the startup databases mentioned previously to correctly identify all programs you want to delete.

Note

When you next reboot your PC, you'll see a message warning that the System Configuration utility has been changed. Check the "Do Not Show This Again" option if you don't want to see this message every time you reboot.

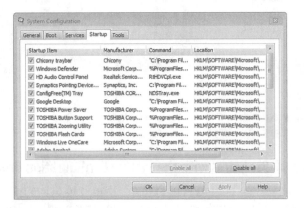

FIGURE 4.8

Managing startup programs with the System Configuration utility.

Deleting Startup Programs with Windows Defender

Let's be honest; deleting startup programs with Registry Editor or the System Configuration utility is a trifle techno-wonky, offputting to non-technical users. A more user-friendly method is afforded by Windows Defender, Microsoft's antispyware program.

Note

Windows Defender is included free with Windows Vista and available for free download for Windows XP users at www.microsoft.com/windows/products/winfamily/defender/.

When you launch Windows Defender, click the Tools button to display the Tools and Settings screen, and then click the Software Explorer option. The Software Explorer screen will display, as shown in Figure 4.9. As you can see, each startup program is listed on the left side of the screen, with information about the currently selected program on the right side.

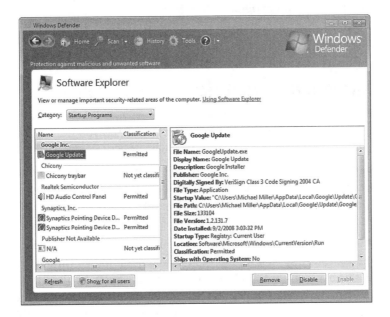

FIGURE 4.9

Managing startup programs with Windows Defender's Software Explorer tool.

What I like about using Windows Defender, as opposed to editing the Registry or using the System Configuration utility, is that you can actually read a little about each program or process before you decide whether to delete it. With the other methods, all you see is a filename, and you don't have any idea what that file actually is or does. With Windows Defender, you can make a more informed decision by learning more about each file.

In general, you want to keep those processes that ship with Windows itself, and question all other autoloading programs. To keep a program from loading automatically, select it in the list on the left, and then click the Disable button. (You can also delete that program from your system by clicking the Remove button, but that's an extreme option best suited for identified spyware or virus programs.)

Tip

Windows Defender assigns a classification to each startup item. If Defender says a program is Permitted, that means that it isn't spyware and is okay to run—although you still might not want it to load automatically.

Note

Defender won't let you disable or remove necessary Windows system utilities.

Removing Programs That Slow Down Your PC

It's not always bundleware that slows down your PC. Some legitimate programs can tax even a well-equipped system, and you may be better off deleting them than trying to work with them.

Identifying these programs takes a bit of detective work. You often don't know what's causing a slowdown until you happen to shut down an offending program and notice that your system is suddenly a bit livelier. It's definitely a trial-and-error process.

As an example, I was battling performance problems (slowdowns and freezes) on my relatively new laptop PC. I followed all of my own advice that I present in this book and still had intermittent sluggishness. While I was in the process of tearing out what hair I had left, it suddenly struck me that there might be *something* running in the background that was causing my problems. I worked through all my background programs one by one until I stumbled on the culprit—my beloved Google Desktop.

Now, Google Desktop does a lot of things, but what I use it for is to index and search the files on my computer's hard disk. To index all these files, it constantly runs in the background finding and sorting what's there. As I discovered, it's this background indexing that was causing my system to slow down.

When I removed Google Desktop from the auto startup list, my system suddenly began to act normal again.

So, as far as I'm concerned, it's adios, Google Desktop!

Another common source of performance problems is, believe it or not, the category of anti-virus programs. I've had particularly bad luck with Symantec's Norton products; over the years, I've found that if I'm experiencing slowdowns and crashes on a PC that's running Norton Anti-Virus, removing Norton more often than not cures my problems. I think it's a matter of the program being overly aggressive and sticking its nose into processes that it shouldn't; as it's checking every last thing a computer does to root out viruses, it keeps those same processes from functioning normally. I can't tell you how many people I've helped with the simple recommendation to remove Norton!

Tip

Let me reiterate. If you have a Norton anti-virus or security product on your computer and you're experience sluggish performance and crashes, *delete the Norton software.* It's likely that this will solve your problems.

Not that Norton is the only culprit in this category. I've also had occasional problems over the years with Symantec's chief competitor, McAfee. For what it's worth, I've had zero problems with Microsoft's Live OneCare suite, nor with the AVG free anti-virus program. These are the two anti-virus programs that I tend to recommend.

In any case, don't assume that just because a program comes from a trusted source doesn't mean that it can't cause problems. Any given program can interact negatively with any other given program, or with a random device driver on your system. It really is a matter of trial and error to discover which program is causing your problems, and then to remove that program from your system—no matter how much you might like that program, otherwise.

Speeding Up Microsoft Outlook

There's one particular program I want to mention, as it's widely used in both the office and home computing worlds. That program is Microsoft Outlook, the email and calendar program included as part of Microsoft Office—and it really can slow down your system.

Here's the deal. All of the email messages in your inbox, your contacts, your appointments, and the like are stored in a single file, typically called OUTLOOK.PST. If this file somehow gets damaged, it can slow down Outlook itself—and, while Outlook is piddling along, your entire system.

Fortunately, Microsoft includes a PST repair utility as part of Outlook—although it's kind of hidden. You run this utility to repair your PST file and, more often than not, speed up the performance of both Outlook and your entire system.

Here's what you need to do; the location of things are slightly different in Outlook 2003 and Outlook 2007:

Note

Outlook can still run with a damaged PST file, it just is more prone to performance issues. Sometimes you may receive an error message when you launch Outlook, saying that the program needs to be checked for problems, but more often than not the only sign of a damaged PST file is sluggish performance.

1. Close Microsoft Outlook.

2. Use My Computer or the Computer folder to browse to the following folder: In Outlook 2007, the folder is C:**Program Files\Microsoft Office\Office12**. In Outlook 2003, the folder is either C:**Program Files\Common Files\System\Mapi\1033** or C:**Program Files\Common Files\System\MSMAPI\1033**.

3. Find and double-click the file **scanpst.exe**; this launches the Outlook Inbox Repair program, shown in Figure 4.10.

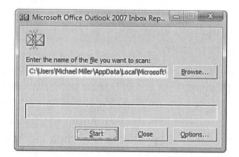

FIGURE 4.10

Repairing your Outlook inbox with the Outlook Inbox Repair tool.

4. Click the Browse button to locate your Outlook inbox file. In Windows Vista, this is probably C:**Users***Username***\AppData\Local\ Microsoft\Outlook\Outlook.pst**. In Windows XP, it's probably C:**Documents and Settings***Username***\Local Settings\Application Data\Microsoft\Outlook\Outlook.pst**.

5. Click the Start button to begin the scan of your PST file. (Depending on the speed of your system, this scan could take anywhere from 5 minutes to a half hour.)

6. At the end of the scan, the utility will tell you if your file contains errors. Assuming this is the case, click the Repair button.

Tip

You can verify the location of your PST file from within Microsoft Outlook. Select Tools, Options to open the Options dialog box; select the Mail Setup tab then click the Data Files button. When the Account Settings dialog box appears, select the Data Files tab and note the location for your Personal Folders.

The Outlook Inbox Repair utility now makes a backup copy of your PST file and then repairs the file itself. You'll see a Repair Complete dialog box when your PST file is fixed—and should experience a noticeable speed improvement when you next open Outlook itself.

The Bottom Line

Two of the most common causes of sluggish PC performance are too many files on your hard drive and too many programs loaded into system memory. Here's the bottom line:

- Because your computer uses hard disk space as virtual memory to supplement the normal system memory, too many files on your hard disk can leave too little virtual memory space, thus slowing down your system.

- To speed up your system, delete all unwanted or unnecessary programs and data files from your computer's hard disk.

- Any program that's running on your PC uses valuable system memory. The more programs loaded into memory—including those that load automatically on startup—the slower your system will run.

- To speed up your system, configure your computer's startup routine to launch only those programs that are absolutely necessary.

- You may also need to remove legitimate programs that interfere with your system's operation, such as some anti-virus programs.

- Microsoft Outlook can also slow down your system if it has a damaged inbox file; use the Outlook Inbox Repair tool to repair your inbox and speed up system performance.

4

5

Optimizing Your Hard Disk

Your hard disk is a critical component of your computer system. Not only does the hard disk store all your program and document files, it also stores the Windows Registry (with all of Windows' configuration settings) and the Windows operating system itself. As you've learned, it also serves as temporary virtual memory when what you need to do exceeds the capacity of your normal system memory.

Therefore, when your hard disk slows down, your entire PC slows down. That's because your computer has to access your hard drive to retrieve those programs, documents, and configuration settings; we're talking dozens of short accesses every minute. So the longer it takes for each hard drive access, even if we're just talking milliseconds per access, the more your computer slows down.

It's obvious, then, that anything you can do to speed up the performance of your hard drive makes your entire system go faster, as well. With that in mind, let's look at some quick and simple ways you can speed things up by optimizing the performance of your computer's hard disk drive.

Defragmenting Your Hard Disk

When your hard drive starts to slow down, one of the most common culprits is a fragmented hard disk. That sounds worse than it is, although disk fragmentation can result in significant performance slowdowns.

Understanding Disk Fragmentation

Disk fragmentation occurs whenever Windows writes files to your hard drive. That's because files aren't saved as single entities. They're broken into smaller chunks for easier handling, and each of these chunks is stored on a separate sector of your hard disk. Because each sector holds exactly 512 bytes of data, a large file could be stored in hundreds or even thousands of separate sectors— and not all together.

When a hard disk is fresh from the factory, all the sectors for a single file can be stored contiguously—that is, all in a row. This makes it easy for the read/write head of the hard disk to access the complete file. But as more files are stored to the hard disk, and as older files are erased, contiguous hard disk space might not be available when saving a new file.

When this happens, the chunks of the file are stored in whatever sectors are available—even if those sectors are widely separated on the hard disk. When a file is fragmented in this fashion, it takes more time for the hard disk's read/write head to access each of the individual chunks and thus assemble the file for use.

It's kind of like taking the pieces of a jigsaw puzzle and storing them in different boxes along with pieces from other puzzles. The more dispersed the pieces are, the longer it takes to put the puzzle together.

So if you notice your system takes longer and longer to open and close files or run applications, it's because these file fragments are spread all over the place—in other words, your hard disk is overly fragmented. You fix this problem when you put all the pieces of the puzzle back in the right boxes, which you do by *defragmenting* your hard disk.

How Disk Defragmenting Works

To improve the performance of your hard disk—that is, to reduce how long it takes to access a file—defragment the disk. This is accomplished by using the Disk Defragmenter utility built in to both Windows XP and Vista.

The Disk Defragmenter rearranges the
chunks of data on your hard disk so that
the data for a single file are stored in contiguous sectors—that is, all together in a
row. To do this, the Disk Defragmenter has
to temporarily store the data from noncon-
tiguous sectors in system memory, erase
those sectors to make room for new data,
and then rewrite the stored data into new,
contiguous sectors.

Tip

Windows' Disk Defragmenter also
rearranges where certain files are
stored on the hard disk. Frequently used files are rewritten
to the first sectors on the disk,
where they can be accessed
more quickly during normal use.

And this is how defragmenting your hard disk speeds up your PC. When necessary data is stored all together, it can be accessed much faster than if your
system has to search all over your hard drive for all the assorted pieces and
parts of the file. For an immediate speed boost, you can't beat a simple disk
defragmentation!

Using the Disk Defragmenter

You use Windows' Disk Defragmenter utility to defragment your PC's hard
drive. In Windows Vista, Disk Defragmenter runs in the background, automatically defragging your hard disk whenever your computer is turned on (and
nothing else is going on). In Windows XP, however, you have to run Disk
Defragmenter manually—which you should do at least once a month. (You
can also run the utility manually in Windows Vista, if you like.)

To run Disk Defragmenter manually, follow these steps:

1. Click the Start button and select All Programs, Accessories, System
   Tools, Disk Defragmenter.

2. If you're running Windows XP, you see the Disk Defragmenter window
   shown in Figure 5.1. Select your hard disk (typically drive C:) from the
   list in the top half of the window. You can then click the Analyze button to determine whether you need to defragment your hard drive, or
   just click the Defragment button to start the defragmenting process.

3. In Windows Vista, you see the Disk Defragmenter window shown in
   Figure 5.2. To defragment your hard disk now, click the Defragment
   Now button.

5

FIGURE 5.1

Using Disk Defragmenter in Windows XP.

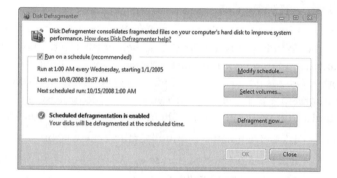

FIGURE 5.2

Using Disk Defragmenter in Windows Vista.

Defragmenting your drive can take awhile, especially if you have a large hard drive or your drive is really fragmented. So, you might want to start the utility and let it run over night or while you're at lunch. But when it's done, you should notice that your PC feels less sluggish.

 Caution

You should close all applications—including your screensaver—and stop working on your system while Disk Defragmenter is running.

Checking Your Hard Disk for Errors

Any time you run an application, move or delete a file, or accidentally turn the power off while the system is running, you run the risk of introducing errors to your hard disk. These errors can make it harder to open files, slow down your hard disk, or cause your system to freeze when you open or save a file or an application.

Fortunately, you can find and fix most of these errors directly from within Windows. All you have to do is run the built-in ScanDisk utility. This simple utility looks for and tries to fix errors on your hard drive—and thus speed up system performance in the process.

How ScanDisk Works

ScanDisk works like other similar "disk fix" utilities. In essence, it performs multiple tests of your hard drive's integrity, and either points out or tries to fix any problems found.

ScanDisk starts by reading the data on your hard drive, sector by sector. If there's a sector that it has trouble reading, ScanDisk attempts to move the data elsewhere, then marks that cluster as bad. Once an area is marked bad, Windows sidesteps it in the future—thus "fixing" your hard drive by disallowing access to bad sectors.

Using ScanDisk to Speed Up Your PC

To use ScanDisk, follow these steps:

1. Click the Start button and select either Computer (Windows Vista) or My Computer (Windows XP).

2. From within Computer or My Computer, right-click the icon for the drive you want to scan, and then select the Properties option from the pop-up menu.

3. When the Properties dialog box appears, select the Tools tab.

4. Click the Check Now button in the Error-Checking section to display the Check Disk dialog box, shown in Figure 5.3.

5. Check both the options (Automatically Fix File System Errors and Scan for and Attempt Recovery of Bad Sectors).

6. Click Start.

5

FIGURE 5.3

Use ScanDisk to check your hard disk for errors.

Windows now scans your hard disk and attempts to fix any errors it encounters. If errors are found (and fixed), your PC's performance should be enhanced.

Using Other Disk-Optimization Tools

Disk Defragmenter and ScanDisk are both built in to Windows and both are quite easy for anyone to use. But they're not the only hard disk utilities available today. Several other companies offer tools to help you optimize your hard drive's performance.

We'll look at the most popular of these tools next.

Diskeeper

Diskeeper is an automatic disk defragmenter that far exceeds Windows' Disk Defragmenter utility. What makes Diskeeper unique is its InvisiTracking technology, which enables it to defragment your hard disk in real time. This ensures that your hard drive never becomes overly fragmented.

Several different versions of Diskeeper are available, with the Home version selling for $29.95. More information can be found at www.diskeeper.com.

Fix-It Utilities Professional

Fix-It Utilities Professional is a collection of more than 40 different utilities designed to speed up your PC's performance. It uses a wizard-based interface to perform various system-optimization routines.

The suite includes utilities for hard drive optimization and repair, disk defragmentation, startup optimization, disaster recovery, virus and spyware protection, file management, file recovery, secure file deletion, and more. It sells for $49.95. More information is available at www.avanquest.com.

Norton SystemWorks

Symantec's Norton SystemWorks, or what used to be called Norton Utilities, is granddaddy of system utility programs. SystemWorks is a collection of utilities, each designed to monitor or repair a specific area of system performance.

SystemWorks is available in three editions: Basic ($49.99), Standard ($69.99), and Premier ($99.99). The Basic edition includes the following optimization utilities:

- CheckIt Diagnostics, which diagnoses hardware problems and helps to optimize memory use
- Norton Cleanup, which deletes unused programs and files from your hard drive
- Norton Disk Doctor, which detects and repairs various hard drive problems
- Norton Speed Disk, which defragments and reorganizes your hard disk
- Norton Startup Manager, which prevents the loading of unwanted applications on startup
- Norton WinDoctor, which cleans and repairs the Windows Registry
- Norton WipeInfo, which lets you permanently delete folders and files from your hard drive
- One-Button Checkup, which performs a combination of system scans at the touch of a single button
- Performance Test, which helps you benchmark the speed of your PC
- Process Viewer, which displays your system's running processes and services
- System Optimizer, which enables you to customize hundreds of Windows settings

The Standard edition includes additional performance-based utilities, and the Premier edition adds antivirus and antispyware protection. Learn more at www.symantec.com/norton/.

5

PC Tools Disk Suite

PC Tools Disk Suite is, as the name implies, a suite of disk management utilities. Included are utilities for file deletion/disk cleanup, disk defragmentation, Windows optimization, hard disk backup and restore, disk partitioning, and (most important) hard disk diagnostics and repair. The hard disk repair feature, shown in Figure 5.4, checks file system structure, scans the disk surface to find and repair bad sectors and disk errors, and displays various information about the status of the hard drive.

FIGURE 5.4
Scanning a hard disk with PC Tools Disk Suite.

PC Tools Disk Suite sells for $39.95. More information is available at www.pctools.com/disk-suite/.

PerfectDisk

PerfectDisk is another freestanding disk defragmenter utility. This utility not only defragments your hard disk but also uses SMARTPlacement technology to place program files on your hard drive based on prior usage patterns. Several different versions of the utility are available; the lowest-priced Professional version sells for $39.99. More information can be found at www.raxco.com.

System Mechanic

System Mechanic is a suite of utilities you can use to speed up and repair your computer system. It includes utilities for hard drive repair, Registry cleaning and repair, disk defragmenting, memory defragmenting, disk/file cleanup, secure file deletion, Windows configuration, hard drive diagnostics, and more.

System Mechanic is available on a subscription basis for $49.95/year. Learn more at www.iolo.com/system-mechanic/standard/.

Tip

In addition to these commercial utilities, many freeware and shareware utilities can help you optimize your system's hard disk. In fact, the number of available software tools is too numerous to mention them all here. I recommend you go to the Tucows download site (www.tucows.com) and check out what's available—many of which are completely free!

WinUtilities

WinUtilities is a collection of tools for optimizing and speeding up your system's performance. It includes utilities for disk/file cleaning, Registry cleaning, Registry backup and restore, startup cleaning, secure file deletion, memory optimization, Windows process/services management, and Windows setting management.

The WinUtilities suite sells for $49.99. Find out more at www.xp-tools.com/winutilities/.

Note

Sometimes even a properly running hard disk can be slow. This is because different hard disks rotate at different speeds. Most hard disks today rotate at 5400 revolutions per minute (RPM), although some older PCs (and even newer notebooks) move at a pokey 4200 RPM. For faster performance, upgrade to a 7200 RPM hard disk—as discussed in Chapter 11, "Adding More Disk Space."

The Bottom Line

The more efficient your hard disk runs, the faster your PC. Here's the bottom line:

- A fragmented hard disk takes longer to access programs and files. You defragment your hard drive using Windows' Disk Defragmenter utility.

- Errors on a hard drive can slow down or even crash your system. You can find and repair hard disk errors with Windows' ScanDisk utility.

- Utilities from other companies can also help you defragment and optimize your hard disk, as well as improve system performance in other ways.

Making Windows Go Faster

Sometimes slow system performance is due to an outside factor, such as a virus or spyware infection. Sometimes it's due to the programs you install and run on your system, or even to a fragmented hard disk. But sometimes sluggish operation is due to the operating system itself—Microsoft Windows.

It doesn't matter whether you're running the older Windows XP or the newer Windows Vista, Windows is a big piece of software that can put huge strains on your system hardware, making even fast PCs run a little slow. Fortunately, you can do some things to speed up how Windows runs on your PC—which we examine in this chapter.

Speeding Up Windows (XP and Vista)

Obviously, a lot of the advice presented elsewhere in the book also affects Windows' overall performance. For example, removing all but the most essential startup programs (as discussed in Chapter 4, "Cleaning Out Unnecessary Programs"), will help Windows not only load faster but run smoother. Defragmenting your hard disk (which we addressed in Chapter 5, "Optimizing Your Hard Disk") also improves Windows' performance.

That said, you can do some specific things to make Windows run faster. We'll start by examining speedups that work for both Windows XP and Windows Vista, and then move on to XP- and Vista-specific speedups in the following sections.

Install the Latest Drivers

Here's a universal speedup for all Windows-based computers. Some devices get speedier over time because their manufacturers come up with upgraded versions of their device drivers. If you want a quick system speedup, check the manufacturers' websites for the latest versions of their hardware drivers. Downloading an updated driver can make that device run significantly faster on your system!

Delete Unused Fonts

Windows includes a lot of built-in fonts, and even more fonts get installed by many of the software programs you use. Know, however, that Windows loads every single one of these fonts into memory. The more fonts you have installed, the more memory they take, and the slower your system will run.

Note

Many of these speedups start from the Windows Control panel—which, by default, operates differently in Windows XP and Windows Vista. A better approach is to display the XP or Vista Control Panel in Classic view, which provides direct access to most operations. The following instructions assume the Control Panel's Classic view.

Tip

You may think that you're safe by letting Windows Update, the auto update utility built into Windows, automatically download new drivers to your system—but you're not. Windows Update doesn't always identify the latest drivers, nor the most functional drivers available. It's a much better practice to download specific drivers from the device manufacturer's website, where you'll find the latest and greatest drivers available.

6

To speed up system performance, especially on PC's with small amounts of RAM, you should delete those fonts you don't use. This will free up memory for more important tasks.

To delete unused fonts from your system, follow these steps:

1. Click the Start menu and select Control Panel.

2. When the Control Panel opens, double-click Fonts.

3. When the Fonts window opens, as shown in Figure 6.1, select the fonts you want to remove, and then press the Del key on your keyboard.

 Caution

Don't go overboard when deleting fonts; many fonts are used by specific documents and templates in various programs. In addition, some fonts are system fonts, used by Windows and other programs to display menu bars, dialog boxes and the like. So make sure a font truly is unused before you delete it! (Alternately, copy any fonts you want to delete to another folder before you delete them, so that you can copy them back if you need them in the future.)

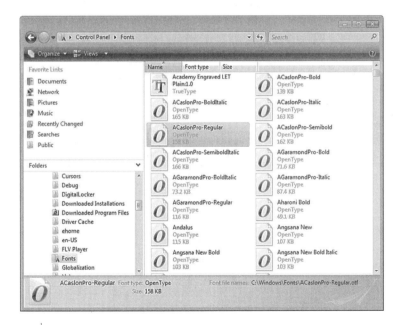

FIGURE 6.1

Deleting fonts in Windows Vista.

The more fonts you delete, the faster your system will run. Bye-bye fonts!

Turn Off System Sounds

Believe it or not, those obnoxious beeps and boops your computer makes for various system operations can actually affect your system's performance—especially during the startup and shutdown operations. You can attain a slight performance gain by turning off Windows' system sounds.

To do this, follow these steps:

1. Click the Start button and select Control Panel.

2. When the Control Panel opens, double-click Sound (in Windows Vista) or Sounds and Audio Devices (Windows XP).

3. When the Sound or Sounds and Audio Devices dialog box opens, select the Sounds tab, as shown in Figure 6.2.

4. Pull down the Sound Scheme list and select No Sounds.

5. Click OK.

That's it—no more sounds!

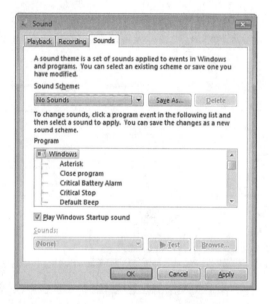

FIGURE 6.2

Turning off system sounds in Windows Vista.

Don't Look for Bootable Media on Startup

If you think your system takes too long to start up (and who doesn't?), here's a way to speed up that startup process. This tip is based on the fact that your computer looks for bootable media in any CD/DVD or floppy disk drives you have installed on your system. This is pretty much just a formality, as you almost always want to boot from your hard drive. If keep your system from looking in these extraneous drives, it will boot up slightly faster.

You make this change outside of Windows, during your computer's pre-Windows boot-up process. The change is actually made to your system's BIOS. Here's how to do it:

1. Reboot your system and wait for a blank screen with a little text on it; the text should tell you how to enter the BIOS or CMOS setup. (You may also need to consult your computer's instruction manual.)

2. Typically, you enter a particular key or key combination. Many computers require you to press the Del or F2 key, although this differs from machine to machine. Press the appropriate key on your computer keyboard.

3. Once you're in the BIOS setup, navigate to the Boot menu and select Boot Sequence.

4. You should now move your hard drive to the top position in this sequence or set it as the "first device."

5. Press the Esc key to record your settings and leave the BIOS setup routine.

> ### Caution
> After you make this change to your system's BIOS, you won't be able to boot from a CD/DVD or floppy disk, which you may need to do in an emergency. To boot from an external disk, you'll need to reverse this process by editing the BIOS and putting your CD/DVD or floppy drive as the "first device" in the boot order.

Optimize Windows' Display Settings

One of the quickest and easiest ways to make Windows run faster is to change several of its display settings. That's because it takes a bit of processing power to display all those fancy graphics onscreen. A plainer display uses fewer system resources, and makes your system run slightly faster.

What sort of resource-eating graphics effects are we talking about? How about effects such as animated windows, sliding menus, and the like—little things, visually, that take big power to create.

6

So if you want a quick visual speedup for your system, follow these steps:

1. Click the Start button and select Control Panel.

2. When the Control Panel opens, double-click System.

3. In Windows XP, this should open the System Properties dialog box, but not so in Windows Vista. In Vista, you need to click the Advanced System Settings link to proceed.

4. When the System Properties dialog box appears, click the Advanced tab, and then click the Settings button in the Performance section.

5. When the Performance Options dialog box appears, select the Visual Effect tab, shown in Figure 6.3.

FIGURE 6.3

Disabling Windows' visual effects.

At this point, the easy option is to check the Adjust for Best Performance option. Doing so disables many of the fancy visual effects and speeds up your system. You do, however, lose the cool effects, but that's the compromise you make for performance.

Alternatively, you can pick and choose which visual effects your system displays (and know that XP has slightly different effects than does Vista). Every one of the effects uses up a certain amount of processing power. The more you leave enabled, the slower your system will run. So to speed up your system incrementally, check only those visual effects that you think are necessary to enhance your computing experience. The more effects you disable, the faster your computer will run.

Reconfigure Processor Priority

Windows' Performance Options dialog box has a second tab that enables even more fine-tuning of your system performance. The Advanced tab, shown in Figure 6.4, presents another option that can speed up your system.

FIGURE 6.4

Editing Windows Vista's advanced performance settings.

The Processor Scheduling section of this tab lets you control how much processor time Windows devotes to an individual program or process. Because your computer's microprocessor has a finite amount of processing power to divide between all the applications and processes that are constantly running, how that power is divided affects what runs faster—your applications or Windows' background processes.

To give the bulk of the processing power to the program running in the foreground, making it run faster, check the Programs option. To split the processing power evenly between all running programs and processes, check the Background Services option—which may make your currently running program appear to run slightly slower.

Eliminate Background Services

Windows XP and Vista, like all operating systems, have a continuous stream of services running in the background. These are process necessary for the running of the operating system or selected applications. Most of these services launch automatically when you start Windows, but not all are required for your system to run properly. You can speed up your system's performance by disabling unnecessary background services.

Tip

In Windows XP, the Performance Options Advanced tab includes an additional Memory Usage section that determines how Windows XP uses system memory. To devote more memory to currently running applications, check the Programs option. On a system without a lot of RAM, this will make your programs run faster. If your system has plenty of memory, however, check the System Cache option, which can speed up your entire system.

While you can disable background services from the System Configuration utility, this option doesn't provide a lot of information about each process, which makes disabling them a bit of a hit or miss proposition. A better approach utilizes Windows' Services console, a "hidden" utility that includes descriptions of all running services. Here's how to do it:

1. Click the Start button and select Run.

2. When the Run dialog box appears, enter **services.msc** and click OK.

3. When the Services console appears, click the Extended tab, shown in Figure 6.5. Doing so displays a list of all services on your system, along with information about each service (in the Description column). The Status column tells you whether the service is currently running ("Started"), while the Startup Type column tells you whether the services starts automatically with Windows or manually.

4. Right-click the service you want to disable from loading on startup and select Properties from the pop-up menu.

5. When the Properties dialog box appears, select the General tab, as shown in Figure 6.6.

FIGURE 6.5
Viewing background services in Windows Vista.

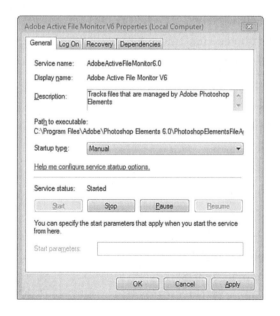

FIGURE 6.6
Disabling a service from loading automatically.

6. Pull down the Startup Type list and select Manual.

7. Click OK.

Note

When you set a service to Manual, it doesn't load on startup but still can be loaded if a particular operation or application requires it.

Obviously, you want to focus on the Automatic services; a Manual service does *not* load automatically on startup. Within the long list of Automatic services, however, how do you know which ones you need—and which you don't?

The simple answer is that you can disable any service that you don't use. For example, if you have a desktop PC (or a notebook that is not a tablet PC), you can for sure disable the Tablet PC Input service. That's an easy one, but you'll probably find more.

While each system is distinct, here's a short list of services that you probably don't need:

- Computer Browser
- DFS Replication
- Distributed Link Tracking Client
- IKE and AuthIP IP Keying Modules
- IP Helper
- IPsec Policy Agent
- KtmRm for Distributed Transaction Coordinator
- Offline Files
- Portable Media Serial Number
- Remote Registry
- Secondary Logon
- SSDP Discovery
- Tablet PC Input
- Terminal Services
- Windows Error Reporting

Caution

If you find that disabling a service causes something not to work on your system, return to the Services console and reenable it.

You may want to experiment with turning various services on and off. Note that not all of these services are available on all versions of the Windows operating system.

Disable File Indexing

Both Windows XP and Windows Vista include a feature that lets you search files on your hard drive. This search feature works by indexing all the files on your hard drive. In other words, Windows extracts information from all the files on your hard disk and creates a searchable keyword index. It's this index that Windows searches when you conduct a query from the Start menu.

Caution

If you disable file indexing, you won't be able to use Windows' built-in search feature to find files on your computer.

There are several problems with using Windows' search feature. First, it isn't that effective or efficient; it doesn't always find what you want, and takes a long time to do it. (Although, to be fair, Vista's search feature is much more effective than the crude one built in to Windows XP.) Second, your system performance really takes a hit while Windows is indexing your hard drive; it takes a lot of memory and processing power to scour all your files. And third, the index itself takes up valuable hard disk space.

Bottom line, using Windows' file indexing dramatically slows down your PC. You can gain a noticeable speed improvement by turning off this feature.

To turn off Windows' file indexing, follow these steps:

1. Click the Start button and select My Computer (Windows XP) or Computer (Windows Vista).

2. When My Computer or the Computer window opens, right-click the C: drive icon and select Properties.

3. When the Properties dialog box appears, select the General tab, shown in Figure 6.7.

4. In Windows XP, uncheck the Allow Indexing Service to Index This Disk for Fast File Searching option. In Windows Vista, uncheck the Index This Drive for Faster Searching option.

5. Click OK.

6. When the Confirm Attribute Changes dialog box appears, select the option to apply the changes to drive C: and all subfolders and files.

Caution

If Windows displays an Access Is Denied warning message, click the Ignore All button.

6

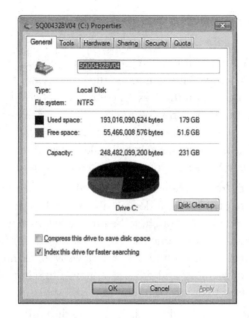

FIGURE 6.7
Turning off file indexing in Windows Vista.

Optimize Virtual Memory

As you recall, Windows uses your hard drive as virtual memory when regular memory fills up. This virtual memory space takes longer to access than does regular random access memory. With that in mind, there are ways you can tweak this virtual memory to improve system performance.

The first thing to do is assign a fixed size to the virtual memory pagefile. By default, Windows resizes the file as needed; unfortunately, this resizing takes time and resources. To create a fixed-size pagefile, follow these steps:

1. Click the Start button and select Control Panel.

2. When the Control Panel opens, double-click System.

3. In Windows XP, this should open the System Properties dialog box, but not so in Windows Vista. In Vista, you need to click the Advanced System Settings link to proceed.

4. From the System Properties dialog box, click the Advanced tab.

Note

Virtual memory space is sometimes called a *swap file, pagefile,* or *paging file.*

5. Click the Settings button in the Performance section.

6. When the Performance Options dialog box opens, select the Advanced tab.

7. Click the Change button in the Virtual Memory section.

8. When the Virtual Memory dialog box appears, as shown in Figure 6.8, uncheck the Automatically Manage Paging File Size for All Drive option.

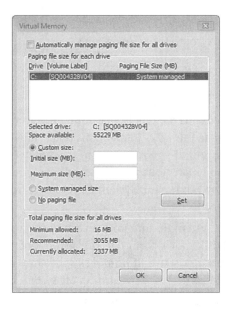

FIGURE 6.8

Managing the size of your system's virtual memory.

9. Select the drive that contains the pagefile, and then check the Custom Size option.

10. Enter a value into the Initial Size box equal to the amount of RAM you have installed on your system. For example, if your system has 2GB (2000MB) of memory, enter 2000 into this box.

11. Enter the same value into the Maximum Size box.

12. Click OK.

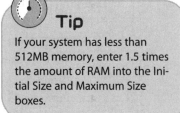

Tip

If your system has less than 512MB memory, enter 1.5 times the amount of RAM into the Initial Size and Maximum Size boxes.

Another way to optimize the performance of your system's virtual memory is to keep the pagefile on your hard drive defragmented. While there's no way to do this from within Windows, you can use Microsoft's PageDefrag utility for this task. You can download PageDefrag (for free) at technet.microsoft.com/ en-us/sysinternals/ bb897426.aspx. Follow the instructions there to fully defragment your system's pagefile.

Tip

You can place your system's pagefile on any drive (or partition within a drive) on your system. A good strategy for speeding up pagefile performance is to move the pagefile off your main hard drive (the one that holds Windows) onto another dedicated (and fast) hard disk.

Turn Off System Restore

This next speedup is *not* one I particularly recommend, because Windows' System Restore feature has tremendous potential value if you have future system problems. Still, if you're willing to risk not being able to restore a recalcitrant system to its previous working condition, you can speed up your PC's performance by not having System Restore take up valuable background system resources.

Not only does System Restore take up a bit of system memory, it also uses up a lot of hard disk space storing all the restore points it creates—up to 15% of your total hard disk space. If hard disk space and memory are at a premium, you can regain some speed by turning off System Restore.

To disable System Restore in Windows XP, follow these steps:

1. Click the Start button and select All Programs, Accessories, System Tools, System Restore.
2. When the System Restore window opens, select the System Restore tab.
3. Select the Turn Off System Restore on All Drives option.
4. Click OK.

Disabling System Restore in Windows Vista is slightly different. Follow these steps:

1. Click the Start button and select All Programs, Accessories, System Tools, System Restore.
2. When the System Restore window opens, click the Open System Protection link.

3. When the System Properties dialog box appears, select the System Protection tab.

4. Uncheck each of the disks listed in the Automatic Restore Points list.

5. Click OK.

Caution

Disable System Restore at your own peril. If System Restore is not running, you won't be able to restore your computer in the event of a system failure.

Speeding Up Windows XP

Although Windows XP and Windows Vista have many similarities (and thus some similar speedups, as you've just learned), some major differences exist between the two operating systems. To that end, let's examine some speedups specific to the older Windows XP operating system.

Reboot Often

Here's something not so good about Windows XP. The longer it stays running without rebooting or shutting down, the less memory you have available. And we all know what insufficient memory does—it slows down your system.

You see, Windows XP is prone to "memory leaks." That is, little pieces of the programs you run stay loaded in system memory, even after those programs have been closed. It's sloppy programming on Microsoft's fault, what some would call a "bug" (although Microsoft doesn't call it that; it doesn't acknowledge the problem much at all), and one that affects anyone who keeps their computer running for days or weeks at a time without rebooting.

Here's the way it works. When you run a program, pieces of that program's code are loaded into your computer's random access memory. You would expect that when you close the program, all those program pieces would be removed from memory; that's the way things are supposed to work. In Windows XP, however, not all the program code gets purged from memory. A few bits and bytes here and there stay lodged in memory, even though they're totally unused.

Now, a few bits and bytes don't amount to much—until they start multiplying. That's because this memory lead problem doesn't affect just one program you run, but rather

Note

Windows Vista appears to have fixed the memory leakage problem that plagued Windows XP. So if you have a Vista PC, there's no need to reboot to free up system memory.

6

most programs you run. So after you open a close a half dozen or so applications, you end up with a significant chunk of memory that you can't use, because old program pieces are still there taking up space.

This problem becomes especially noticeable if you don't regularly shut down your computer at the end of each working day. If you're like most users, you leave your computer running for days, weeks, even months at a time without shutting it down or rebooting. And all the time your computer is running, more and more of your memory becomes lost to this memory leak problem.

In other words, the longer your computer stays up and running, the more bits of old programs end up lodged in memory—and the less memory you have available to run other programs. This is what slows down your system.

The solution is simple. Every time you close Windows, either by turning off or rebooting your system, the clogged up pieces of program are purged from memory, and you get a clean start on the restart. (Until, of course, you start opening and closing new programs again!)

So if you find your Windows XP computer slowing down day after day, do the simple thing and reboot it once every few days. (Click the Start button and select Turn Off Computer; when the Turn Off Computer dialog box appears, click Restart.) Doing so purges all occupied memory and get your computer running faster again—until you start loading more programs, unfortunately.

Don't Browse Network Folders

Some computer performance relates to an individual operation. That is, you can speed up the performance of some individual operations, regardless of the overall system performance.

One such operation that you can speed up is the opening of folders. In case you haven't noticed it, there's always a slightly delay when you double-click a folder to open it. That's because Windows XP automatically searches for network folders and printers every time you open the My Documents or Documents folders, and this takes time.

To speed up folder opening, you can turn off this network folder browsing. Follow these steps:

1. Click the Start button and select Control Panel.

2. When the Control Panel opens, double-click Folder Options.

3. When the Folder Options dialog box appears, select the View tab, shown in Figure 6.9.

4. Scroll down through the Advanced Settings list and uncheck the Automatically Search for Network Folders and Printers option.

5. Click OK.

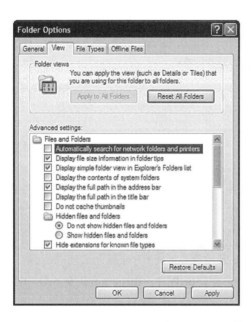

FIGURE 6.9

Turning off Windows XP's network folder browsing.

Note that you must reboot your computer for this change to take effect.

Improve Windows XP's Swap File Performance

Previously, we learned how to improve performance by tweaking the configuration of Windows' virtual memory. In Windows XP, an additional performance improvement can be had by making sure that all your RAM is used before the swap file is utilized—especially if you have more than 256MB of memory installed on your system. Follow these steps:

1. Click the Start button and select Run.

2. When the Run dialog box appears, enter **msconfig.exe** and click OK.

3. When the System Configuration utility appears, select the System.ini tab, as shown in Figure 6.10.

4. Click the plus sign next to the 386enh item to expand that listing.

5. Click New.

6. In the resulting box, enter **ConservativeSwapfileUsage=1**.

7. Click OK.

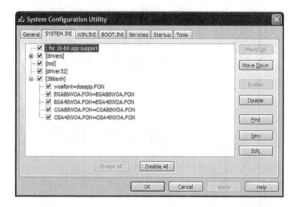

FIGURE 6.10

Speeding up Windows XP swap file use.

You must reboot your PC for this change to take effect.

Speeding Up Windows Vista

Unlike Windows XP and previous operating systems, Windows Vista is fairly streamlined in terms of performance. That means that there isn't a lot you can do to tweak it to make it faster—although some tweaks do exist, as you'll soon learn.

Disable Windows Vista's Aero Interface

Windows Vista is a more demanding operating system than Windows XP, especially when it comes to graphics display. This is due to Vista's new graphics engine, which is used to render the fancy-schmancy Aero interface.

If you're new to Vista, know that Aero is a glass-like 3D interface; the translucent windows give a sense of depth when individual windows are stacked on top of each other. Unfortunately, if you have an older or lesser-powered computer, it may not have the graphics horsepower necessary to run Aero efficiently.

If you think that the Aero interface is affecting system performance, you can turn it off and revert to the Windows Vista Basic interface. Of course, the Basic interface doesn't look as pretty—but it will respond much faster in day-to-day operation, especially on low-end machines.

To disable the Aero interface, follow these steps:

1. Click the Start menu and select Control Panel.

2. When the Control Panel opens, double-click Personalization.

3. When the Personalize Appearance and Sounds window opens, click Windows Color and Appearance.

4. When the Windows Color and Appearance window opens, click the link Open Classic Appearance Properties for More Color Options.

5. When the Appearance Settings dialog box appears, as shown in Figure 6.11, select Windows Vista Basic from the Color Scheme list.

6. Click OK to apply the new theme.

 Note

To display Vista's Aero interface, your PC's video card must support DirectX 9 with Pixel Shader 2, have a minimum of 64MB graphics memory and 1280 x 1024 resolution, and offer 32 bits per pixel, Windows Display Driver Model (WDDM) support. You must also be running Windows Vista Home Premium, Ultimate, Business, or Enterprise editions. You can't display the Aero interface if you're running Windows Vista Home Basic.

FIGURE 6.11

Changing from the Windows Vista Aero to the Windows Vista Basic interface.

The Basic interface should feel a bit faster than the Aero interface, especially if you have a slower system to begin with.

Remove Windows Vista's Sidebar

Windows Vista adds a neat feature called the Sidebar, shown in Figure 6.12. The Sidebar is a pane on the side of the desktop that helps to organize mini-applications that Microsoft calls *gadgets*. Gadgets can deliver a variety of information and services, and can either be docked on the Sidebar or float above the desktop.

Tip

For a less-radical change, uncheck the Enable Transparency option in the Windows Color and Appearance window. This turns off Aero's see-through feature while still retaining other key elements of the interface; it's the transparency effect that hogs the most memory.

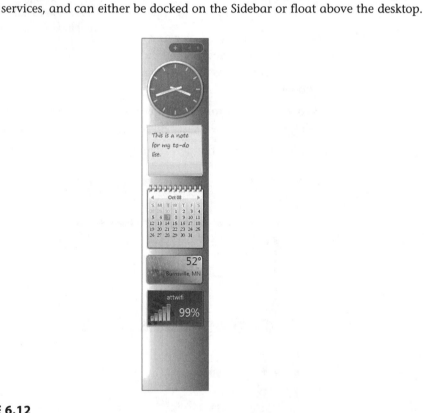

FIGURE 6.12

The Sidebar in Windows Vista.

The only problem with the Sidebar is that it takes up valuable system resources. If you want to add a bit of speed back to your system, turn off the

Sidebar (and its corresponding gadgets). To do so, right-click anywhere on the Sidebar and select Close Sidebar from the pop-up menu. It's gone!

Tip

To redisplay the Sidebar, click the Start button and select All Programs, Accessories, Windows Sidebar.

Turn Off Windows Vista's User Account Control

In previous versions of Windows, it was too easy for any user to inadvertently install dangerous software. Windows Vista makes it harder to do anything wrong, by applying a new feature called *User Account Control* (UAC). Unfortunately, UAC works by displaying a series of "nag" dialog boxes that keep asking you if you *really* want to do whatever it was you wanted to do. To many users, UAC is less protection than it is a nuisance, making you take longer to do everyday operations.

The solution to the UAC problem is to turn it off. Here's how:

1. Click the Start menu and select Control Panel.

2. When the Control Panel opens, double-click User Accounts.

3. When the User Accounts window opens, click Turn User Account Control On or Off.

4. When the next window appears, as shown in Figure 6.13, uncheck the Use User Account Control option.

5. Click OK.

Caution

Disabling UAC makes your system less secure than when UAC is operating. Make sure you monitor which programs you download and install on your PC; you no longer have UAC there to protect you against obvious malware.

FIGURE 6.13

Disabling Windows Vista's User Account Control.

Turn Off Unnecessary Windows Vista Features

When Windows Vista is installed on a PC, it also installs a bunch of utilities that you may or may not ever use. Unfortunately, most of these features automatically load into system memory when Windows loads, which is a recipe for poor system performance.

Fortunately, Windows lets you disable unnecessary or unwanted utilities from the operating system. Doing so keeps the utilities from automatically loading—but doesn't delete them from your hard drive, so they're still there in case you ever need them.

To turn off these unwanted features, follow these steps:

1. Click the Start menu and select Control Panel.

2. When the Control Panel opens, double-click Programs and Features.

3. When the Programs and Features window appears, click Turn Windows Features On or Off (in the leftmost panel).

4. When the Windows Features dialog box appears, as shown in Figure 6.14, uncheck those you want to disable. (You may need to click the + sign beside some features to see all related subfeatures.)

5. Click OK to apply your changes.

FIGURE 6.14

Disabling unwanted features in Windows Vista.

Which of these features do you need? It all depends. If you never play Windows built-in games, such as Solitaire and Chess Titans, you can uncheck the Games feature. If you don't have a tablet PC, you can uncheck the Tablet PC Optional Components feature. If you don't use Windows Meeting Space, you can uncheck that feature. And so on.

Tip

If you later do want to use one of these features, you can always reopen the Windows Feature dialog box and recheck that feature.

Just remember—every feature you uncheck will speed up your system performance just a tad. The more unnecessary features you disable, the faster your system will run.

Use ReadyBoost

Our last Windows Vista speedup deserves more space than we can devote in this chapter. That's because a very effective way to speed up Windows Vista is to provide it with more temporary memory, which you can do using a USB flash drive and Vista's new ReadyBoost feature. Turn to Chapter 10, "Adding More Memory," to learn more.

The Bottom Line

Windows XP and Windows Vista are both operating systems that use a lot of system resources. Fortunately, you can reduce this resource use—and speed up performance—by making a series of configuration tweaks. Here's the bottom line:

- Both Windows XP and Vista can be speeded up by turning off graphics elements that require excessive use of system resources.
- Both operating systems can also benefit by disabling unnecessary background services and features.
- The file indexing required by Windows' search feature is something else that slows down most systems. Turn off file indexing to speed up your PC.
- Windows XP has a memory leak issue that results in less usable memory being available over time. The quick solution is to reboot your XP machine every few days.
- Windows Vista's biggest resource hog is its Aero interface. Revert from Aero to the Windows Vista Basic interface to speed up your system.

6

PART

Power Speedups for Power Users

Cleaning Up the Windows Registry

I n the previous section of this book, we discussed some relatively non-technical ways to speed up your PC. In this section, we get slightly more technical—stuff that regular folks can still do to increase performance, but that requires a bit more technical confidence to achieve.

First up are a bunch of speedups that involve something called the Windows Registry. Don't worry, no screwdrivers or wrenches are required yet; the Registry is nothing more than a big file that you can edit with relatively easy-to-use software tools.

Understanding the Windows Registry

Here's something that's pretty obvious to any computer user: Windows is a complex and sophisticated piece of computer software. The operating system itself encompasses literally tens of thousands of individual system files—all of which have to be managed and monitored, as do all the devices that Windows is tasked with managing. It's a lot of information to manage.

Windows tracks all these thousands of individual configuration settings via a big database file called the Windows Registry. The Registry is where Windows turns to when it needs to find out anything about any part of the system. The Registry houses all manner of settings for everything from window color and translucency to the brand and model number of printer you're using. This type of centralized configuration storage makes it easy for Windows to find precise settings when necessary.

The Registry also has a big impact on your PC's speed. It all comes down to what is stored in the Registry and how the Registry is configured. An overly cluttered Registry can slow down performance, while tweaking certain Registry settings can speed up performance. For that reason, learning how to clean up and tweak the Registry is an essential skill for anyone trying to speed up a Windows XP or Vista computer.

How the Registry Works

Every time you make a configuration change, that information is automatically written to the Registry. Change the system time, and the Registry is updated; change your desktop wallpaper, the Registry is updated; change the home page in Internet Explorer, the Registry is updated. The Registry is also updated whenever you install a new software program or hardware device. And it all happens automatically, in the background.

When Windows needs to do anything—open a program, display a dialog box, you name it—it accesses the Registry to obtain the proper configuration information. In this sense, the Registry functions like a control center for your entire computer system; it defines how every part of your system looks and works.

Organizing the Registry

The Registry is organized into five major sections, called *hives*. Each hive is stored in its own system file on your PC's hard disk.

These hives include the following:

- **HKEY_CLASSES_ROOT:** Contains information about registered applications, including file associations and OLE object classes. (This hive displays the same settings as the HKEY_LOCAL_MACHINE\Software\Classes key.)
- **HKEY_CURRENT_USER:** This hive is a subset of the HKEY_USERS hive, pertaining to the current user of the PC. It contains all attributes for the desktop environment and network connections.

- **HKEY_LOCAL_MACHINE:** Contains most of the settings for your PC's hardware, system software, and individual applications.

- **HKEY_USERS:** Contains subkeys corresponding to the HKEY_CURRENT_USER hives for all users of the PC, not just the current user.

- **HKEY_CURRENT_CONFIG:** Contains information gathered when Windows first launches, such as settings pertaining to your PC's display and printers. The data stored in this hive is not permanently stored on disk, but rather is regenerated each time your PC boots.

Note

The Windows Registry was first introduced in Windows 95. Before that particular version of Windows, two system files kept track of much of the same information—win.ini and system.ini. As more objects became installed in the operating system, however, these files became huge and unwieldy—and contributed significantly to the slowing of Windows. Starting with Windows 95, therefore, all the information formerly stored in these two files (and more) was moved to the Registry, which is much more organized and easier to manage than the previous files.

Each hive is further organized into a variety of keys and subkeys that can be represented by a series of folders and subfolders. For example, if you want to find configuration information for which programs Windows loads at launch, you would look in the following key: HKEY_LOCAL_MACHINE\SOFTWARE\Microsoft\Windows\CurrentVersion\Run.

The settings or data for each individual key or subkey is called the *value.* Each value in the Registry is defined by a value name (often called just the value), the type of data used for that entry, and the value of that data.

Editing the Registry

Most of the time you won't need to bother with the Registry—it operates in the background, automatically updated whenever you change a Windows setting or install a new piece of software or hardware.

Tip

Most experts recommend that you make a backup of the Registry before you make any changes to it. Fortunately, backing up the Registry is as simple as setting a System Restore point before you make an edit. The System Restore point contains a back up of the Registry; if you have problems following a Registry edit, you can simply restore the Registry to its pre-edit state using the System Restore utility. (Learn how to use System Restore in Chapter 2, "Before You Start: Protect Your Data."

However, there will come the occasion when you experience a particularly vexing system problem that can be fixed only by editing a particular value in the Registry.

Launching the Registry Editor

You edit the Registry with a built-in utility imaginatively called the Registry Editor. To launch Registry Editor, follow these steps:

1. Click the Start button and click Run.

2. When the Run window appears, enter **regedit** in the Open box.

3. Click OK.

As you can see in Figure 7.1, the Registry Editor window has two panes. The left pane displays all the Registry's hives and keys. All keys have numerous subkeys. The right pane displays the values, or configuration information, for each key or subkey. You display the different levels of subkeys by clicking on the + next to a specific item.

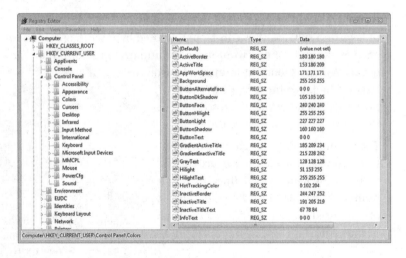

FIGURE 7.1
Editing the Windows Registry with the Registry Editor.

Editing and Adding Keys, Subkeys, and Values

You edit a particular value by highlighting the subkey in the left pane and then double-clicking the value in the right pane. This displays the Edit Value (or Edit String) window, like the one shown in Figure 7.2. Enter a new value in the Value Data box, and then click OK.

Caution

Registry settings are changed as you make the changes. There is no "save" command in the Registry Editor. There is also no "undo" command. So be very careful about the changes you make—they're final!

FIGURE 7.2

Editing the value of a key.

To add a new value to a subkey, right-click the subkey and select one of the New, Value options from the pop-up menu. Type a name for the new value, and then double-click the value to display the Edit Value (or Edit String) window. Enter the new value in the Value Data box, and then click OK.

You also can add new subkeys to the Registry. Just right-click the key where you want to add the subkey, and then select New, Key from the pop-up menu. A new subkey (with a temporary name) appears. Type a name for the new subkey, and then press Enter.

To delete a subkey or value, right-click the item and select Delete. Remember, however, that all changes are final. Once a subkey is deleted, it's gone!

Cleaning Up the Registry for Faster Performance

When it comes to the Windows Registry, here's what slows down your system. Over time, all the different programs you install and settings you configure create lots and lots and lots of entries in the Registry—even after you uninstall the programs or no longer need the settings. That contributes to Registry "bloat" with lots of unnecessary or orphaned entries. And the larger the

Registry is, in terms of both file size and number of entries, the longer it takes for Windows to load it on startup—which slows down your system.

The fix for this problem is deceptively simple: Delete all the orphaned and unnecessary Registry entries. That's easier to say than to do, however. How do you know which entries are necessary and which aren't? Plus, do you really want to do all that work by hand, using the Registry Editor?

How Registry Cleaners Work

Fortunately, various third parties have recognized this issue and come up with their own solutions, in the form of Registry cleaner utilities. These programs automatically scour your Registry for redundant, invalid, or orphaned entries, and delete them. The process is easy as pie.

What kind of impact does a Registry cleaner actually have? It depends, to some degree, on how "clean" your Registry was to begin with. If a cleaner finds only a dozen or so entries to delete (out of the thousands of valid entries), the performance impact is minimal. But if you have a

Caution

There is the slight chance that a poor-quality Registry cleaner program may incorrectly identify a working entry as an unnecessary one, and thus delete a setting that Windows needs to run. For that reason, you should set a restore point (using System Restore) before cleaning your registry. You can always go back to that precleaner restore point if your system has problems after the cleaning.

greater number of useless entries (or a smaller number of total entries), a Registry cleaner will have a larger percentage impact on your system's performance. So you might notice a very small change in speed or a very large one, depending.

Choosing a Registry Cleaner

A large number of Registry cleaners are available today. The best of these include the following:

- CCleaner (www.ccleaner.com), a free utility that offers various system maintenance operations, including deleting temporary files and log files in addition to cleaning the Registry

Tip

I recommend you choose a cleaner with backup and restore functions. This lets you undo any changes made by the cleaner, in case the program accidentally deletes something it shouldn't.

- EasyCleaner (personal.inet.fi/ business/toniarts/ecleane.htm), a free dedicated Registry cleaner

- Registry Healer (www.zoneutils.com/ regheal/), a shareware Registry cleaner with optional $19.95 registration fee

- Registry Mechanic (www.pctools. com/registry-mechanic/), one of the most popular Registry cleaners, costing $29.95 for a three-computer license

- RegSeeker (www.hoverdesk.net/ freeware.htm), another free dedicated Registry cleaner

Caution

Beware of so-called Trojan applications that masquerade as legitimate Registry cleaners. These malware programs typically are pushed via pop-up windows that purport to alert you of Registry problems and urge an immediate download. Once installed, they operate as spyware or adware on your system. No legitimate Registry cleaner promotes itself in this fashion.

- Tuneup Utilities (www.tune-up.com/products/tuneup-utilities/), a $49.95 suite of tune-up utilities that include disk defragmenting, file cleanup, and Registry cleaner

- Uniblue RegistryBooster (www.liutilities.com/products/registrybooster/), a $29.95 dedicated Registry cleaner

- WinCleaner (www.wincleaner.com), another dedicated Registry cleaner that sells for $29.95

Using a Registry Cleaner

Most Registry cleaners work in a similar fashion, scanning your Registry for entries that don't lead anywhere. This can be done automatically (the cleaner deletes every bad entry it encounters) or manually (you're asked whether you want to delete each individual entry it finds). Because most users don't know what's good and what's bad, the automatic operation is generally recommended.

Figure 7.3 shows one of the more popular cleaners, CCleaner, in action. You start the

Caution

In some rare instances, Registry cleaners can accidentally delete entries and DLLs that are used (if infrequently) by some programs. For this reason, make sure you create a System Restore point before running the cleaner utility; you can always restore your system to that point if any problems occur after cleaning.

7

scan by clicking the Scan for Issues button. Problem entries are then listed in the rightmost pane. To delete all identified entries, leave everything checked and click the Fix Selected Issues button. Alternatively, you can manually examine all the entries and uncheck those you don't want to remove.

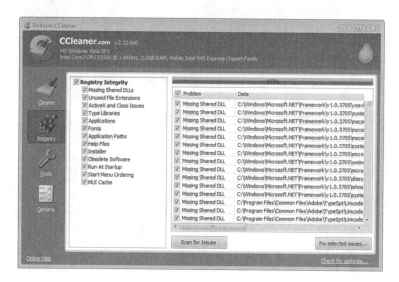

FIGURE 7.3
Cleaning the Windows Registry with CCleaner.

Tweaking the Registry

Now that you know how to clean and edit the Windows Registry, let's examine a handful of Registry tweaks that can speed up your PC. They're easy to do—as long as you're comfortable using the Registry Editor.

Speed Up Windows' Menus

Want to make Windows' menus display more quickly? That's what you get when you enable this Registry tweak that removes the slight delay that is normally present between clicking a menu and Windows displaying that menu.

To perform this tweak, follow these steps:

 Caution

Just another reminder that editing Registry settings can result in unexpected system behavior. Make sure you set a System Restore point before attempting any of these Registry tweaks!

7

1. Open the Registry Editor.

2. Navigate to the HKEY_CURRENT_USER\Control Panel\Desktop key.

3. Right-click the MenuShowDelay item and select Modify.

4. In the Edit String dialog box, change the current value (typically 400) to something a bit lower—something around 100 typically works well.

5. Click OK.

Caution

If you set the MenuShowDelay value too low, menus will open if you merely move your mouse over them. You need a value somewhere above 0; otherwise, it will make Windows difficult to use.

You can now close the Registry Editor and see how fast your menus open.

Close Programs Faster on Shutdown

Tired of waiting… and waiting… and waiting while your computer shuts down or reboots? Part of that time is spent waiting on Windows to automatically close any programs you have open. Fortunately, you can reduce that waiting time, by tweaking the Windows Registry. Just follow these steps:

1. Open the Registry Editor.

2. Navigate to the HKEY_CURRENT_USER\Control Panel\Desktop key.

3. Right-click the WaitToKillAppTimeout item and select Modify.

4. In the Edit String dialog box, change the value to 1000.

5. Click OK.

6. Now right-click the HungAppTimeout item and select Modify.

7. In the Edit String dialog box, change the value to 1000.

8. Click OK.

9. Now navigate to the HKEY_USERS\.DEFAULT\Control Panel\Desktop key.

10. Right-click the WaitToKillAppTimeout item and select modify.

11. In the Edit String dialog box, change the value to 1000.

12. Click OK.

13. Navigate to the HKEY_LOCAL_MACHINE\System\CurrentControlSet\Control key.

14. Right-click the WaitToKillServiceTimeout item and select Modify.

15. In the Edit String dialog box, change the value to 1000.

16. Click OK.

The next time you shut down your system, it shouldn't take quite so long.

Disable Low Disk Checking

Windows constantly checks to see whether there's enough free space on your hard drive. If there isn't, it displays a low disk space warning. The problem is, all this disk space checking uses up system resources, and you probably know if your disk space is low, anyway.

You can speed up your PC by turning off this low disk space checking. Here's how to do it:

1. Open the Registry Editor.

2. Navigate to the HKEY_CURRENT_USER\Software\Microsoft\Windows\ CurrentVersion\Policies key.

3. If the Explorer key exists, select it. If not, right-click in the rightmost pane and select New, Key. Name this new key **Explorer**, and then select it.

4. Right-click in the rightmost pane and select New, DWORD (32-bit) Value.

5. Name the new DWORD **NoLowDiskSpaceChecks**.

6. Right-click the new NoLowDiskSpaceChecks item and select Modify.

7. In the Edit DWORD dialog box, change the value to 1.

8. Click OK.

Move the Windows Kernel into Memory

Anything that runs in system memory runs faster than if it runs from your hard disk. To that end, you can speed up Windows itself by moving the Windows kernel into RAM, by executing this Registry tweak:

1. Open the Registry Editor.

Note

A DWORD is a special type of data value used for some Registry entries.

Caution

You should only move the Windows kernel into RAM if your PC has 256MB or more of system memory.

7

2. Navigate to the HKEY_LOCAL_
   MACHINE\SYSTEM\
   CurrentControlSet\Control\Session
   Manager\Memory Management or
   HKEY_LOCAL_MACHINE\
   SYSTEM\CurrentControlSet\Session
   Manager\Memory Management
   key.

Caution

If you experience system problems after performing this tweak, re-edit the value of DisablePagingExecutive back to 0.

3. Right-click the DisablePagingExecutive item and select Modify.

4. In the Edit DWORD dialog box, change the value to 1.

5. Click OK.

You must reboot your system for this tweak to take effect.

The Bottom Line

The Windows Registry contains thousands of configuration settings that enable Windows to run properly. It's no surprise that tweaking and cleaning the Registry can have a big impact on your PC's performance. Here's the bottom line:

- Because the Registry is a large file that must be loaded whenever Windows launches, any way to reduce the size of that file can speed up your PC.

- The quickest way to speed up Registry performance is to use a Registry cleaner program that identifies and deletes unnecessary entries from the Registry.

- Additional performance gains can come from tweaking individual Registry entries, using the Registry Editor utility.

7

When All Else Fails: Reinstalling Windows from Scratch

et's face it. Over time, your computer system gets "gunked up." That is, you get so many programs and utilities and such loaded onto your hard disk and into system memory that the whole shebang starts running slower and slower and slower. Too much gunk in your system and things slow to a crawl.

Now, you can try to remove some of that gunk manually—which is what we've discussed in several of the previous chapters. But sometimes there's just too much gunk and you can't get rid of it all. That's when you need to do something more extreme.

What's the most extreme thing you can to do clean out a gunked up system? How about wiping your hard drive clean and reinstalling Windows from scratch? I know, it sounds extreme—and it is—but this last-ditch approach can work wonders for cleaning up a bloated system, or one unduly infected by viruses and spyware.

8

When Extreme Measures Are Called For

The solution proposed in this chapter is a rather extreme one. Instead of taking a scalpel to your performance issues, this is more of a blunt axe approach. You don't carefully excise a handful of programs and files, but instead get rid of everything that's installed on your hard drive by doing what's called a *clean install* of the Windows operating system.

The advantage of this approach is that you start with a completely clean system—no gunk. The disadvantage, of course, is that a clean system doesn't have all your favorite stuff on it, so you'll have to do a lot of reinstalling and reconfiguring after the fact. But a clean system should run faster than a gunked-up one, and that's what you're looking for.

Given the extreme nature of this particular speedup, when should you consider reinstalling Windows from scratch? Here are some common scenarios that might warrant this approach:

- **Your system is recovering from a computer virus infection—or you can't seem to recover from said infection.** Computer viruses are tough. Although most antivirus programs do a good job of disinfecting your system, some of the nastier viruses are quite difficult to get rid of. If you've tried cleaning your system but still have symptoms of infection, the only solution may be to wipe your hard disk clean and start over from scratch—virus free, of course.

- **Your system has been frequently and severely hit by spyware intrusions—and you can't get rid of them.** Spyware is sometimes more difficult to get rid of than viruses. Some spyware programs do an excellent job of hiding from antispyware programs, and of replicating themselves when you think you've deleted them. If spyware consistently recurs after you've scrubbed your system with one or more antispyware programs, starting with a clean hard disk may be your only solution.

- **You've tried to clear unwanted startup programs from your system, but they keep popping up again.** Cleaning unwanted startup programs from your system is often difficult; these programs can hide in the most unlikely places. If you

 Caution

Don't confuse hard-to-remove spyware with a new spyware intrusion. If spyware recurs after you've visited a file-sharing site, it's more likely that you've downloaded new spyware rather than that the old spyware has come back to life.

can't find all these startup programs, or if deactivating them doesn't seem to work (that is, they keep coming back after you've turned them off or deleted them), the only way to get rid of them may be to wipe them off in the process of a clean install of Windows.

■ **You've tried all the other speedups suggested so far, and your system is still running sluggish.** Yeah, that's why this is called a "last-ditch" approach. Everything else you've tried to this point doesn't work, and you're at wit's end. Well, performing a clean install is kind of a "drop back 10 and punt" solution, but when you don't know what's slowing down your system, sometimes punting is just the thing that's called for.

While this is a radical solution to performance problems, it's not all that rare. Believe it or not, some users do a clean install of Windows on brand-new PCs, in order to remove all the bundleware that comes preinstalled on new systems. A clean installation gives you a copy of Windows unencumbered by unwanted programs, utilities, and trialware. It also removes all the unnecessary stuff that you accumulate in months and years of computer use. In short, reformatting your hard drive and reinstalling Windows is an effective way of hitting the reset button and letting you start over with a clean—and fast—system.

What's Involved in a Clean Install

So what's involved in this so-called radical solution? Although it's not that hard to do (even non-technical users can perform a clean install), what happens is a bit drastic.

In short, your hard drive is wiped clean by reformatting. Everything on the disk—programs, data files, and the Windows operating system itself—is effectively deleted, and you're left with a blank, like-new hard disk. Like I said, it's an extreme solution.

Onto that newly blank hard drive, then, is placed a clean installation of the Windows operating system. By *clean*, I mean an installation that includes only those elements you need and excludes all the excess garbage that your computer manufacturer may have included when you first purchased the system. You end up with Windows and Windows only installed on your hard drive.

But what about all your programs and documents? Like I said, they're wiped off the hard drive during the clean install process. This is why you need to back up all your document files before you reformat, typically to an external hard disk. You can then reinstall your programs from their original installation disks (assuming you have them) and restore your documents from the backup drive. You reinstall only those programs you want and restore only those documents you need—which means you should end up using less hard disk space than you did previously.

Before You Reinstall...

Before you perform a clean installation of Windows, you need to do a few things. Here's what I recommend.

Caution

Don't confuse a manufacturer's "restore" CD with the official Microsoft Windows installation disc. The restore CD restores your computer's hard disk to the way it shipped from the factory—complete with all that unwanted bundleware that was installed when you first purchased your PC. It does *not* create a clean installation of Windows on your hard drive.

Obtain the Windows Installation Disc

First, make sure you have your Windows installation CD or DVD. This might sound easier than it actually is, because not all computer manufacturers supply you with the official Microsoft installation media. (It saves them a few bucks to leave this out of the box.)

If your computer manufacturer supplied the Windows installation disc, great. If not, you might try calling or emailing to see whether they'll ship you one. If not, you'll need to purchase a new copy of Windows—presumably Windows Vista—for the new installation.

Locate Program Installation Discs

Next, you want to locate all the installation discs for the programs you want to reinstall on your system. (Remember, all your existing programs will be deleted when you reformat the hard drive; to use those programs again, you have to reinstall them from scratch.) Likewise, if you originally downloaded the programs, you'll need to redownload them to your reformatted hard drive.

Caution

Before you upgrade from Windows XP to Windows Vista, make sure your computer hardware meets Vista's more restrictive specifications, detailed at www.microsoft.com/windows/windows-vista/get/system-requirements.aspx. Not all older PCs can run Windows Vista.

Worse comes to worst, you may have to repurchase one or more programs for which you can't find the installation discs. This may not be all bad, especially if you have an older version of the program; a newer, upgraded version of the program might be available that may run faster on your system.

Tip

If you have to download a software program, you may be able to obtain an "unlock" key for the program, so that you don't have to pay for it again. Check the software manufacturer's website to access your previous account and get more information.

Back Up All Your Files

Finally, you need to back up *all* your data and configuration files from your hard drive to some sort of backup devise. I recommend purchasing an external hard drive equal to or larger in size than your computer's internal hard drive just for this purpose. You can move all these files to the external hard drive and then back to the reformatted internal drive when you're done with this process.

What's the best way to copy all you files to the backup drive? I recommend using the File and Transfer Settings Wizard in Windows XP, or Windows Vista's similar Easy Transfer utility. Both of these programs work in a similar fashion, letting you copy all important data files, user files, and configuration settings to a backup disk, and then restoring them to the reformatted disk when you're ready.

Backing Up in Windows XP

To use Windows XP's File and Transfer Settings Wizard, follow these steps:

1. Click the Start button, and then select All Programs, Accessories, System Tools, Files and Settings Transfer Wizard.

2. When the wizard launches, click the Next button.

3. When the Which Computer Is This? screen appears, check the Old Computer option, and then click Next.

4. When the Select a Transfer Method window appears, as shown in Figure 8.1, select how you want to

Caution

If you've made a backup of a file that has been infected with a computer virus or spyware, restoring that backup file will infect your newly clean system. Make sure to run anti-spyware and anti-virus utilities on your backup media before you perform any restoration.

8

transfer the files. If you're copying files to an external hard disk, select that disk, and then click Next.

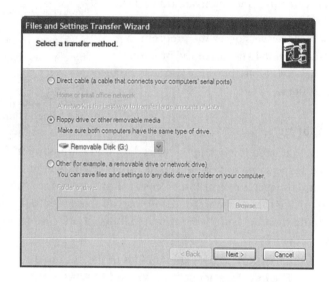

FIGURE 8.1

Selecting your backup medium in the Files and Settings Transfer Wizard.

5. When the What Do You Want to Transfer? screen appears (as shown in Figure 8.2), select Both Files and Settings, and then click Next.

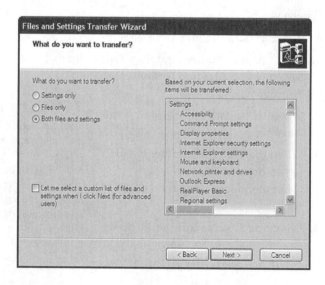

FIGURE 8.2

Selecting what to back up from your hard drive.

6. The wizard now collects everything it needs to copy to the new PC. This takes several minutes, after which you'll be prompted to begin the transfer. Follow the onscreen instructions to complete the procedure.

Caution

The Files and Settings Transfer Wizard transfers files and settings only from the currently active user. So if you have more than one user assigned to your old PC, you'll have to run the wizard again for each user of the computer.

Backing Up in Windows Vista

To use Windows Vista's Easy Transfer utility, follow these steps:

1. Click the Start button and select All Programs, Accessories, System Tools, Windows Easy Transfer.

2. When the Easy Transfer welcome screen appears, click the Next button to proceed.

3. If you have any programs currently running on your PC, you'll be prompted to close them. Click the Close All button to proceed.

4. When the Which Computer Are You Using Now? screen appears, as shown in Figure 8.3, click My Old Computer.

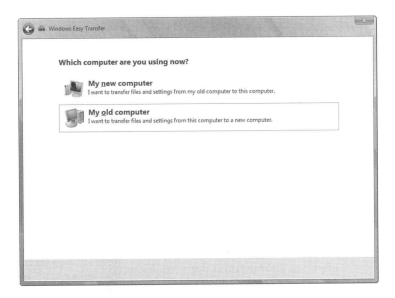

FIGURE 8.3

Telling Easy Transfer that you're using your old PC.

5. You're now asked if you're using an Easy Transfer Cable. Click No.

6. Next, the screen in Figure 8.4 asks you how you want to transfer your files—over your network or via CD, DVD, or other removable media. Click the appropriate option to proceed.

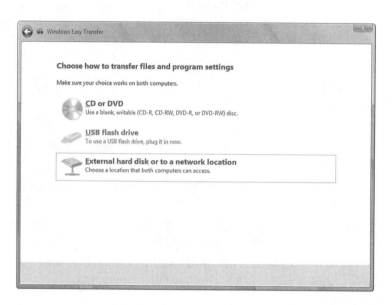

FIGURE 8.4

Choosing how you want to transfer your files and settings.

7. If prompted to select a location to save your files and settings, make the selection.

8. When the screen shown in Figure 8.5 appears, select the All User Accounts, Files, and Settings option. This transfers everything that can be transferred, for all users of your PC.

9. Easy Transfer now prompts you for your user account, on both computers. Enter your account name and click Next.

Note

How long it takes to copy your files and settings depends on how many files you're copying. Generally speaking, the more files you have to transfer, the more time it takes. Whether you're using the Transfer Files and Settings Wizard or Easy Transfer, you're probably talking anywhere from half an hour to several hours to complete the process.

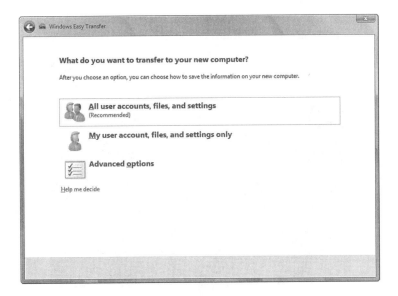

FIGURE 8.5

Selecting which items to transfer.

Easy Transfer estimates the transfer size and begins copying the files and settings you specified from your computer to your external hard drive. You'll then be prompted to move the hard drive to your new PC and then copy the files from that device or media to your new PC. Obviously, you hold off on this until after you perform the clean install.

Performing a Clean Install of Windows XP

Windows XP and Windows Vista each handle clean installations in their own unique fashions. We'll start with the Windows XP clean install, and then discuss the Windows Vista operation.

If you're running Windows XP on your computer and have a Windows installation CD, make sure you've backed up all your data, and then follow these instructions:

1. Close Windows and turn off your PC.
2. Insert the Windows XP CD into your CD-ROM drive and restart your PC.

 Caution

If you can't boot your system from the Windows XP CD, you need to reconfigure your CMOS BIOS so that your CD drive is the boot path. You do this by rebooting your PC, pressing the correct key to enter the CMOS configuration utility, finding the boot sequence setting, and adding your CD drive to the boot sequence *before* the hard disk. With this reconfigured, you should now be able to boot from the Windows XP CD.

3. When you see the onscreen message Press Any Key to Boot from CD, press any key on your keyboard.

4. After a minute, you'll see the Welcome to Setup screen, shown in Figure 8.6. Press Enter to set up Windows XP now.

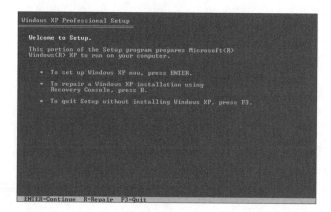

FIGURE 8.6

Starting a clean installation of Windows XP.

5. When the License Agreement appears, read it (if you want), and then press F8 to proceed.

6. The next screen, shown in Figure 8.7, tells you that you already have a version of Windows installed on your system. Press the Esc key to continue with the clean install.

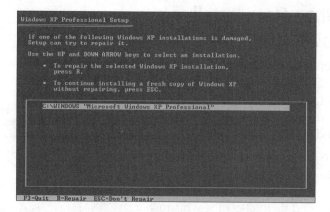

FIGURE 8.7

Press Esc to perform a clean install.

7. The next screen, shown in Figure 8.8, shows you the existing partitions on your hard drive. Select the drive where you want to install Windows (typically drive C:) and press Enter.

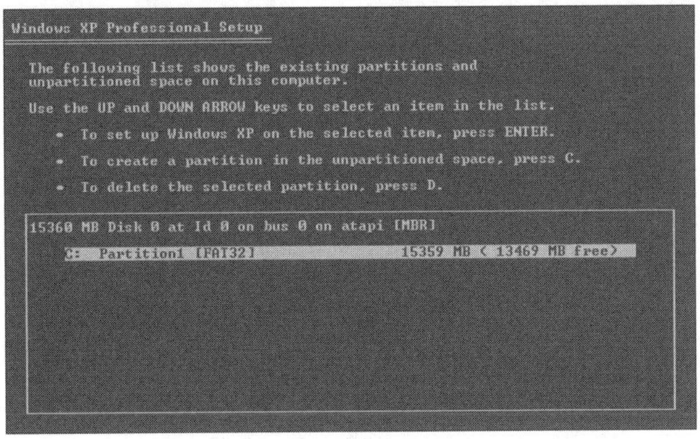

FIGURE 8.8

Selecting where to install Windows XP.

8. The following screen, shown in Figure 8.9, again warns you that you already have Windows installed on this partition. Press C to continue.

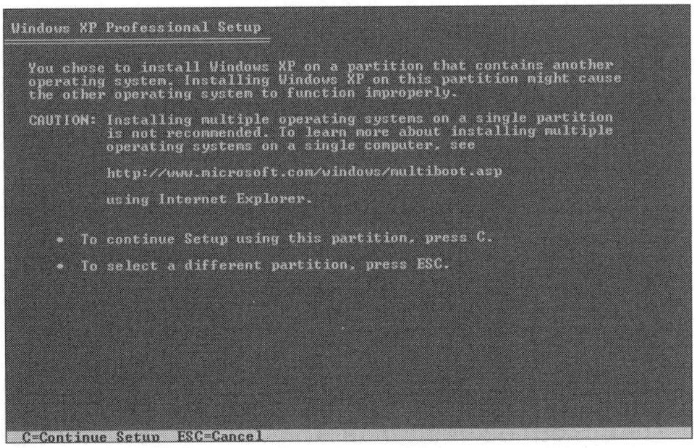

FIGURE 8.9

Continuing with the clean install.

9. Next, you're prompted to format the Windows XP partition, as shown in Figure 8.10. Select the Format the Partition Using the NTFS File System option and press Enter.

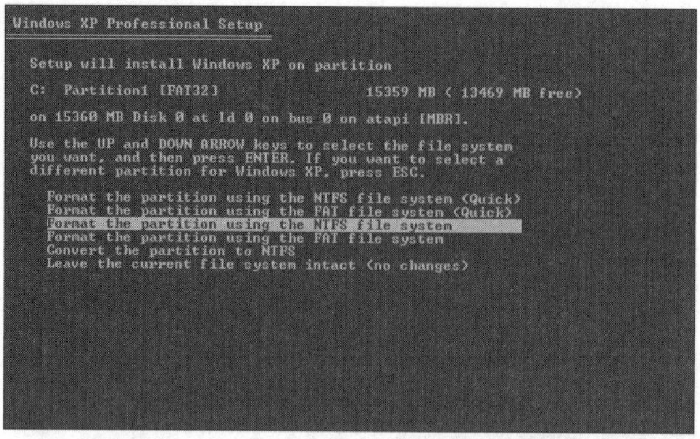

FIGURE 8.10

Getting ready to format your hard drive.

10. You're now prompted to begin the reformatting. Press F to continue.

The installation program now begins to format your hard disk and then install the Windows XP operating system. At some point you'll need to make some configuration choices and input a variety of information—including that long product key located on the back of the Windows XP CD. Just follow the onscreen instructions and be sure you have a few thick magazines to read while the installation program does its thing.

When the installation is complete, you'll need to reinstall your favorite programs and copy all your files and settings from your external backup disk. Read on to the "After the Clean Install: Reinstalling Programs and Data" section, later in this chapter, to learn more.

Performing a Clean Install of Windows Vista

Performing a clean install of Windows Vista is similar but different than with Windows XP. Make sure you've backed up your files and settings and that you have your Vista installation DVD in hand, and then follow these instructions:

> **Note**
>
> Your computer will probably reboot at least once during the installation process. If you're then prompted to press any key to boot from the CD or DVD, ignore this request to continue the installation process. Otherwise, the installation process will start from the top again.

1. Close Windows and turn off your PC.

2. Insert the Windows Vista DVD into your CD/DVD drive and restart your PC.

3. If prompted to press a key to boot from the DVD, do so.

> **Caution**
>
> Microsoft won't let you perform a clean install from an upgrade version of Windows Vista. You can do a clean install only from a full version of the installation DVD.

4. As shown in Figure 8.11, you're now prompted to confirm the installation language, time and currency format, and keyboard or input method. Do so, and then click the Next button.

FIGURE 8.11

Entering language configuration information.

5. When the screen shown in Figure 8.12 appears, click Install Now.

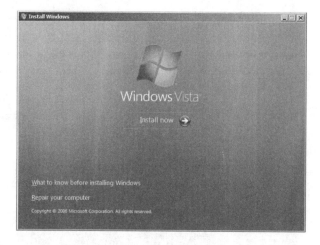

FIGURE 8.12

Beginning a clean install of Windows Vista.

6. As shown in Figure 8.13, you're now prompted to enter the Windows product key, which is found on the installation disc package. Enter the key, check the Automatically Activate Windows When I'm Online option, and then click Next.

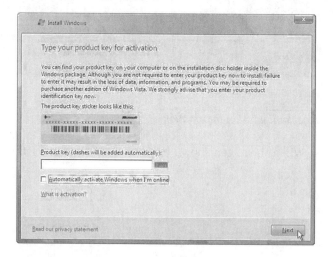

FIGURE 8.13

Entering the Windows Vista product key.

7. You're now asked to select which version of Windows you're installing. Make your choice, and then click Next.

8. Windows now displays the end user agreement. Read if you like, check the I Accept the License Terms options, and then click Next.

9. As you can see in Figure 8.14, you're now prompted to select what type of installation you're making. Select Custom to proceed.

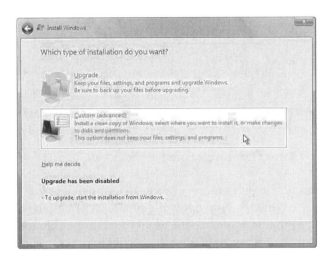

FIGURE 8.14

Selecting the Custom installation option.

10. You're now prompted to select where you want to install Windows. Don't select a drive just yet. Instead, click the Drive Options (Advanced) option.

11. The screen changes to that shown in Figure 8.15. Select your primary hard drive (typically drive C:), click the Format option, and then click Next.

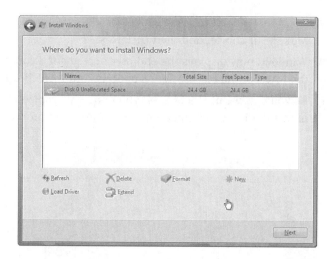

FIGURE 8.15

Selecting the hard drive to format and install Windows Vista.

The installation program now begins to format your hard disk and then install the Windows Vista operating system. When all the files are copied, you'll be prompted to make the usual configuration choices. Just follow the onscreen instructions to finalize the installation.

When the installation is complete, you'll need to reinstall your favorite programs and copy all your files and settings from your external backup disk. Read on to learn how.

After the Clean Install: Reinstalling Programs and Data

While the clean install process is a little time consuming, it's pretty simple. What you receive in its wake is a clean hard drive with an ungunked copy of Windows installed. That's it; there are no programs or data files cluttering things up—yet.

The next step in this process is to restore to your clean hard drive all the files and settings you previously backed up, and then reinstall copies of your favorite programs—and *only* those programs. (That's right, here's where you keep things clean by not installing those unnecessary programs that only served to take up disk space before.)

Restoring Files and Settings in Windows XP

On a Windows XP machine, you use the File and Settings Transfer Wizard to restore your data files and settings from your external hard disk back to your main reformatted hard drive. Here's how to do it:

1. Click the Start button and select All Programs, Accessories, System Tools, Files and Settings Transfer Wizard.

2. When the wizard launches, click the Next button.

3. When the Which Computer Is This? screen appears, as shown in Figure 8.16, check the New Computer option, and then click Next.

4. When the next screen appears, asking whether you have a Windows XP CD, select I Don't Need the Wizard Disk option, and then click Next.

5. When the Where Are the Files and Settings? screen appears, select how you've stored the files, and then click Next.

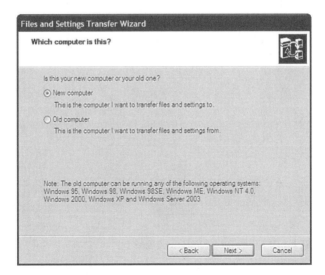

FIGURE 8.16

Restoring files and settings on a Windows XP PC.

That's it. The wizard now automatically transfers the files and settings to your new computer. All you have to do is sit back and wait for the whole thing to finish. When it's done you might have to reboot your computer, but then it will be up and running—and looking and acting just like you're used to!

Restoring Files and Settings in Windows Vista

On a Windows Vista PC, you use the Easy Transfer utility to copy your data files and settings from your external backup drive back to your reformatted internal hard disk. Here's how to do it:

1. Click the Start button and select All Programs, Accessories, System Tools, Windows Easy Transfer.

2. When the Easy Transfer welcome screen appears, click the Next button to proceed.

3. When the next screen appears, as shown in Figure 8.17, click Continue a Transfer in Progress.

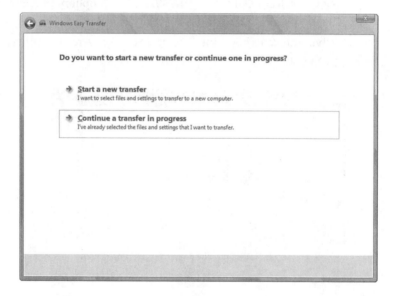

FIGURE 8.17

Restoring your files and settings in Windows Vista.

4. When the Where Did You Copy Your Files? screen appears, as shown in Figure 8.18, select Removable Media.

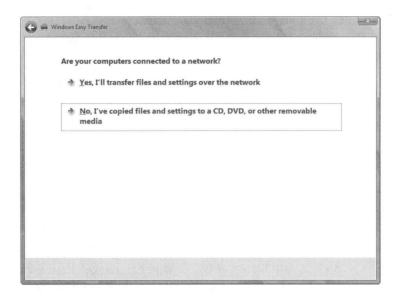

FIGURE 8.18
Locating your copied files and settings.

5. When the Locate Your Saved Files screen appears, select the external drive where your data files and settings are stored.

6. When prompted, select the usernames you want to use for your new Windows installation.

7. On the next screen, select the destination drive for these files and settings, (typically drive C:).

8. When the final screen appears, click Start to begin the transfer.

The restoration process now begins. When it's done, your computer should be up and running with all your old data files and Windows settings.

Reinstalling Your Favorite Programs

The last thing you need to do is reinstall those programs you want to continue using. Obviously, you'll need each program's installation discs—or, in the case of downloaded programs, the download URL and (if required) a download activation key. If you don't have the original discs or if the software publisher doesn't let you perform multiple downloads of the same program, you may need to purchase a new version of that program. In any case, do whatever you need to do to reinstall the programs you're likely to use on a daily basis—but not those you'll never use going forward.

Tip

Always check for updates and newer versions when reinstalling an older program. You might as well get the latest and greatest version of the program—with all the latest bug fixes included!

The Bottom Line

If your system is severely gunked up and still slow after trying the other solutions presented in this book, you can de-gunk it and likely speed it up by performing a clean install of the Windows operating system. Here's the bottom line:

■ A clean installation of Windows reformats your hard drive, deletes all existing data and programs, and reinstalls Windows without any bundleware.

■ Before you do a clean install, make sure you back up all your data files and settings by using either the Files and Settings Transfer Wizard (Windows XP) or the Easy Transfer utility (Windows Vista). It's best to make this backup to an external hard disk.

■ To perform a clean install, you need a full (not upgrade) copy of the Windows installation CD or DVD.

■ After the clean install, you'll need to reinstall your favorite software programs and restore your files and settings from your backup hard disk to your PC's main hard drive.

Upgrading Your PC for Speed

Preparing for a Computer Upgrade

I f your PC is more than a year or two old, you can probably improve its performance by upgrading one or more internal components. That might mean adding more memory, a bigger hard disk, a faster video card, or even a more powerful central processing unit (CPU).

Some of these upgrades are relatively easy to do. For example, adding memory requires you to plug a new chip into your system's motherboard, whereas upgrading the video card is no more difficult than unplugging the old card and plugging in the new one.

Other upgrades require more technical expertise. (The CPU upgrade, in particular, is not for the technically timid.)

That said, if you're comfortable with digging around inside your PC's system unit, know that replacing one or two internal components often costs considerably less than purchasing a brand-new PC. With that in mind, read on to learn how to upgrade your way to a speedier computer.

Before You Upgrade: Getting to Know Your Computer System

It helps to know what you're doing before you try to do it. That's why I think it's a good idea to get to know what's both outside and inside your computer's system unit—what it does and how it does it—before you start removing and replacing things.

Note

In this and following chapters, we focus on upgrading a desktop PC, which can be done with comparative ease. It is less easy—if not downright impossible—to upgrade anything inside a notebook PC, save for the memory and (on some units) the hard drive. For that matter, we don't discuss notebook upgrades in this chapter.

What's on the Back

The back of your PC's system unit is covered with all types of connectors. This is because all the external components of your computer system connect to your system unit, and they all have to have a place to plug in.

Because each component has its own unique type of connector, you end up with the assortment of jacks (called *ports* in the computer world) that you see in Figure 9.1. The back of your PC might look somewhat different than the one pictured here, depending on the manufacturer, but this should help you identify the major connectors.

What's Inside

When we're talking about internal upgrades to your PC, we're talking about what's inside the system unit case. To do that, you have to open the case and take a peek around inside.

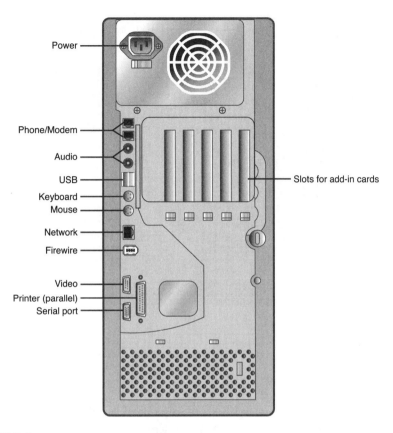

Power

Phone/Modem

Audio

USB

Keyboard

Mouse

Network

Firewire

Video

Printer (parallel)

Serial port

Slots for add-in cards

9

FIGURE 9.1

The back of a typical system unit—just look at all those different connectors!

To remove your system unit's case, look for some big screws or thumbscrews on either the side or back of the case. (Even better, read your PC's instruction manual for instructions specific to your unit.) With the screws loosened or removed, you should then be able to either slide off the entire case or pop open the top or back, as shown in Figure 9.2.

 Caution

Always turn off and unplug your computer before attempting to re-move the system unit's case—and be careful about touching anything inside! Not only can you shock yourself, but if you have any built-up static electricity, you can seri-ously damage the sensitive chips and electronic components with an innocent touch. You can guard against static discharge by using an anti-static wrist strap, or by simply touching the power supply as soon as the case is opened—with the power turned off, of course!

FIGURE 9.2

Removing the case on a PC's system unit.

When you open the case on your system unit, you see all sorts of computer chips and circuit boards. The really big board located at the base of the computer, (into which everything else is plugged) is called the *motherboard*, because it's the "mother" for your microprocessor and memory chips, as well as for the other internal components that enable your system to function. This motherboard, like the one shown in Figure 9.3, contains several slots, into which you can plug additional *boards* (also called *expansion cards*, or just *cards*) that perform specific functions. Different computers use different types of motherboards, so the layout will differ from PC to PC.

 Caution

If expansion cards aren't inserted correctly, your entire system could fail to function. In addition, if a card is configured using switches or jumpers, setting these in the wrong positions might cause that card—or your entire system—to seriously malfunction.

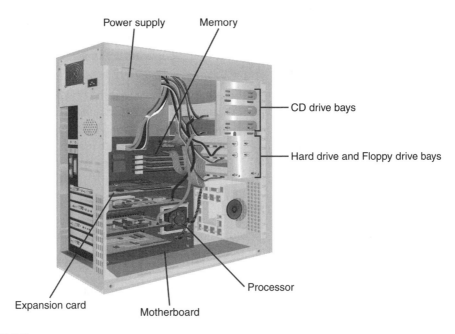

Power supply   Memory

CD drive bays

Hard drive and Floppy drive bays

Processor

Expansion card   Motherboard

FIGURE 9.3

The inside of a typical system unit—a big motherboard with lots of add-on boards attached.

Does an Upgrade Make Sense?

Paradoxically, it's easier to upgrade a newer PC than it is an older one. Of course, if you have a newer PC, you have less need to upgrade. In fact, if your computer is *too* old, you'll find upgrading both problematic and overly expensive; when you add up the costs of the new components you want to add, you'll probably find that it's cheaper to buy a new PC—especially with today's low PC prices.

How old is too old? For some time now, techies have invoked the "three years and out" rule: The rule of thumb is, if your PC is more than three years old, don't bother upgrading. These days I might stretch the three years to four or perhaps five, but there's a point to be made: Really old PCs often don't have the oomph necessary to accept newer, higher-performing components. It's also possible that some components of your old PC might be obsolete. After all, if you can't find new components that physically match your older ones, an upgrade is out of the question.

Cost is also a factor. As low priced as new PCs are these days, you don't want to put too much money into an old machine when a few bucks more will buy you a brand-new system. Should you spend $300–$400 on upgrades when you can buy a new (and much faster) PC for $600 or so? Probably not.

Of course, some minor upgrades are both feasible and affordable, even if your PC is more than three or four years old. This includes the upgrade with which we lead off this chapter—replacing a PC's video card. Replacing a CPU or motherboard is more questionable, in terms of cost, but still worth considering.

What Can You Upgrade?

When it comes to speeding up your PC, what are the most popular upgrades? Here's the short list of upgrades that make the biggest impact on your system's performance:

- **Memory:** Adding more memory to your system not only increases the speed at which your applications run, it also lets you run more apps at the same time. A memory upgrade is one of the least expensive upgrades you can do, typically less than $50. (Learn more about upgrading memory in Chapter 10, "Adding More Memory.")

- **Hard disk:** A larger hard disk not only adds more storage capacity to your system, it also speeds up system performance by increasing the amount of space you can devote to virtual memory. In addition, adding a *faster* hard drive will also speed things up considerably. Adding either a new external or internal hard drive will run $100 or more, depending on the capacity of the new drive. (Learn more about upgrading your hard disk in Chapter 11, "Adding More Disk Space.")

- **Video card:** A faster video card lets your system more quickly display three-dimensional graphics and provides smoother playback for visually demanding PC games. A new video card will run you between $50 and $400, depending on the card's video processing power. (Learn more about upgrading your video card in Chapter 12, "Upgrading to a Faster Video Card.")

- **CPU:** This is the most technically involved upgrade you can undertake, but can provide the biggest improvement in system performance. The CPU is the engine behind everything your PC does. A faster CPU means a faster PC, period. Upgrading the CPU chip can run from $50 to $200. If you have to upgrade the entire motherboard (which is sometimes necessary), expect to pay $100 or more above the individual CPU price. (Learn more about upgrading your CPU in Chapter 13, "Upgrading Your System's CPU.")

Note

All the prices here and elsewhere in this book are approximate, and subject to change. In general, the cost of PC equipment decreases over time, and if you shop around a little you'll get a better deal than if you buy from the first store you walk into. So don't take these prices as gospel—do your homework to find the best bang for your buck when you're ready to upgrade!

For what it's worth, I think that most non-technical users get the biggest bang for the buck by upgrading their PC's memory. A hard disk upgrade won't noticeably speed up most systems, although the ease (and low cost) of adding an external hard drive makes this upgrade difficult to argue against. A video card upgrade is really only necessary if you're running games or applications that tax your current system. And a CPU upgrade is what you do when nothing else works—or if you're an inveterate tweaker.

The Bottom Line

If you're really serious about speeding up your PC, consider upgrading one or more key internal components. Here's the bottom line:

- Upgrading your system's memory will speed up the way all applications run.
- Upgrading your system's hard disk will provide more virtual memory for a slight speed improvement.
- Upgrading your system's video card will speed up the display of graphics-intensive games and applications.
- Upgrading your system's CPU will speed up everything your PC does.

Adding More Memory

Every computer comes with a bunch of built-in electronic memory. This is where your computer temporarily stores program instructions, open files, and other data while it's being used.

The more memory your computer has, the faster your applications will run—and the more applications (and larger files) you can have open at one time. If you don't have enough memory in your system, your computer will appear sluggish and possibly freeze up from time to time.

So here's one of the most effective ways of speeding up your PC: Add more memory!

Understanding Different Types of Memory

There are actually four different types of computer memory: read-only memory, random access memory, flash memory, and virtual memory. Each has its own unique function within your system.

Random Access Memory—Your PC's Main Memory

The main memory on your computer is called *random access memory* (RAM). This main memory is used to temporarily store the programs and data that your computer is using at any given moment. The RAM has to be able to access this data in *nanoseconds* (billionths of seconds), which is considerably faster than the *milliseconds* (thousandths of seconds) that this data can be read from your system's hard disk, where it is stored for the long term.

RAM is electronic memory created by a number of memory chips that reside on your computer's motherboard. It's volatile memory—that is, it gets completely erased whenever your computer is shut off; nothing is held in RAM long-term.

RAM is upgradable, by adding more or larger-capacity memory chips. The more RAM that's available on a machine, the more instructions and data that can be stored at one time—and the faster the PC will run.

Note

All memory is measured in terms of *bytes*. One byte is equal to approximately one character in a word processing document. A unit equaling approximately one thousand bytes (1,024, to be exact) is called a *kilobyte* (KB), and a unit of approximately one thousand (1,024) kilobytes is called a *megabyte* (MB). A thousand megabytes is a *gigabyte* (GB).

Note

Random access memory gets its name because the data stored there can be read in random order. That is, it takes no more time to get to the one-millionth location in memory as it does to get to the first location.

Know, however, that the maximum amount of RAM you can add to your computer depends on your PC's operating system. For example, the 32-bit versions of Windows XP and Vista have a top limit of 4GB of RAM, whereas 64-bit Windows can use up to 128GB of RAM. So if you already have 4GB of RAM on your 32-bit Windows machine, there's no more upgrading to be done.

Read-Only Memory: Permanent Storage for Important Instructions

RAM isn't the only type of memory on your system. Also important is *read-only memory* (ROM), which is used to permanently store key operating instructions for your system. Unlike RAM, which can be both read from and written to (over and over again), ROM can only be read from; you can't write new information to ROM.

The way it works is that the computer manufacturer loads these key instructions into a special ROM chip on your system's motherboard. It's non-volatile memory, in that the instructions stored there are not erased when your computer is shut off; they're always there for use when you next turn on your PC.

ROM is also non-upgradable memory. There is no need to upgrade or expand your system's ROM; more ROM will not speed up your PC.

Note

The operating instructions loaded into ROM are actually a piece of software called the *basic input/output system* (BIOS). This BIOS serves as the permanent interface between your computer's operating system (Windows) and your computer hardware. It must be read before Windows itself is loaded into random access memory.

Flash Memory—External Memory Storage

Flash memory, sometimes called flash RAM, is a type of non-volatile memory used in both computers and in other electronics devices, such as digital cameras. Unlike traditional computer RAM, which is wiped clean when the power is turned off, the contents of a flash memory device don't get erased when the host unit powers down. Flash memory data is always there, ready to be addressed whenever the power is turned back on.

In computers, flash memory is typically external memory. Flash memory devices include so-called USB memory sticks, SD and CompactFlash memory cards, and similar devices. You insert the external device into the appropriate slot on your computer, and the memory on that device is made available for your PC to use. In fact, if you have a Windows Vista PC, it can directly access the flash memory in an external device to supplement your system's built-in RAM.

Virtual Memory—Supplemental Memory on Your Hard Disk

Here's something most computer users don't know. If your computer doesn't possess enough RAM, its microprocessor can use the physical storage space on your machine's hard disk to supplement the main electronic memory. When used in this fashion, the hard disk space becomes *virtual memory*.

While virtual memory is important, especially on computers with low amounts of RAM, this method of data retrieval is slower than retrieving instructions and data from electronic memory. Although it's better in the long-term to add more RAM to your system, using virtual hard disk memory is a good short-term solution for many users.

How Memory Affects PC Speed

It's a fact: The more memory you have installed on your computer, the faster it will run. But why is that?

How Your PC Uses Memory

At its most basic, your computer works by feeding information stored on your hard disk to the microprocessor (also called a *central processing unit*, or CPU) for processing. The CPU is the brains of the system, while the hard drive stores all the data.

The problem with this model is that your hard drive is much, much slower than the CPU. If the CPU literally accessed the hard drive to retrieve every piece of data it needs, your system would operate very slowly.

To speed things up, therefore, a temporary buffer is introduced into the flow. This buffer—your computer's RAM—reads data from the hard disk and stores it for a time until the CPU needs it. Because accessing electronic memory is much faster than accessing a physical hard disk, this speeds up your PC's performance.

Using Virtual Memory

So the more RAM you have installed on your computer, the more data that can be temporarily stored for your CPU's use. But if you don't have enough memory on your system, where is the excess data stored?

As you learned previously, when your system's main memory fills up, the overflow goes back to your hard disk, in the form of virtual memory. The temporary data, instead of being written to electronic memory, is written to your computer's hard drive. Unfortunately, reading and writing to hard disk is much slower than reading and writing to electronic RAM, so system performance suffers.

How More Memory Speeds Up Your PC

Here's the deal. If you have a small amount of RAM on your system—say, 256MB or less—Windows will constantly swap data to and from the virtual memory space on your hard drive, which is slow. If you have a larger amount of RAM installed—more than 2GB, for example—there's enough room in RAM for everything you need to do, which means you experience virtually none of that slow hard disk swapping.

Bottom line? If you have too little memory, your system will run slow—particularly with memory-hungry applications (such as photo- and video-editing programs) and really large documents. If you increase the amount of memory on your system, you'll notice a definite increase in your PC's speed.

How Much Memory Do You Need?

The amount of memory you need depends on which operating system you're using (Windows Vista is more demanding than Windows), which programs you're running (photo/video editors and games are more demanding than web browsers and word processors), and the size of the documents you typically create (big presentations and long videos require more memory than small spreadsheets and letters).

Table 10.1 details my recommendations.

Table 10.1   Memory Requirements

Operating System	Typical Applications	Minimum Memory	Recommended Memory
Windows XP	Word processing, web browsing, email	512MB	1GB
Windows XP	Large presentations, photo editing, video editing, graphics-intensive games	1GB	2GB
Windows Vista	Word processing, web browsing, email	1GB	2GB
Windows Vista	Large presentations, photo editing, video editing, graphics-intensive games	2GB	4GB

Adding Instant Memory to Windows Vista with ReadyBoost

If your PC is running Windows Vista, you can get an instant memory increase—without opening up the case—via Vista's new ReadyBoost technology. With ReadyBoost, you can use a flash memory device to temporarily increase the amount of RAM on your personal computer. Insert one of these devices into the appropriate slot on your PC, and your system's memory is automatically increased—and your system's performance is automatically improved.

How ReadyBoost Works

When you activate ReadyBoost, Windows duplicates the overflow data that might otherwise be sent to your computer's hard drive virtual memory. This duplicate data is then sent to the inserted flash memory device.

 Note

ReadyBoost is available only with Windows Vista. Windows XP does not have a similar feature.

Windows then uses the data stored in the flash device's RAM, instead of accessing the data on the slower hard disk. Because a flash memory device is approximately 10 times faster than hard disk-based virtual memory, you'll notice an immediate speed boost.

 Note
Even with ReadyBoost activated, Windows continues to write the data sent to the flash memory device to your system's hard disk, as a backup.

In short, the RAM on the flash memory device is added to the available RAM on your computer's motherboard. This gives you that much more memory to run applications and open documents.

Speeding Up Your PC with ReadyBoost

To use ReadyBoost, you first have to insert an external memory device into one of your PC's open slots. If you have a USB memory drive, like the one in Figure 10.1, insert it into a USB slot. If you have a flash memory card, insert it into the appropriate card slot.

FIGURE 10.1
Use a USB memory drive, like this SanDisk Cruzer Micro, to add instant memory to any Windows Vista computer.

You should now be prompted as to how you want to use that device, as shown in Figure 10.2. Select Speed Up My System, and your notebook will automatically access available memory on the device.

You can configure Vista to use all or just part of the available memory on the USB drive for your system's RAM. Just open the Start menu and select Computer. When the Computer window opens, right-click the USB drive and select Properties. From the Properties dialog box, shown in Figure 10.3, select the ReadyBoost tab and adjust the slider to select how much space to use.

Note

Windows Vista ReadyBoost supports USB flash memory drives, as well as CompactFlash (CF) and Secure Digital (SD) memory cards. It can handle devices that hold between 256MB and 4GB of RAM.

FIGURE 10.2

Enabling ReadyBoost to use external memory.

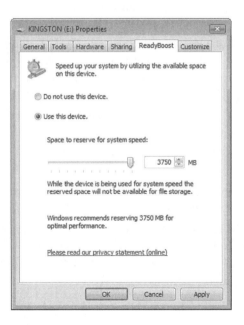

FIGURE 10.3

Configuring how much memory to use.

When you're done using the flash memory device, or if you no longer need the speed boost, simply remove the device. When the flash memory device is removed, Windows returns to using just the regular RAM installed on your system.

Note

Any data still in use when the flash memory device is removed is now read from the hard disk, where it was duplicated during the ReadyBoost process. No data is lost.

Adding More Memory to a Desktop PC

ReadyBoost on Windows Vista PCs aside, if you want to truly increase the amount of memory on your computer, you have to do a little physical work. That means installing new memory chips—which isn't nearly as difficult as you think.

In this section you learn how to upgrade the memory on a desktop computer—the kind with a separate system unit, monitor, and keyboard. If you have a notebook or laptop computer, you can skip this section and read ahead to the "Adding More Memory to a Notebook PC" section, instead.

Choosing the Right Memory Module

The easy part of increasing your computer's memory is performing the installation—for which you need only a screwdriver. The hard part is determining what type of memory you need to buy. That's because there are a bunch of different types of memory available. You need to figure out what type of memory your computer uses to buy the right RAM for your system.

All memory today comes on modules, such as the one shown in Figure 10.4. Each module contains multiple memory chips. The capacity of each chip adds up to the total capacity of the memory module. The memory modules plug into memory sockets located on your PC's motherboard; installation is actually quite easy.

Depending on the age and type of your computer, your PC could be using one of four different types of memory modules:

> ■ **SIMM (Single Inline Memory Module):** This is an older type of computer memory, where chips were mounted on only one side of the module (hence the *single* in the name). SIMMs have not been used in computers since the late 1990s.

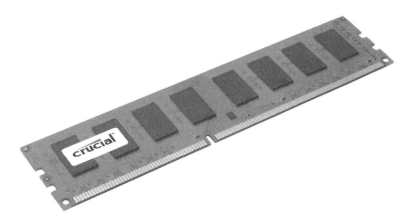

FIGURE 10.4

A typical memory module, which plugs into the memory socket on your PC's motherboard. (This one happens to be a DDR3 DIMM, courtesy of Crucial.)

10

- **DIMM (Dual Inline Memory Module):** Unlike the single-sided SIMMs, DIMMs have memory chips mounted on both sides of the module, and come in both 168-pin and 184-pin versions. DIMMs are the most popular memory modules in use today. If you have a full-sized consumer desktop PC, this is probably the type of memory that is used.

- **SO DIMM (Small Outline DIMM):** This is a module about half the size of a standard DIMM module, used primarily in notebook PCs and small form-factor desktops. SO DIMMs are available in 72-pin, 144-pin, and 200-pin versions.

- **RIMM (Rambus Inline Memory Module):** RIMMs use 184-pin connectors and are slightly faster than comparable DIMMs. RIMMs also cost at least twice as much DIMMs. For that reason, they're not widely used in most consumer-oriented PCs, although you might find them in higher-end servers and workstations.

You'll need to consult your PC's instruction manual (or look up your PC's model number in a manufacturer's website cross-listing) to determine the type of module your machine uses. And, although it's important to get the right type of module for your specific PC, you shouldn't worry about accidentally inserting the wrong module into the wrong type of slot. It's physically impossible to insert a memory module into a slot that doesn't match it, pin-wise.

 Note

Some types of memory modules have to be installed in pairs. Consult your instruction manual or manufacturer's website for more details.

Choosing the Right Type of Memory Chip

Not only do you have to specify what type of memory module your system uses, you also have to specify what type of RAM chip is installed on the module. There are several different types of memory chips in use today:

Note

DDR2 SDRAM is faster than the original DDR SDRAM. DDR3 is faster still, and DDR4 is ever faster.

- ■ **DRAM** (Dynamic RAM)
- ■ **SDRAM** (Synchronous Dynamic RAM)
- ■ **DDR SDRAM** (Double Data Rate SDRAM)
- ■ **DDR2 SDRAM** (Double Data Rate 2 SDRAM)
- ■ **DDR3 SDRAM** (Double Data Rate 3 SDRAM)
- ■ **DDR4 SDRAM** (Double Data Rate 4 SDRAM)
- ■ **RDARM** (Rambus DRAM)
- ■ **FPM DRAM** (Fast Page Mode DRAM)
- ■ **EDO DRAM** (Extended Data Out DRAM)
- ■ **BEDO DRAM** (Burst EDO DRAM)

The differences between these chip types are technical and not of interest to most users. The key thing is to recognize what type of chip is used in your particular PC.

SIMM modules typically use either FPM or EDO DRAM chips. RIMM modules use RDRAM chips. Most DIMM modules use either SDRAM or DDR DRAM chips. The newer your PC, the more likely it is to use the more advanced DDR2, DDR3, or DDR3 chips. Consult with your PC's instruction manual to determine what type of RAM your system uses.

Choosing the Right Memory Size

RAM today is typically available in 128MB, 256MB, 512MB, and 1GB increments. So, for example, if you want to add 1GB of RAM to your system, you could buy one 1GB module, two 512MB modules, four 256MB modules, or eight 128MB modules. To make the most efficient use of your system's vacant memory slots, it's always best to add the smallest number of larger-capacity modules possible.

Shopping for Memory Upgrades

Where can you buy the correct memory for your desktop PC? Lots of places.

You should be able to purchase memory modules directly from your computer's manufacturer, at your local computer store, or directly from the memory manufacturers:

- Crucial Technology (www.crucial.com)
- Kingston (www.kingston.com)
- PNY (www.pny.com)

All of these manufacturers provide lots of charts and tables and "configurators" (like the one shown in Figure 10.5) to help you find the right type of memory for your particular PC model. You'll need to know your computer's manufacturer and model number. The configurator should then direct you to the specific memory your need for your machine.

FIGURE 10.5
Using Crucial's RAM Memory Advisor to determine what type of memory to buy for your PC.

Performing the Upgrade

Once you've figured out what type of memory to buy, it's time for the actual upgrade. Fortunately, this is pretty much a "plug-and-go" installation, with no undo configuration necessary.

Just follow these steps:

1. Close Windows and power off your PC.
2. Disconnect your PC from its power source.

Caution

It's important to protect against electrostatic discharge while you're installing memory. Use an antistatic wristband or take other precautions to make sure you don't fry your new RAM before you get to use it.

3. Open the system unit case, per the manufacturer's instructions.

4. Locate your system's memory slots on your system's motherboard—the big computer board located at the bottom or side of your system unit. Figure 10.6 shows you what you should be looking for.

Note

If you don't have an open memory slot on your PC, you'll have to remove an old lower-capacity memory module and replace it with the new higher-capacity module.

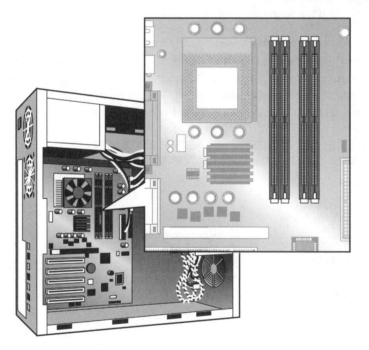

FIGURE 10.6

Locating the memory slots on your computer's motherboard.

5. Insert the new memory module into an open memory slot. Note that each type of module inserts into its slot a little differently. DIMMs and RIMMs insert fairly traditionally, as you can see in Figure 10.7. You release the clips at either end of the slot, line up the module, press it firmly down into the slot, and then flip the end clips back into place. (Some force may be necessary.) The older SIMMs, however,

Caution

When you're installing RIMM modules, you cannot leave any RIMM sockets empty. Any empty slots must be occupied by a *continuity module* (sometimes called a *continuity RIMM*), which looks like a standard RIMM but with no memory chips installed.

insert into the slot at a 45-degree angle, as shown in Figure 10.8. After the module is in place, you then push it up to lock it into a vertical position.

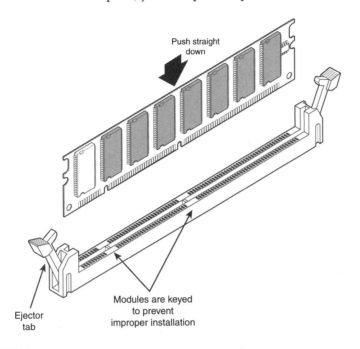

FIGURE 10.7

Inserting a DIMM module.

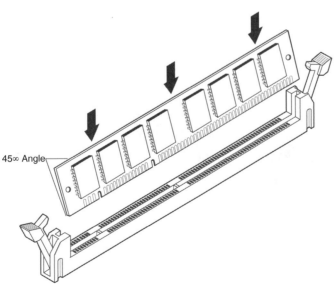

FIGURE 10.8

SIMMs insert at an angle, then click upward into place.

6. Reinstall the system unit's cover, reconnect your PC to an AC power supply, and power it up.

And that's all you need to do. Your PC should recognize the new memory when it reboots—and run much faster than what it did before.

Caution

If your system displays any sort of error message when you start it up, you'll need to enter the BIOS setup program and reconfigure your system settings manually for the proper amount of memory now installed.

Adding More Memory to a Notebook PC

Believe it or not, upgrading memory on a notebook PC is even easier than it is on a desktop machine. That's because you don't have to open up your notebook case to make the upgrade; it all happens in a little compartment on the bottom of your PC.

Shopping for Notebook Memory

As with desktop memory, you shop for notebook memory by plugging in the manufacturer name and model number into a "configurator" program on the memory manufacturer's website. Most notebook RAM comes in modules, like the one shown in Figure 10.9, that look like little credit cards. You have to get the exact type of memory used by your particular PC, whatever that might happen to be.

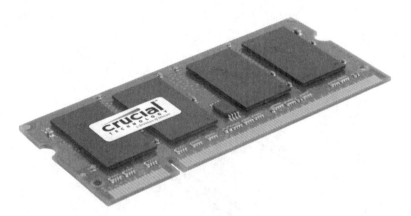

FIGURE 10.9

A DDR2 SO DIMM notebook memory module from Crucial.

Memory upgrades vary in cost depending on factors such as the type of memory that your computer system uses and the amount that you intend to purchase. You should be able to purchase memory modules directly from your computer's manufacturer, at your local computer store, or from any of the memory manufacturers noted previously in this chapter.

Performing the Upgrade

Memory is typically added to a notebook PC through an easily accessible compartment on the bottom of the unit. A small Philips screwdriver is all you need to remove the door to this compartment; then the memory itself simply snaps into place.

Just follow these steps:

1. Close Windows and power off your notebook.

2. Remove your notebook's battery.

3. Locate and open your notebook memory compartment, as shown in Figure 10.10. This should be on the bottom of your notebook case.

4. Insert the new memory module or card, per the manufacturer's instructions. Most memory modules insert into the socket at a slight angle, as shown in Figure 10.11. Apply pressure to each end of the module to fully seat it into the slot. After the module is in place, you then push the socket downward until it locks back into position.

5. Reinstall the cover to the memory compartment, reinsert the battery, and power up your notebook.

Note

On some notebooks you may need to remove an old lower-capacity memory card in order to add a new higher-capacity one.

Most notebooks will automatically recognize the new additional memory when you reboot. You should notice an immediate speed improvement when you next use your notebook.

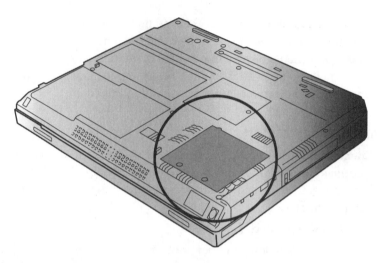

FIGURE 10.10

The memory compartment on the bottom of a notebook PC.

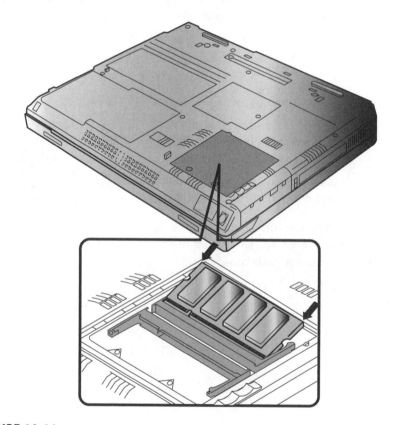

FIGURE 10.11

Inserting a memory module into a notebook PC.

The Bottom Line

You'd be surprised at the speed improvement you can gain by upgrading the amount of memory installed on your PC. Here's the bottom line:

- Your computer temporarily caches programs and data in random access memory. The more memory installed, the more data that can be cached and the faster your system will run.

- If you're running Windows XP, go for at least 512MB memory (1GB is better). If you're running Windows vista, go for at least 1GB of memory (2GB is better).

- You can add extra memory to a PC running Windows Vista PC by inserting a USB or flash memory device into an open slot.

- Desktop PC memory is upgraded by installing new memory modules into the memory slots on the motherboard inside your PC's system unit.

- Notebook PC memory is upgraded by inserting new memory modules or cards into the memory compartment on the bottom of the notebook PC.

- Your computer should recognize the upgraded memory when you reboot—and should show an immediate performance boost.

10

Adding More Disk Space

In the preceding chapter, you learned how adding more random access memory (RAM) can speed up your PC. You also learned how your computer sometimes uses your hard disk as virtual memory, to supplement your system's main memory.

If you don't have enough free space on your hard drive, you might not have enough virtual memory to ensure speedy operation. In addition, an overly stuffed hard drive takes longer to open and close the programs and documents you use every day.

Because your computer's original internal hard disk will tend to fill up over time, you may want to consider adding a second hard drive to your system—or replacing the original hard drive with a bigger one. Not only will more hard disk space speed up your system, however slightly, it will also give you more valuable storage space for your programs and files. And, given the low price of hard drives today, it's not a big investment!

How Hard Disk Storage Affects Your PC's Speed

Before you grab your screwdriver and start poking around inside your PC's system unit, let's stop for a second and examine just how it is that your hard disk affects the performance of your entire computer system. Because it does, you know.

Supplementing RAM with Virtual Memory

The first way your hard disk affects system performance revolves around the topic of virtual memory. As you've learned previously in this book, virtual memory is hard disk space used as overflow or supplemental memory to your computer's main electronic memory. Virtual memory compensates, in a way, for having too little RAM on your system; data and instructions that might otherwise be temporarily written to RAM are instead written to your PC's hard drive.

For virtual memory to be effective, you must have enough free hard disk space. (It also helps if your hard disk is fully defragmented and free from errors.) If your hard disk space is running low, that means that there's less space to devote to virtual memory—and the less total memory (main plus virtual) you have, the slower your computer will run.

Enabling Access to Programs and Data

The other way that your hard drive can adversely affect system performance concerns all the programs and documents that are read from and written to your hard disk in the course of a computing day. It's a simple math problem: The faster your system can move this data to and from your hard drive, the speedier your PC will be.

The challenge comes when your hard disk becomes too full. A full hard disk has to spread the bits and pieces of each file in different sectors of the drives, because there typically aren't enough free sectors all together to allow contiguous storage. This results in disk fragmentation, which as you recall can really slow down hard disk performance; it takes longer to retrieve and reassemble a file from all across your hard disk than it does from a contiguous area.

 Note

Learn more about disk defragmentation in Chapter 5, "Optimizing Your Hard Disk."

Understanding Hard Drive Capacity

The goal, therefore, is to have a big enough hard drive so that there's enough space both for virtual memory and for storing your documents and programs in contiguous sectors, thus avoiding disk defragmentation. But how do you know how much free space you have on your hard disk—and how much capacity do you need?

Viewing the Capacity of Your Hard Drive

The answer to the first question is easy. To view the overall and used capacity of your hard drive, just follow these steps:

1. Click the Start button and select either Computer (Windows Vista) or My Computer (Windows XP).

2. In Windows Vista, you can view the capacity of a drive by clicking that hard drive's icon. As you can see in Figure 11.1, the space used is shown graphically at the bottom of the window, with space free and total size also displayed.

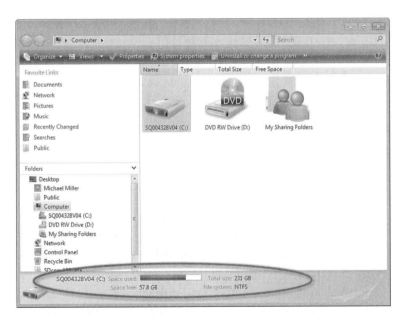

FIGURE 11.1

Viewing basic disk capacity in Windows Vista.

3. In both Windows XP and Vista, you can see more detail by right-clicking the hard drive icon and selecting Properties from the pop-up menu. When the Properties dialog box appears, make sure the General tab is selected. As you can see in Figure 11.2, this displays a pie chart of your drive's used and free space, along with details as to capacity (in gigabytes).

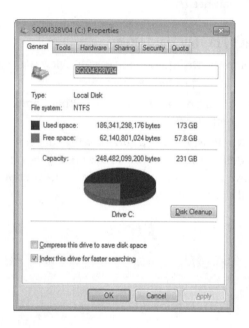

FIGURE 11.2
Viewing detailed disk capacity in Windows Vista.

Determining the Ideal Hard Disk Capacity

As to the question of how much free space is enough, you should leave at least 20% of your total space free for use as virtual memory and other essential operations. So if you have an 80GB hard drive, you need to leave 16GB free.

That said, the total amount of hard disk space you need depends on how much stuff you need to store on it. If all you do is browse the Web and read email, you can make due with a relatively small hard drive. On the other hand, if you store a ton of digital photos or music, or run some very large programs, you need more hard disk space. How much is something you have to determine based on your own specific needs.

Shopping for a New Hard Drive

If you don't have enough hard disk space on your computer, you can make more space by deleting programs and files you don't use or by purchasing a new hard drive. You can go with an external hard drive to supplement your main internal hard drive, or you can replace your existing internal drive with a larger capacity model. (We examine all these options later in this section.)

Of course, it pays to do your research before you buy any type of new hard drive. You need to understand the relevant specifications to make an informed buying decision—and to get the right hard drive for your system. This information, typically available somewhere on the drive's packaging, tells you how much data the disk can hold, how fast it can access that data, and the type of interface the drive uses. (Faster is better, of course—and more expensive.)

Of these specs, you'll want to focus your attention on form factor, size, speed, and price. Given the low prices of hard drives today, you'll probably want to spend a few extra bucks to get a larger-capacity drive. If you're using disk-intensive applications (such as PC games or audio/video-editing programs), you'll also want to spring for the faster 7,200 RPM models. And, of course, price is always a factor; make sure you make the price/performance compromise that works best for your specific needs.

Internal or External?

The first question to answer is whether you want an external or internal hard drive. Naturally, if you want to replace your existing hard drive, you're talking an internal model. But if you want to supplement your existing drive rather than replace it, an external drive is probably the best way to go; all you have to do is connect said external drive to a free USB or FireWire port on your PC, it's that easy.

Replacing an existing drive has its advantages, however. Although it's a bit more work (and involves digging around inside your PC's system unit), it results in simpler operation. That's because you only have to deal with a single drive when installing programs, opening and saving files, and the like. Get a big enough C: and you don't need to bother with a D: drive as well.

That, of course, is the drawback of adding a supplemental external drive. You now have to split your programs and files between two drives (C: and D:); you may also have to move some of your existing files from your original drive to the new one. It can get a bit confusing if you're not well organized, even if the initial installation is much simpler.

11

So which is best for you? If you don't mind getting your hands dirty, technically speaking, and don't want to bother with moving files from one disk to another, go with a replacement internal drive. If you want a simple installation, however, and don't mind dealing with two drives in day-to-day operation, add an external drive instead.

Capacity

Now let's get down to specifications, starting with capacity. Disk drive size is typically measured in gigabytes (GB) and terabytes (TB). A terabyte is equal to 1,000 gigabytes.

The bigger the drive, of course, the higher the price. As of fall 2008, you can purchase new drives ranging in capacity from 80GB to 2TB. Prices run from less than $100 to more than $500. For example, as I write this book, Best Buy is selling a 500GB Western Digital external drive for $99 and a 1TB Seagate drive for $299. Expect prices to be similar or even lower by the time you read this.

Caution

Another drawback to adding a second hard drive is that you still have to deal with any issues regarding your current internal drive. If your current drive is slow, fragmented, or damaged, or has a spyware/virus infection, those problems remain even if you supplement your capacity with an external hard drive.

Caution

It's actually possible to buy too big a hard drive—on older PCs, anyway. If you're running Windows 95 or earlier, your operating system will only support drives up to 32GB in size. If you're running Windows 98 or any later operating system (including Windows XP and Windows Vista), you can use drives that exceed the 32GB limit.

Spin Rate

Spin rate measures the speed at which the platters spin, in revolutions per minute (RPM). Faster-spinning drives result in faster data transfer rates (discussed next); most drives today spin at either 5,400 RPM or 7,200 RPM, and some high-performance drives reach 10,000 RPM. The slower speed is acceptable for traditional office use, but you'll want a faster drive if you're doing a lot of audio- or video-related tasks.

Data Transfer Rate

The *data transfer rate* is the speed at which the system copies data from the hard drive to your computer (and vice versa). This spec is typically measured in megabits per second (Mbps). As with most of these specs, faster is better.

Tip

Make sure the data transfer rate of your new hard drive matches the specs of your computer—although, in most cases, if you get a faster hard drive than your system can handle, it can be configured to run at a slower mode to ensure compatibility.

Access Time

The next spec to consider is *access time* or *seek time*, which is the amount of time it takes for the heads to locate a specific piece of data on the hard drive. Manufacturers typically specify the "average access time," because the actual seek time varies depending on the location of the heads and where the next bit of data is stored. A faster access time (smaller number) is better, naturally.

External Connection Type

When you're looking at an external drive, you can typically choose between USB and FireWire connections. Most low-priced external drives today feature USB connections. Some higher-end drives have both USB and FireWire.

Today's USB connections adhere to the USB 2.0 specification, which promises a 480Mbps transfer speed. Note the word *promises*; USB connections rarely exceed 280Mbps sustained speeds.

Tip

For most purposes, either USB or FireWire will do a good job on the average system. However, if you're using your hard disk for video editing or similar high-demand tasks, the faster FireWire 800 connection might be necessary.

There are actually two different types of FireWire connections in use today. The older (and more common) FireWire 400 has a maximum transfer speed of 400Mbps, whereas the newer FireWire 800 doubles that to nearly 800Mbps.

Table 11.1 compares the specs of these interfaces, in terms of data transfer rates—faster is always better.

11

Table 11.1   USB Versus FireWire Transfer Rates

Connection Type	Data Transfer Rate (Maximum)
USB 2.0	480Mbps
FireWire 400	400Mbps
FireWire 800	800Mbps

Internal Interface Type

When you're looking at an internal drive, there are several different interfaces available that control the communication between your hard drive to your PC:

- **ATA** (Advanced Technology Attachment). An ATA drive uses a parallel connection with a 40-pin connection. These drives are quite common and easy to install and configure. Standard ATA drives transfer data at 16.6Mbps; variations of the ATA standard include ATA-100 (also known as Ultra ATA), which has a data transfer rate of 100Mbps, and ATA-133, which has a data transfer rate of 133Mbps.

- **SATA** (Serial ATA). This is a more advanced version of ATA, using a serial connector rather than a parallel one. The parallel connector enables faster data transfer rates, in theory up to 300Mbps.

- **SCSI** (Small Computer System Interface). This is a more expensive, difficult-to-configure interface primarily used in systems designed for high-end audio/video editing.

In most instances, you'll replace your existing drive with a drive that uses the same interface. So if your PC has an ATA drive, you should buy a new ATA drive. If it has an SATA drive, you should replace it with another SATA drive.

Note

Some vendors use the terms *PATA* (parallel ATA), *IDE* (*Integrated Drive Electronics*), or IDE/ATA to describe ATA drives.

Tip

If you're working with an older PC, you might encounter some additional, now-obsolete interfaces, such as ST-506, ESDI, and MCA-IDE. If your system uses any of these interfaces, it's an antique; junk the thing and buy a new PC!

RAID or Not to RAID?

If you want to get really fancy, you can install multiple hard disks on your system in what is called a *RAID*—a redundant array of independent disks. RAID technology lets you use two or more hard disk drives simultaneously; your data is divided and replicated between the multiple disks for increased reliability and input/output performance.

Some manufacturers sell high-end external drives that contain multiple disks configured in a RAID array. For internal drives, you have to install the multiple disks yourself and then configure them in the RAID array.

I won't go into RAID arrays in depth here; they're mainly for higher-end, higher-capacity systems, such as network storage servers. However, if you have extreme data storage needs (say, for a home media server), you should consider a RAID array for both safety and performance reasons.

Disk Drive Manufacturers

When you're looking for a new hard disk, it pays to stick to the major manufacturers. Here are some of the companies that specialize in magnetic storage media:

- Iomega (www.iomega.com)
- LaCie (www.lacie.com)
- Maxtor (www.maxtor.com)
- Seagate (www.seagate.com)
- Western Digital (www.westerndigital.com)

Both external and internal hard drives can be found at most computer and consumer electronics stores, including Best Buy and Circuit City.

Adding a New External Hard Drive

The easiest type of hard drive to install is the external variety. These drives typically install via either USB or FireWire, and supplement the storage space on your main internal hard drive.

11

Connecting the New Drive

Installation of an external hard drive is relatively simple. Just follow these steps:

1. Plug the new drive into a live electrical outlet.

2. Connect the drive to an open USB or FireWire port on your PC, as shown in Figure 11.3.

3. If your new drive came with an installation CD (and it probably did), insert the CD into your CD-ROM drive and run the installation program. (Sometimes the installation program is actually on the hard drive itself, and will automatically run when you connect the drive.) Otherwise, Windows should recognize the new drive and automatically install the proper device drivers.

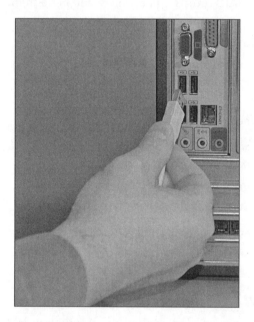

FIGURE 11.3

Connecting an external hard drive via USB.

Your new external drive assumes the next highest available drive letter on your system. So, for example, if your current hard drive is the C: drive, the new external drive will be the D: drive. (If your CD-ROM drive was formerly the D: drive, it will now become the E: drive. When it comes to letters, your system likes to group similar types of drives together.)

Freeing Up Space on Your Existing Drive

Once you have the new external hard drive connected, you can install any new programs to that drive, as well as save new documents to that drive. But that doesn't make your existing internal disk any less congested.

What you have to do now is free up some disk space on your internal drive by moving files from there to your new external hard disk. The best candidates for relocation are data files—Word documents, Excel spreadsheets, digital photographs, music tracks, and the like. It's relatively easy to open up two Computer or My Computer windows and drag and drop entire document folders from the old drive to the new one. The more files you move, the more disk space you free up and the faster your computer should run.

You can also relocate software programs from the old drive to the new one, but this is a bit more work. If you want to move a software program, you have to uninstall the program from the current hard drive and reinstall it on the external drive. This is a good idea only if you have the original software installation discs—and if you don't have to reregister a program when you reinstall it.

The one thing you definitely *can't* move to your new external drive is the Windows operating system. Windows has to be located on your computer's first (internal) hard drive, so don't even think about moving it.

11

Upgrading an Existing Internal Hard Drive

It's one thing to add an external hard drive to your system. It's quite another to replace your existing hard drive; not only do you have to deal with opening up your PC's system unit and making a lot of connection, you also have to somehow transfer your existing data and software programs (and the Windows operating system) from the old drive to the new.

Planning the Upgrade

Physically, replacing the drive is as simple as taking the old one out of your system unit and plugging the new one into the same spot. The big challenge in replacing a hard drive is how to transfer your existing stuff from the old drive to the new one.

One approach is to back up all your data and programs from your old drive, and then restore them to your new drive after it has been installed. This is a big pain in the rear, but it works.

A better approach is to install the new hard drive in your system unit as your master drive, but keep the old drive installed as your second, or slave, drive. When you do this, you can then copy all the data and programs from the old (now slave) drive to your new (master) drive. Plus, you get the benefit of having two hard drives on your system—and every little bit of storage space helps!

If you take this approach, I recommend purchasing a software program to help you with the disk-copying chores. The best of these programs are Acronis True Image (www.acronis.com), Symantec's Norton Ghost (www.symantec.com/norton/ghost), and Paragon's Drive Copy (www.paragon-software.com/home/dc-personal/). These programs automate the process of creating an exact mirror of your old drive on your new drive, including the operating system and all your data and applications.

Getting to Know the Hard Drive

It helps to know what you're dealing with before you get inside the case, so open up your new hard drive and take a look at it.

The back of the drive unit is where you make all your connections. As you can see in Figure 11.4, most internal hard disk drives include power and data connectors, as well as a set of jumpers that determine how the drive will be used in your system. Familiarize yourself with these connectors before you perform the upgrade.

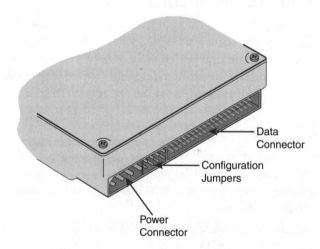

FIGURE 11.4

The back of an internal hard drive.

Replacing the Drive

If you want to replace your old internal hard drive with a newer, bigger model, make sure you have a Philips screwdriver handy and that your system unit is in a comfortable workspace. You might even want to grab a small flashlight to help you see into all the nooks and crannies inside your PC.

Caution

Static electricity can zap critical components when you're working inside the system unit. Use an anti-static wrist strap or similar device to protect against static discharge when touching anything inside your PC.

The following instructions assume you install the new hard drive alongside the old one, to make it easier to transfer data from the old drive to the new one. Follow these steps:

1. Close Windows and power off your PC.

2. Disconnect your PC from its power source.

3. Open the system unit case as per the manufacturer instructions.

4. Set the drive selection jumper on the new hard drive as per Figure 11.5. You typically have three options: *master, slave,* and *cable select.* Because this will be your second hard drive (initially), you'll probably select slave—unless, that is, your system is set up to automatically determine which drive is which, in which case you'll select the cable select setting. You'll have to consult the hard drive's instructions to determine where the drive selection jumper is located, and how to position it. (It's different with every manufacturer.) Often, the jumper settings are silkscreened on the drive itself, so be sure to check it first!

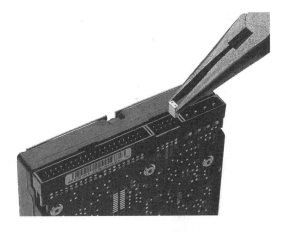

FIGURE 11.5

Use a pair of needle nose pliers or a pair of tweezers to move the jumper block into the correct position.

5. Locate an empty drive bay in your system unit and position the drive next to the bay. *Don't* slide the drive into the bay just yet.

6. Connect the internal power cable to your new hard drive, as shown in Figure 11.6.

7. Connect the internal data cable to the hard drive. (You use the same cable to connect the slave drive and the master drive; the slave connector

Tip

Cable select is the preferred setting for most newer PCs, especially those capable of running ATA-100 and faster modes. You can also check the jumper setting on your existing hard drive. If it's set for cable select, use this setting for your new drive, too. Otherwise, use the slave setting.

is typically color-coded gray, where the master connector is color-coded black.) Make sure you line up the colored stripe on the data cable with pin 1 on the drive's data connector.

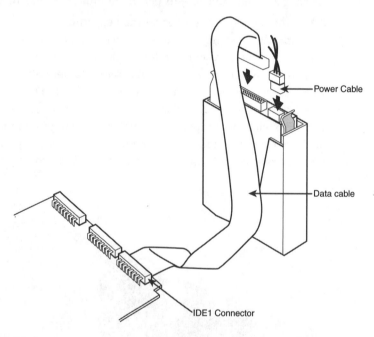

Power Cable

Data cable

IDE1 Connector

FIGURE 11.6

Attaching the power and data cables to the hard drive.

8. Slide the new drive into the drive bay. If necessary, fasten the drive into the bay with the supplied screws; most newer drives should just snap into place.

9. Reinstall the system unit cover and reconnect the PC to its power source.

10. Power on your PC. When your system starts up, press the correct key to enter the BIOS setup utility.

11. Use the arrow keys to move to the section of the utility that holds the hard disk configuration information and select the Auto Detect or Auto Detect Drives option.

12. Save your configuration changes, exit the BIOS setup utility, and allow your computer to continue the startup process.

Caution

If your drive bays are enclosed in a metal cage, you'll need to remove the cage before inserting the new drive. In addition, if you're trying to fit a 3.5-inch drive into a 5.25-inch bay on an older PC, you'll need to use a frame adapter to make the thing fit. (If your new drive didn't come with a frame adapter—actually a set of rails—you can buy it separately.)

13. If your hard drive came with its own installation program, run it now to prepare your hard drive for use. If it didn't, you may need to partition and format the drive before you can use it. If this is the case, read on to the next section.

14. When the new drive is up and running, run the drive-copy software to copy the contents of your old drive to your new drive. (You may first need to reinstall Windows from the original installation CD or DVD.)

15. Get back inside your system unit and change the jumper settings on your old drive to the slave setting, and then change the jumper settings on your new drive to the master setting.

16. Assuming that your new hard drive is working fine as your main C: drive, reformat your old hard drive (which should now be your D: drive) to wipe off all the old data, applications, and operating system.

Caution

You might want to wait a few days or weeks before reformatting your old drive, just to make sure that all your programs and data have been successfully transferred to the new drive.

Your new hard drive should now mirror the operation of your old drive, but with more free space. You can now use your old hard drive for additional data storage.

Upgrading Hard Disk Storage on a Notebook PC

The preceding section described how to upgrade the hard disk on a desktop PC. You can also upgrade the hard drive on many (but not all) notebook PCs. It isn't easy, but it is possible.

Tip

As with desktop PCs, the easier approach is to connect a supplemental external hard drive to your notebook, typically via USB.

11

If you're lucky, your notebook's hard drive slides into a modular bay on the side or bottom of your notebook, as shown in Figure 11.7. If this describes your notebook, replacing the hard disk is as easy as following these steps:

1. Completely power off your PC.
2. Unplug the notebook from the electrical outlet and remove the internal battery.
3. Slide out the old hard drive.
4. Slide in the new hard drive.

Caution

When you replace a computer's main hard drive, you lose access to all programs and data on the old hard disk. You'll need to reinstall Windows and all your programs onto the new hard drive. You should also back up all your documents and files from the old hard drive, if you can, and then restore them to the new drive.

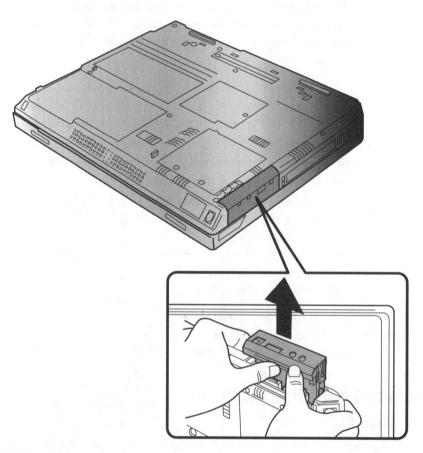

FIGURE 11.7

A modular hard drive bay on a notebook PC.

Some notebooks let you access the hard drive via a panel on the bottom of the machine, as shown in Figure 11.8. This type of arrangement makes replacing the hard drive quite similar to replacing system memory. After you've powered off the PC and removed the battery, remove the cover to the hard drive compartment and then disconnect and remove the old drive.

Tip

Not sure how to get to your notebook's hard drive? Consult your notebook's instruction manual or technical information on the manufacturer's website.

Connect the new hard drive inside the compartment, and then refasten the door to the compartment.

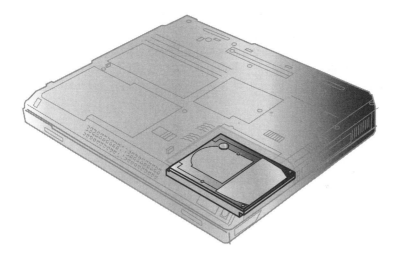

FIGURE 11.8

A hard disk compartment on the bottom of a notebook PC.

If you're not so lucky, and some of us aren't, replacing your notebook's hard drive is an internal procedure. If you're technically adept, you'll need to disassemble your notebook's case to gain access to the motherboard, which is directly underneath the keyboard assembly. Locate the hard drive and remove any screws connecting the hard drive to its mounting cage. Remove the ribbon cable that connects to the hard drive, and then carefully slide the drive out of the notebook. To install the new hard drive, simply reverse this procedure.

11

The Bottom Line

Although it's true that system memory has the biggest impact on your computer's performance, an overworked hard drive can also slow things down to some degree. Here's the bottom line:

■ Your hard drive not only has to access programs and data, it also serves as virtual memory to supplement your system's main memory. If your hard drive is too full, it will slow down your system's performance.

■ The easiest way to add hard disk storage is to connect an external hard drive via USB.

■ You can also replace your system's internal hard drive with a larger model, although this involves some technical work inside your PC's system unit.

■ If you have a notebook PC, it's possible that it can be replaced with a larger model, by sliding it out of a compartment in the notebook case.

11

Upgrading to a Faster Video Card

Upgrading certain internal system components can increase the speed of your PC. We've already discussed how to upgrade memory (Chapter 10, "Adding More Memory") and hard disk capacity (Chapter 11, "Adding More Disk Space"); now it's time to turn to your system's video performance.

Like upgrading memory, installing a new video card is relatively easy—assuming that you're comfortable opening up your desktop's system unit, that is. And, if you're trying to run graphics-intensive applications, this simple upgrade can make your system look and feel a lot faster than you're used to.

How the Wrong Video Card Can Slow Down Your PC

The images you see on your computer monitor are generated inside the computer, via a specialized video card or chip on your motherboard (sometimes called a *video adapter*, *graphics adapter*, or *display adapter*). This card generates video images at a specified resolution, which is a measurement of how detailed your picture is. (The higher the resolution, the sharper the picture—and the more items you can fit onscreen.)

What benefit might you get from upgrading your computer's video card? Many of today's state-of-the-art applications require a fast video card with lots of onboard video memory to generate the rapidly changing three-dimensional graphics associated with the applications, and of Windows Vista itself. It takes a lot of horsepower to make all those objects appear to move around realistically onscreen in real time.

What applications are most difficult to display? Here's a short list:

- Graphics-intensive PC games, especially those games with highly realistic 3D images
- Video-editing programs, such as Adobe Premiere and Pinnacle Studio
- Windows Vista's Aero interface

> **Tip**
>
> Programs are graphics intensive when they have to *create* new three-dimensional graphics and video effects. Programs that merely reproduce existing graphics—such as displaying digital photographs or playing DVD movies—do not require near as much graphics horsepower, and will benefit less from a video card upgrade.

If your video card isn't up to snuff, you might find any of these apps—or the Windows Aero interface—not displaying properly onscreen. The graphics might lack translucency or 3D effects; objects might not move smoothly across the screen; it's possible that the entire interface might freeze up or not run at all. However it manifests itself, insufficient graphics power can noticeably slow down your PC.

Here's why. Many low-end PCs come with (surprise!) low-performance video cards (or low-end video capability built right in to the motherboard), which just aren't capable of displaying high-resolution graphics, fast-moving game images, and moving video from DVDs and digital movies. In fact, some PCs don't even have dedicated video cards, instead relying on a motherboard-based graphics chip to do the job—or not, as the case may be.

12

So if your video display has a tendency to shudder and jerk, if it can't run some of the latest graphics-intensive games, or if it can't display all of Windows Vista's fancy Aero graphics without getting bogged down, it's time to think about getting a higher-performance video card.

Shopping for a New Video Card

Fortunately, upgrading your video card is pretty much as easy as removing the old one and replacing it with a new one. You do, however, want to pay attention to some key specifications when you're shopping for a new card.

Resolution

Your video card generates images at a specific resolution, typically measured in terms of pixels. While higher resolution is generally better, especially if you have a larger (19-inch or bigger) monitor, make sure the resolution of your card matches the resolution of your monitor. If a video card generates a higher resolution than your monitor is capable of, all you may see onscreen is gibberish.

Caution

Before you buy a new video card, make sure that you can actually upgrade your system's video. Some low-end PCs come with the video adapter integrated into the motherboard—which means there's no video card to change out. Fortunately, most systems with onboard video still let you add a separate video card, which then disables the built-in video capabilities. (You may have to enter your PC's CMOS BIOS setup to disable the onboard video.)

Note

The following specs are useful for the average home or business user. However, if you're a really hardcore PC gamer or a graphics professional, there are even *more* video specifications that you need to look at—much more technical than I can go into here.

Memory

All video cards contain some amount of video RAM (VRAM), which supplements your system's main memory and is used to temporarily store graphics information while images are being assembled for display. The more memory on your video card, the faster high-resolution images (moving images, in particular) can be displayed.

How much memory is enough? For casual computing and gaming, I recommend at least 256MB of video RAM. For more serious PC gaming and speedy rendering of 3D graphics, you need a minimum of 512MB video RAM. Obviously, more VRAM is better; you should buy a card with as much onboard memory as you can afford.

3D Acceleration

A *graphics accelerator* is a special chip on the video card that assumes the task of drawing shapes onscreen. This enables faster rendering of graphics objects. A graphics accelerator specifically designed to render 3D graphics is sometimes called a *3D accelerator*. If you're an avid gamer, you need a card with a 3D accelerator to handle the graphics demands of today's graphics-intensive games.

You can tell a 3D video card by looking at the card's *frame rate* spec, which measures the number of frames per second of 3D animation that the card can reproduce. Cards with 3D accelerator chips have faster frame rates than other types of video cards.

DirectX Support

DirectX is an evolving standard that defines a variety of application programming interfaces (APIs) for handling video rendering. To run Windows Vista Aero, your video card must support the DirectX 9 graphics standard. To play most of today's graphics-intensive games, your video card should support the more advanced DirectX 10 (or later) standard.

Connectors

Different types of computer monitors use different types of connectors. All CRT monitors and some LCD monitors use a traditional analog video (VGA) connector. Some LCD monitors use a digital (DVI) connector. Most video cards include a VGA connector; some include both VGA and DVI connectors.

In addition, some video cards include additional connections for connecting your PC to TV sets and home theater systems. These can include a single composite video jack, a higher-resolution S-video jack, or even higher-resolution three-cable component video connectors. If you're using your computer to connect only to a standard computer monitor, you can ignore these connections and focus on the VGA and VCI connections. (Figure 12.1 shows a video card with the three most common types of connectors: VGA, DVI, and S-video.)

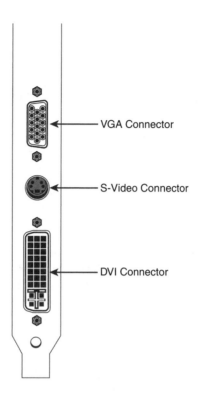

VGA Connector

S-Video Connector

DVI Connector

FIGURE 12.1

A video card with VGA, DVI, and S-video connectors.

If you have the choice, go with a DVI connection—even though a DVI cable will cost substantially more than a comparable VGA cable. (Assuming that your monitor has a DVI connection, of course; not all do.) This digital connection is slightly faster than the older analog VGA connection, and provides higher resolution, at least in theory.

Slots

A desktop PC can have three different types of expansion card slots inside the system unit, as shown in Figure 12.2:

12

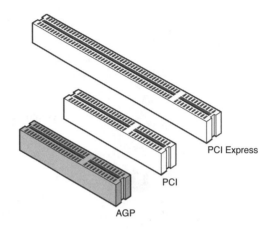

FIGURE 12.2

The three most common slot types for video cards—PCI, AGP, and PCI Express.

- **PCI** (Peripheral Component Interconnect), an older and slower standard. PCI lets your video card transfer data at a maximum rate of 133MBps.

- **AGP** (Accelerated Graphics Port), a newer and faster standard that is being phased out in favor of the even newer PCI Express. AGP lets your video card transfer data at up to 2.12GBps.

- **PCI Express** (also called PCIe), the newest expansion card standard. The PCIe 1.1 standard can transfer data up to 8GBps, and the newer PCIe2.0 standard doubles that maximum transfer rate to 16GBps.

Most newer computers use PCI Express, whereas computers more than three years old or so are likely to include both PCI and AGP slots. Today's fastest video cards are PCIe cards. If you have an older computer without a PCIe slot, go with an AGP card instead.

Video Card Manufacturers

When you're shopping for a new high-performance video card, look for models from the following companies:

- ASUSTeK (www.asus.com)

- ATI by AMD (ati.amd.com)

 Tip

If you're a hardcore gamer, your choice of video card is simple: Go with any card that uses an nVidia chipset. nVidia makes the highest-performing video chips out there, and many game designers optimize their software to work best with the nVidia chipset. To learn more about nVidia chips— and which cards use them— check out the nVidia website, at www.nvidia.com.

- BFG Technologies (www.bfgtech.com)
- PNY Technologies (www.pny.com)
- XFX (www.xfxforce.com)

Making the Upgrade

Upgrading your video isn't that hard to do. Yes, it's a little technical, in that you have to open up your system unit to do it. But beyond that, it's really just a matter of swapping out your old card for a newer one. Pull one out, push one in; that's all there is to it. The technical part comes after you've installed the card—you have to tell Windows that you're changing cards and then reconfigure your system to get the most out of your new card.

How do you upgrade your system's video card? Follow these steps:

1. From within Windows, click the Start button and click Control Panel.

2. When the Control Panel opens in Windows XP, click System. In Windows Vista, click System, and when the next window opens, click Advanced System Settings.

3. When the System Properties dialog box appears, select the Hardware tab and click the Device Manager button.

4. When the Device Manager opens, click the Display Adapters item, select your video card, and click the Uninstall button (or select Action, Uninstall).

5. Close Windows and power off your system.

6. Power off your monitor.

7. Disconnect both your PC and your monitor from their power sources.

8. Open your PC's system unit case, per the manufacturer instructions.

9. Locate your existing video card; it should have a cable running from the part that sticks out the rear of your system unit to your computer monitor, as shown in Figure 12.3. Disconnect this cable.

Caution

Static electricity can zap critical components when you're working inside the system unit. Use an anti-static wrist strap or similar device to protect against static discharge before touching the video card or other internal components.

12

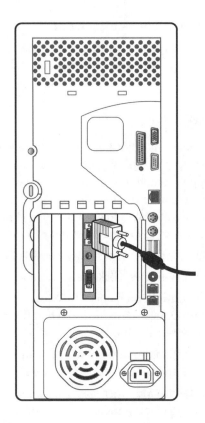

FIGURE 12.3

Locating your existing video card.

12

10. Remove the screw on the back of the system unit holding the old video card in place. Save the screw—you'll need to use it again.

11. If there are any cables running to the video card from other devices inside the system unit (such as your sound card or DVD drive), label them with masking tape or a sticker, and then disconnect them form the video card.

12. Remove the old video card from its slot and set it aside.

13. Insert the new video card into the now-open slot.

14. Reconnect any cables you disconnected previously (in step 11).

15. Use the screw you saved in step 10 to fasten the new card into place.

16. Reattach the cable that connects your monitor to the new video card.

17. Reinstall the system unit cover and reconnect the PC to its power source; while you're at it, go ahead and plug your monitor back in, too.

18. Power on your monitor, and then restart your computer.

19. Run the installation software that came with your new video card, or use the Windows Add Hardware Wizard to install the proper drivers for the new card.

Caution

If you don't see what you're supposed to see onscreen after installing the new video card, you might have to restart your computer and enter Windows' Safe mode, with VGA display, in order to install the proper video drivers.

That's it—as far as the basic installation goes. You now have to reconfigure Windows to use the full capabilities of your new video card.

Configuring Your Display Properties

You configure your video card from within Windows, by following these steps:

1. Click the Start menu and select Control Panel.

2. When the Control Panel opens in Windows XP, click Display. In Windows Vista, click Personalize, and when the next window opens, click Display Settings.

3. When the Display Settings or Display Properties dialog box appears, as shown in Figure 12.4, use the Screen Resolution or Resolution slider to select the desired resolution. Use the highest resolution that your monitor can display.

Tip

Assuming that you're running Windows on a 15-inch or bigger monitor, I recommend choosing a resolution of at least 1024×768.

4. Pull down the Color Quality or Colors list to select the desired color level. You should be able to use the highest 32-bit level.

5. Click OK to apply the new settings.

12

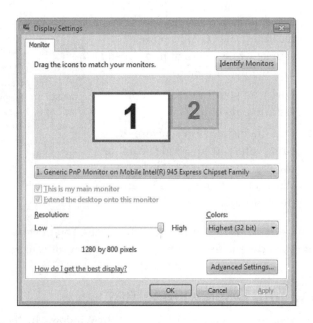

FIGURE 12.4
Configuring your video card from the Windows Vista Display Settings dialog box.

That's it. Your new video card is now installed and configured. You should see an immediate improvement in video display performance.

The Bottom Line

If your PC is slowing down when displaying graphics-intensive applications, you can speed it up by upgrading to a more powerful video card. Here's the bottom line:

- Rapidly-moving and three-dimensional graphics require significant graphics horsepower to create onscreen.
- A new graphics card with at least 512MB of onboard video RAM can speed up your system's onscreen display.
- When shopping for a new video card, look for a PCI Express 2.0 card with DVI connection.
- To upgrade your video card, you must first remove your old card and then replace it with the new one.
- To configure Windows for the new card, use the Display Settings (Windows Vista) or Display Properties (Windows XP) dialog box; dial in the highest resolution and color quality your card and monitor support.

Upgrading Your System's CPU

The core component of any computer system is its central processing unit (CPU) or microprocessor. The CPU affects the speed of everything your computer does; a faster CPU equals a faster PC.

Unlike the upgrades we've discussed in the previous chapters, upgrading your system's CPU is not for the technically faint of heart. Depending on your particular system, replacing your PC's CPU is complicated and carries some degree of risk. I recommend it only for the more technically savvy.

That said, upgrading to a more powerful CPU can result in significantly faster performance in everything your PC does. So if you're up to the task, read on to learn how to upgrade your way to a speedier computer.

Understanding the CPU

Back in Chapter 9, "Preparing for a Computer Upgrade," we took a peek inside the system unit of a typical desktop PC. Well, buried somewhere on that big motherboard is a specific chip that controls your entire computer system. This chip is called the central processing unit, and it's the brain inside your system. The CPU processes all the instructions necessary for your computer to perform its duties. The more powerful the microprocessor chip, the faster and more efficiently your system runs.

What a CPU Does

CPUs carry out the various instructions that let your computer compute. Every input and output device hooked up to a computer—the keyboard, printer, monitor, and so on—either issues or receives instructions that the CPU then processes. Your software programs also issue instructions that must be implemented by the CPU. This chip truly is the workhorse of your system; it affects just about everything your computer does.

If your PC has issues running demanding programs, such as photo- and video-editing applications, it's probably because the CPU isn't powerful enough. Everyday computing tasks, such as browsing the web and doing basic word processing, don't require much in the way of CPU power. But when you're doing heavy-duty computing tasks—manipulating large photos and videos, for example, or crunching big numbers on big spreadsheets—a more powerful CPU is a necessity to keep your system from getting bogged down.

Note

Upgrading your CPU should be a last-resort speedup. You'll most often get better results by upgrading your system's memory and hard disk—and, in fact, probably should do both of these before attacking the CPU.

Factors That Affect CPU Speed

What makes one CPU faster than another? It's all in the microprocessor chip's construction; there are multiple factors that affect the CPU's speed, as detailed in Table 13.1.

13

Table 13.1   CPU Properties

Property	Description
Clock speed	The number of operations that can be performed per second; measured in gigahertz (Ghz).
Architecture	Describes the natural unit of data used by the CPU, typically measured in bits. Some CPUs run dual- or quad-cores, which essentially provide the power of multiple processors in a single device.
Numeric coprocessor	Enables the CPU to directly perform floating-point numeric computations.
Number of instruction pipelines	Enables the CPU to "look ahead" to future instructions to make the best use of its power.
Internal cache RAM	Internal high-speed memory built in to the chip.
Data path	The largest number that can be transported into the chip in a single operation.

Of these factors, the CPU's clock speed is probably the key spec. Looking at clock speed is similar to looking at the horsepower of a car engine as an approximate measure of power; all other things being equal, a faster clock speed means faster execution and better performance.

Also important is the CPU's architecture. Most CPUs today utilize either 32-bit or 64-bit designs; a 64-bit CPU is noticeably faster than a 32-bit CPU when running software specifically designed for 64-bit operation.

Equally important, most newer CPUs utilize a multiple-core design, which incorporates two or more microprocessors running in tandem for greater speed. A dual-core CPU has two microprocessors, effectively doubling the CPU's power; a quad-core CPU has four microprocessors.

 Note

CPU speed is measured in megahertz (MHz) and gigahertz (GHz); 1GHz is equal to 1,000MHz. So a CPU with a speed of 1MHz can run at one million clock ticks per second, while a 1GHz CPU can run at one *billion* ticks per second!

Shopping for a New CPU

Different computers have different types of microprocessor chips. There are two main manufacturers of CPUs for Windows-compatible computers: Intel and AMD. Although chips from these two companies perform similar functions, you can't replace one with another.

13

Compatibility Is an Issue

When shopping for a new CPU, make sure that it's compatible with your computer and motherboard. It's not near as simple as plugging in a new expansion card or memory chip. CPUs are not interchangeable; instead, CPUs are specific to particular motherboards.

With that in mind, you need to pay particular attention to the CPU's socket. You can't plug a chip of one socket type into a different type of socket. For example, if you have a PC built for an older Pentium 4 CPU, you can't plug a newer dual core CPU into the old socket. You're normally limited to upgrading within a given family of CPU chips. You can upgrade to a CPU with a greater clock speed, but not to one with a completely different architecture.

Determining Your Current CPU and Motherboard

The first step, therefore, in shopping for a new CPU is determining what CPU you currently have in your computer. Fortunately, both Windows XP and Windows Vista let you examine which CPU is installed in your system.

Here's how you do it in Windows XP:

1. Click the Start button, and then click Control Panel.
2. When the Control Panel opens, click the System icon.
3. When the System Properties dialog box appears, select the General tab, as shown in Figure 13.1. The Computer section of this tab tells which processor you have and how much memory (RAM) you have installed.

In Windows Vista, the process is somewhat different:

1. Click the Start button, and then click Control Panel.
2. When the Control Panel opens, click the System icon.
3. The System window, shown in Figure 13.2, now appears. Your system's processor (along with other information) is detailed in the System section of this window.

You may also need to know what type of motherboard your system uses, to determine which chips can work with that motherboard. Unfortunately, you can't find this information within Windows. Instead, you must look on the motherboard itself for a manufacturer and model number. You can then check with the motherboard's manufacturer (or search online) to determine the type of *socket* used for the CPU, as well as the maximum clock rate supported. This information will tell you what type of new CPU you can use in your system.

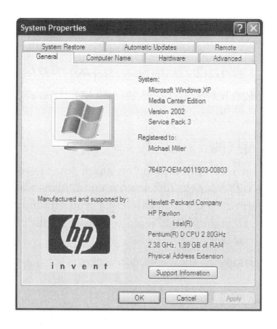

FIGURE 13.1

Use the System Properties dialog box in Windows XP to find out what processor your computer is running.

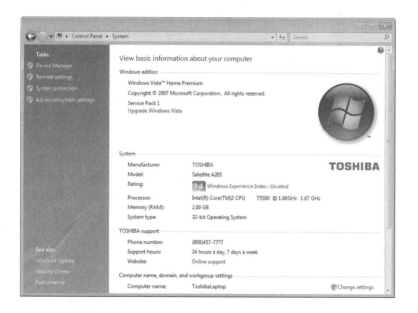

FIGURE 13.2

Use the System window in Windows Vista to view your PC's processor information.

Even better, some systems display the manufacturer and model number of the motherboard when booting. This information typically appears near the bottom of the all-text screen before Windows loads. Press your keyboard's Pause button to better read this info.

Note

The maximum clock rate is sometimes referred to in CPU specs as the Front Side Bus or FSB.

Finding a Compatible CPU

When you have this information on hand, you can search for CPUs that are compatible with your existing motherboard. Remember, you're looking for a microprocessor chip that you can easily plug into the socket used by your current CPU—and you can only replace your CPU with another CPU that uses the same type of socket.

Table 13.2 details the most common socket types in use today.

Table 13.2   CPU Socket Types

Socket Type	CPUs Supported	Clock Speeds Supported
Socket 370	Celeron, Pentium III	66MHz, 100MHz, 133MHz
Socket 462	Athlon, Athlon XP, Duron, Sempron	200MHz, 266MHz, 333MHz, 400MHz
Socket 478	Celeron, Celeron D, Pentium 4, Pentium 4 Extreme Edition	400MHz, 533MHz, 800MHz, 1066MHz (1GHz)
Socket 775	Celeron D, Pentium 4, Pentium 4 Extreme Edition, Pentium D, Pentium Extreme Edition, Core 2 Duo, Core 2 Extreme, Core 2 Quad	533MHz, 800MHz, 1066MHz (1GHz)
Sockets 754, 939, 940, AM2, F	Most newer AMD models: Sempron, Athlon 64, Athlon 64 X2, Athlon 64 FX, Opteron	All speeds

If you can't find a compatible CPU or want to upgrade to something more powerful, you have the option of replacing the entire motherboard on your PC. Although this approach lets you upgrade to any number of CPUs (including those using more advanced designs), it's a much more technical upgrade process—as you'll learn later in this chapter. For most users, replacing the chip itself (and not the motherboard) is the preferred approach.

Tip

When shopping for a CPU, look for a model sold in retail packaging. A retail-boxed CPU typically includes an appropriate fan/heatsink with the necessary thermal grease already applied. CPUs sold into the OEM market often include only the CPU and not the accompanying fan/heatsink—which means more effort for you.

Performing a CPU Upgrade

If you've obtained a new CPU that's compatible with your motherboard's existing CPU socket, replacing your old CPU with the new one really isn't that difficult.

Preparing for the Upgrade

What do you need to upgrade your CPU? It's a short list of things:

- The new CPU
- Philips screwdriver
- Flat-head screwdriver
- Antistatic wrist band
- Thermal compound (designed specifically for computer use)

Note

Thermal compound (sometimes called thermal grease) aids in the transfer of heat between the CPU and the heat sink and prevents overheating.

Performing the Upgrade

Once you've assembled your simple toolkit, here's how to replace the CPU:

1. Turn off your PC and disconnect it from the power source.

2. Disconnect all external peripherals connected to your PC, including your monitor, keyboard, mouse, and printer.

3. Remove the case to your PC's system unit, as per the manufacturer's instructions.

Caution

Static electricity can blow out your new CPU before you get it installed in your PC. Protect against static discharges by wearing an antistatic wrist strap while performing the upgrade.

4. Locate your current CPU on the motherboard. The CPU should be located below a large heat sink, which resembles a piece of finned metal with a cooling fan mounted on top, as shown in Figure 13.3.

5. Disconnect the cable connecting the heat sink's fan to the motherboard.

13

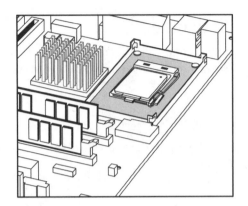

FIGURE 13.3

Locating the CPU on the motherboard—it's below the heat sink.

6. Remove the heat sink. This may be accomplished by unlocking some sort of locking mechanism, or by unscrewing two or more supporting screws.

7. Remove the CPU itself by lifting up the locking lever that holds it into place, as shown in Figure 13.4. You can then lift the CPU up and out of its slot.

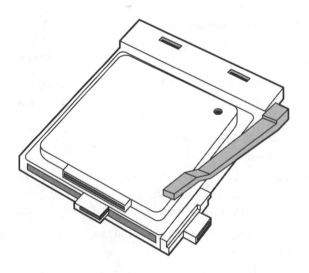

FIGURE 13.4

Removing the existing CPU.

8. Insert the new CPU into the slot vacated by the old CPU. Make sure you push down on the locking lever to lock the new CPU into position.

Caution

Don't apply too much thermal compound, or it could squeeze onto the motherboard. Only a small amount is necessary!

9. Apply a small amount of thermal compound on the top of the CPU.

10. Reinstall the heat sink onto the motherboard.

11. Reconnect the wire connecting the heat sink's fan to the motherboard.

12. Consult the motherboard's instruction manual to determine whether you need to reconfigure any jumpers or switches on the motherboard to recognize the new CPU. If so, make the changes now.

13. Replace the system unit's case.

14. Reconnect all of your system's external peripherals.

Tip

To confirm that your computer recognizes the new CPU, enter the BIOS setup menu during the boot process, navigate to the hardware component menu, and view the CPU information presented there. It should match the information provided by the CPU's manufacturer.

15. Reconnect your PC to its power source and power it up.

That's it. Your computer should recognize the new CPU during the boot process and operate normally—albeit slightly faster than you're used to.

Replacing Your Entire Motherboard

If you want to upgrade to a newer CPU design, you can't just plug the new chip into your old socket. Instead, you have to replace the entire motherboard with a new one designed for the new CPU.

That's because each model motherboard is designed to work with a specific type of CPU. All the circuits, ports, slots, and devices designed into and connected to the motherboard are specially selected to perform their best with a specific CPU. If you change the CPU, not only will all those pieces and parts not perform optimally, some simply won't work at all.

So, in some instances, replacing the entire motherboard is the only solution when you want to upgrade to a faster CPU. But let me say upfront that this is not an easy upgrade, and is not recommended for nontechnical users; it can also be nearly as costly as buying a new PC, especially if you plan on upgrading memory and other components at the same time. As such, I'll outline the

13

general steps involved but not supply in the specific details; if you have the technical expertise, you'll know how to fill in the blanks.

Preparing for the Upgrade

What do you need to upgrade the motherboard in your PC? Here's the short list:

- New motherboard
- New CPU (if the motherboard didn't come with a CPU already installed; most do)
- CD or DVD that came with the new motherboard (it should include all necessary drivers for motherboard components)
- Philips screwdriver
- Flat-head screwdriver
- Antistatic wrist band
- Windows installation CD or DVD—full version, not upgrade version

Wait a minute—why do you need a Windows installation disc to replace your motherboard? It's because Windows doesn't like you to make major hardware changes like this, and you actually have to repair your Windows installation to recognize the new motherboard. (I told you this wasn't a simple upgrade!)

Making the Upgrade

So what's involved in a motherboard upgrade? Here are the general steps:

1. Power down your PC and disconnect it from its power source.
2. Disconnect all external peripherals from the PC.
3. Remove the system unit case, as directed by the manufacturer.
4. Disconnect all internal cables and wires that connect to the existing motherboard. Label each cable to make it easier to reconnect to the new motherboard.
5. Remove any expansion cards plugged into the motherboard.
6. Remove the memory modules from the existing motherboard.

Tip

If you're not comfortable with the technical details involved in a motherboard upgrade, you may want to take your PC to a qualified technician to do to the job for you.

Caution

When replacing your PC's motherboard, you want to protect against static discharges by wearing an antistatic wrist strap.

13

7. Remove all the screws that attach the motherboard to the system unit case.

Tip

While the system unit case is relatively empty, use a can of compressed air to clean out the inside of the case.

8. When it is completely disconnected, remove the motherboard from the system unit and set it aside.

9. Insert the new motherboard into the system unit case, making sure to line up the screw holes in the motherboard with the matching holes in the system unit case.

10. Attach the motherboard to the case with the necessary screws (being very careful not to scratch the surface of the motherboard with the tip of the screwdriver).

11. If the new CPU came separate from the new motherboard, insert the CPU into its slot in the motherboard now.

12. Insert the old memory modules into the new motherboard.

13. Insert the old expansion cards into the new motherboard.

14. Reconnect all the internal cables to the new motherboard.

15. Reinstall the case for the system unit.

16. Reconnect all external peripheral devices to the system unit.

17. Reconnect the system unit to the power source.

18. Power up your computer and, during the initial part of the boot process, enter the BIOS setup menu. (You may be prompted to do this, or you may have to enter the setup menu manually by pressing Del or some similar key when prompted during the boot process.)

19. In the BIOS setup menu, navigate to the "integrated peripherals" screen and disable any devices not connected to your system.

20. Exit the BIOS setup.

21. You now have to tell Windows about your new motherboard. Resume the boot process by inserting the Windows installation CD or DVD into your system's CD/DVD drive.

22. When prompted, select the option to set up Windows.

23. When prompted, select the option to begin a repair installation. Your system will now reinstall Windows, but without reformatting your hard drive or replacing any of your existing data. Windows reinstalls all system files and redetects all the hardware on your system—including your new motherboard.

13

24. When the reinstallation is complete, you'll be prompted to reactive Windows. This requires a new activation code, which you need to acquire from Microsoft. Follow the onscreen instructions to call Microsoft (toll free) and obtain the new activation code.

After this long and involved process, your computer should be up and running just like a new PC. Congratulations on a job well done!

The Bottom Line

When you want to elevate your PC to next-generation performance, you have to replace the engine that drives the machine—your PC's central processing unit. Here's the bottom line:

- CPU speed and design affect a PC's total performance. A faster CPU equals a faster PC.
- You can replace your system's CPU with a faster model of the same design. You can't, however, switch CPU types.
- Replacing a CPU also involves removing and then reinstalling the heat sink and fan connected to the existing CPU.
- If you want to upgrade to a more powerful CPU design, you have to replace your system's entire motherboard—which is not a job for the technically timid.

Internet and Network Speedups

Cleaning Up Your Web Browser

S o far in this book, we've covered various solutions to a sluggish PC. But not all computer slowness is the fault of your computer hardware and software. Sometimes it's what you're doing with your PC that's slow.

Case in point: web browsing. Your computer might be fast as greased lightning when you're doing word processing or photo editing or whatever, but when you head out to the Web, everything slows down to a snail's pace. You might think it's your PC that's slow, but really it's your web browser.

Of course, slow web browsing can also be caused by a slow Internet connection, and we'll get to that in the next chapter. But for now let's focus on the web browser itself, and the many ways it can slow down your browsing experience.

How to Slow Down a Web Browser

Your web browser is what you use to surf pages on the World Wide Web. It's a software program, not much different from a word processor or spreadsheet application, designed specifically to display HTML pages on the Web. Like any software program, it contains numerous configuration settings—some of which affect the speed at which web pages are displayed.

A typical HTML web page contains a mix of text, graphics, and other elements. Text is easiest to display; not a whole lot involved with that. Graphics, however, can take longer to display, primarily because image files can be quite large. These large files take longer to download and thus longer to display in your web browser.

Other page elements can include audio and video files, along with bits of JavaScript code. JavaScript is typically used to insert "applets" (small applications) into a web page; these applets often contain elements hosted on other websites. For example, a page might display a clock created with JavaScript; the code for the clock is on the web page itself, while the engine and graphics for the clock are hosted on another site. Because of this dual-hosting nature of some JavaScript code, these applets can often take longer to display than elements hosted natively.

Naturally, the more elements on a web page, the longer it will take your browser to display them. It's not just a matter of download size; all those elements must be rendered for display by the browser, and this rendering takes computing horsepower and time. It's no surprise that bigger web pages can really slow down some browsers.

Here's something else that can slow down your browser: having multiple tabs open at the same time. Yes, most modern browsers are designed with a tabbed interface, the better to load multiple web pages simultaneously. But all those web pages have to be downloaded, rendered, and stored in memory. It's just more work for the browser—and an overworked browser can be quite sluggish.

Note

Microsoft's Internet Explorer is the web browser of choice for most Windows users, and that's what we focus on in this chapter—in particular, Internet Explorer version 7. If you use another browser, such as Firefox, Safari, or Google Chrome, many of the same speedups also apply, although the specific instructions will differ somewhat.

Tip

Some web browsers are faster than others—and Internet Explorer is probably the slowest of all, in terms of how long it takes to load web pages. If you think IE is slow on your system, you might want to try a faster browser, such as Mozilla Firefox (www.mozilla.com/firefox/) or Google Chrome (www.google.com/chrome/).

Note

Not all sluggish web browsing is caused by the web browser. If you also have problems downloading files or retrieving your email, you could be plagued by a slow Internet connection. Learn more in Chapter 15, "Reconfiguring Your Internet Connection."

14

Fortunately, many of these issues can be overcome by some simple configuration changes—or, in the most extreme case, a tweak to the Windows Registry. Read on to learn how to speed up your browser—and make surfing the Web go a lot smoother!

Cleaning Up Your Cache and Cookies

We'll start with the easy speedups first—and the easiest of them all concern your browser's temporary cache and cookies.

Clearing Your Cache

You might not know this, but your web browser stores a temporary copy of each web page you visit. This is called a *cache*, and it takes up space on your hard disk. Although the cache is designed to speed up browsing (your browser simply accesses the local cache when you want to revisit a recent page), too big of a cache can slow your browser to a crawl.

You see, over time your browser keeps adding web pages to the cache file—and these pages aren't deleted automatically. So the more web pages you visit, the bigger the cache on your hard disk. And too large a cache file puts a drain on your web browser, because your browser has to sort through the cache every time you load a web page, looking for a cached version of that page. A bigger cache takes longer to reference.

The solution to cache-based sluggishness is to clean out the cache. In essence, what you do is delete the cache file; this "empties" the cache, frees up valuable hard disk space, and makes it much easier for your browser to search for previously cached pages. Fortunately, this is easy to do—even if it must be done manually.

Here's how you clean out the cache in Internet Explorer 7:

1. Click the Tools button and select Delete Browsing History.
2. When the Delete Browsing History dialog box appears, as shown in Figure 14.1, click the Delete Files button.
3. When prompted for confirmation, click Yes.

This deletes the temporary cache file on your computer and should speed up browser performance.

FIGURE 14.1

Deleting Internet Explorer's temporary cache file.

Clearing Your Cache Automatically

If you don't want to delete the cache on a regular basis, Internet Explorer can automate the process for you. All you have to do is enable the option that automatically clears the cache when you close the browser.

Follow these steps:

1. Click the Tools button and select Internet Options.

2. When the Internet Options dialog box appears, select the Advanced tab.

3. In the Settings list, scroll down to the Security section and check the option Empty Temporary Internet Files Folder When Browser Is Closed.

4. Click OK.

Changing the Size of Your Cache

You can also change the size of the Internet Explorer cache. The smaller the cache, the speedier Internet Explorer will be.

Here's how to change the cache size in Internet Explorer 7:

1. Click the Tools button and select Internet Options.

2. When the Internet Options dialog box appears, select the General tab.

3. Click the Settings button in the Browsing History section.

4. When the Temporary Internet Files and History Settings dialog box appears, as shown in Figure 14.2, set the Disk Space setting to the desired number.

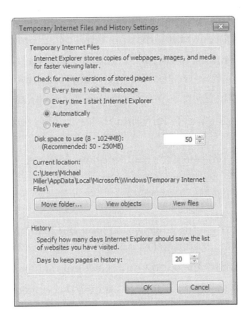

FIGURE 14.2

Configuring the size of the browser cache.

What's the right size? While you can set a cache as small as 8MB, I recommend something in the 50MB range. Anything much smaller is less than useful, and anything much larger just takes up disk space and slows down your browser.

Deleting Cookies

Just as your browser stores a temporary copy of each web page you visit, it also stores information about those pages, in the form of *cookies*. A cookie is a small file, created by a website but stored on your PC, which contains information about you and your activities on that website. For example, a cookie file for a particular site might contain your username, password, credit card information, and the most recent pages you visited on that site. The cookie file created by a site is accessed by that site each time you visit in the future, and the information used appropriately.

14

Aside from the privacy concerns of all these websites tracking your activities, cookies can also slow down your web browser. That's because, over time, you accumulate a *lot* of cookies. These files, although small, can take up significant amounts of hard disk space; in addition, your browser must sort through them all to find the cookies it needs when accessing a specific site. The more cookie files on your hard drive, the harder your browser has to work.

As with your browser's cache file, the solution to cookie-induced sluggishness is to delete all your cookies. It's quite easy to do in Internet Explorer:

1. Click the Tools button and select Delete Browsing History.

2. When the Delete Browsing History dialog box appears, click the Delete Cookies button.

3. When prompted for confirmation, click Yes.

Avoiding Cookies

You can also configure Internet Explorer not to store some or all types of cookies, by adjusting the browser's privacy level. Here's how you do it:

1. Click the Tools button and select Internet Options.

2. When the Internet Options dialog box appears, as shown in Figure 14.3, select the Privacy tab.

3. Adjust the slider to the privacy level you want, and then click OK.

Internet Explorer 7 has six levels of cookie management, ranging from accepting all cookies to declining all cookies. At one extreme is the Accept All Cookies option, which does what it says it does—it stores all cookies from all websites. At the other extreme is the Block All Cookies option, which doesn't store a single cookie. In between are four other levels that store specific types of cookies; the default level is Medium, which pretty much blocks all advertising-related cookies and deletes any cookies that contain personal information when you close Internet Explorer.

 Caution

You might think that turning off all cookies would be the way to go, but this might cause problems with some frequently visited websites. That's because some sites store useful information in their cookies, such as your username, password, and such—all of which makes the site easier to use.

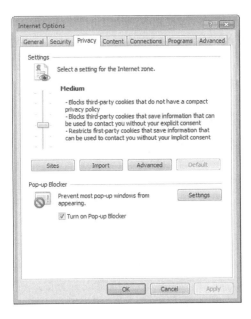

FIGURE 14.3
Configuring cookie and privacy options in Internet Explorer.

Reconfiguring Key Settings

Internet Explorer is a web browser that has lots of built-in features, some of which can slow down the display of web pages. Given that you may or may not need all of these features, turning a few of them off can speed up your web browsing. We'll look at those features that most affect your browsing experience next.

Don't Display Graphics

Here's a big one that may or may not appeal to you. Many web pages are overloaded with photos and other images; these images are big files that can take a long time to download and display, especially if you have a slow web connection. You can speed up the loading graphics-intensive pages by simply turning off the graphics. That leaves you with a text-only web page, of course—but that page will load a lot faster than it did with all the images intact.

14

To turn off the display of images in Internet Explorer, follow these steps:

1. Click the Tools button and select Internet Options.

2. When the Internet Options dialog box appears, select the Advanced tab (shown in Figure 14.4).

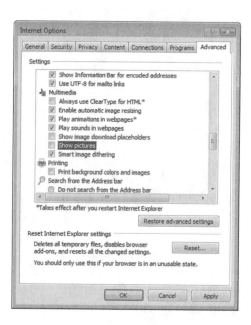

FIGURE 14.4

Speeding up IE by turning off graphics.

3. Scroll down to the Multimedia section and uncheck the Show Pictures option.

4. Click OK.

Tip

While you're at it, you can further speed up web page display by unchecking the Play Animations in Webpages and Play Sounds in Webpages options.

Disable ClearType

Internet Explorer 7 uses Windows' ClearType technology to smoothly render type at all sizes. Some users have reported that ClearType has slowed down the performance of Internet Explorer on their systems. To disable ClearType, follow these steps:

1. Click the Tools button and select Internet Options.

2. When the Internet Options dialog box appears, select the Advanced tab.

3. Scroll down to the Multimedia section and uncheck the Always Use ClearType for HTML option.

4. Click OK.

Turn Off the Phishing Filter

Internet Explorer 7 includes a security feature called the Phishing Filter. This feature is designed to identify and warn you about so-called phishing websites—sites that pretend to be official sites but actually exist solely to steal your personal information. Unfortunately, the Phishing Filter can sometimes slow down web browsing, as it takes a bit of time to search the list of known phishing websites. You can speed up your browsing by turning off the Phishing Filter.

Here's how to do it:

1. Click the Tools button and select Phishing Filter, Turn Off Automatic Web Site Checking.

2. When prompted, click OK.

> **Caution**
>
> If you turn off the Phishing Filter, you need to be more vigilant about clicking links in emails and on web pages to avoid becoming the victim of phishing schemes.

Disable RSS Feeds

Here's a feature of Internet Explorer 7 that few people use yet slows down everyone's browsing. I'm talking about IE7's RSS feeds feature, which enables you to subscribe to RSS feeds from blogs and news sites and automatically display new postings and updates in the browser.

If you don't use the RSS feeds feature (and you probably don't), you can disable it and speed up your normal web browsing. Follow these steps:

1. Click the Tools button and select Internet Options.

2. When the Internet Options dialog box appears, select the Content tab.

3. Click the Settings button in the Feeds section.

4. When the Feed Settings dialog box appears, as shown in Figure 14.5, uncheck every option.

5. Click OK.

FIGURE 14.5
Disabling RSS feeds in Internet Explorer 7.

Uninstalling Unnecessary Add-Ons

Some of what slows down Internet Explorer are add-ons to the main program. These auxiliary programs require more computing power than the browser does by itself, and sometimes access third-party websites that require additional downloads. You can speed up your browsing by disabling the least essential of these add-ons.

Remove Third-Party Toolbars

Many websites like to install their own toolbars for Internet Explorer. While these toolbars—especially from sites such as Google and Yahoo!—make using those sites easier (a one-button affair, in many cases), they also put an extra load on Internet Explorer, which can make your browsing seem sluggish.

To remove unwanted toolbars from Internet Explorer 7, follow these steps:

1. Click the Tools button and select Toolbars.

2. Uncheck those toolbars you want to disable.

 Caution

Although Google and Yahoo! toolbars are legitimate, some toolbars are actually a form of spyware, designed to report your browsing activity back to some mothership on the Web. Therefore, you might need to run an antispyware program to completely get rid of these malware toolbars.

14

You may also be able to remove some toolbars using Windows' Add/Remove Programs features. To do this, open Control Panel and select either Add/Remove Programs (Windows XP) or Programs and Features (Windows Vista); select the toolbar program from the list and click the Remove or Uninstall button.

Remove the SSVHelper Class Add-On

Here's a somewhat esoteric plug-in that has been known to slow down IE's browsing performance. The SSVHelper Class plug-in is a nonessential part of the Java plug-in (which itself is fairly necessary). To display this plug-in, follow these steps:

1. Click the Tools button and select Manage Add-Ons, Enable or Disable Add-Ons.

2. When the Manage Add-Ons dialog box appears, as shown in Figure 14.6, select Java(tm) Plug-In SSV Helper.

FIGURE 14.6

Managing add-ons in Internet Explorer 7.

3. Select the Disable option.

4. Click OK.

14

Remove Other Add-Ons

When you open the Manage Add-Ons dialog box, you see a full listing of all the add-ons currently running in Internet Explorer. You may need all of these add-ons, you may not. For example, you might find that a particular website has installed an add-on to view content on its site, but that add-on is not necessary when visiting other sites; that add-on is a prime candidate for removal.

Determining which add-ons to keep and which to disable is mainly a matter of trial and error; there are no universal recommendations. I might be perfectly happy disabling the Shockwave Flash add-on (I *hate* unwanted Flash animations!), but other users might balk at not having any Flash animations display in their browsers. The key is whether you frequently visit sites that use a particular add-on; if not, you might as well disable it—and help speed up your browsing!

Browsing Faster with an Alternate DNS Service

Even the fastest broadband connection can feel slow if it takes a long time to pull up each website you want to visit. This problem is due to something called the Domain Name System (DNS) and slowness in your ISP's DNS server—and can be corrected.

What Is a DNS Server—and How Does It Affect Connection Speed?

Every website is hosted on a web server, which is a fancy type of computer connected to the Internet. To identify the millions of such servers, each server has its own unique address, called an IP address, which looks something like this: 192.111.222.333.

Of course, you don't type this address into your web browser when you want to visit a website. What you type is the URL or website address, which looks something like this: www.websiteaddress.com. The URL, then, is an alias for the site's true address.

What a DNS server does is link the site's easy-to-remember URL with its hard-to-remember IP address. For example, www.google.com is the URL for the server located at the 209.85.153.104 IP address. When you enter the URL www.google.com in your web browser, that URL request is sent to a DNS server that looks up that URL's IP address and then routes the request to the server located at 209.85.153.104. (You can test this by entering the IP address directly into your browser; it should take you directly to the associated website.)

When you connect to the Internet via your Internet service provider (ISP), your URL requests are sent to that ISP's DNS server. That's a simple enough process—until your ISP's DNS server starts to get bogged down. When that happens, it takes longer for the DNS server to look up the IP addresses for the URLs you enter.

Unfortunately, many ISP DNS servers are notoriously slow. The result is that it takes longer to load any web page you want to visit. It's not the connection that's slow, it's the ability of your ISP to look up the web pages you want to view.

Choosing a Third-Party DNS Service

You can work around this issue by directing your URL requests to a different DNS server. To that end, several sites offer alternative DNS services, promising faster lookups and thus faster web browsing.

Note

Some third-party DNS services offer additional features, such as parental controls, phishing protection, and more-reliable DNS lookup services.

To use a third-party DNS service, you have to configure your web browser to route your URL requests to the new server. We'll get to that in a moment. First, let's look at some of the third-party DNS services available. Table 14.1 provides the detail, including the information you'll need to reconfigure Windows for that service. All of these services are free, although you may have to subscribe to gain full access.

Table 14.1   Free DNS Services

Service	URL	Preferred DNS Server	Alternate DNS Server
BrowseSafe	www.browsesafe.com	66.11.234.70	66.11.234.71
DNS Advantage	www.dnsadvantage.com	156.154.70.1	156.154.71.1
OpenDNS	www.opendns.com	208.67.222.222	208.67.220.220

Configuring Your System for an Alternate DNS Service

To use an alternate DNS service, you have to reconfigure Windows to send all URL requests to the new DNS server. It's a network-related procedure, and works slightly differently in Windows XP than in Windows Vista.

Here's how you reconfigure Windows XP to use an alternate DNS service:

1. Click the Start button and click Control Panel.
2. When the Control Panel opens, click Network Connections.
3. When the Network Connections window opens, right-click the icon for your connection and select Properties.
4. When the Properties dialog box appears, select Internet Protocol (TCP/IP) and click the Properties button.
5. Select the Use the Following DNS Server Addresses option.
6. Enter the DNS service's preferred DNS server address into the Preferred DNS Server box.
7. Enter the DNS service's alternate DNS server address into the Alternate DNS Server box.
8. Click OK.

To reconfigure Windows Vista for an alternative DNS service, follow these steps:

1. Click the Start button and click Control Panel.
2. When the Control Panel opens, click Network and Sharing Center.
3. When the Network and Sharing Center opens, click Manage Network Connections (in the Tasks list).
4. When the Network Connections window opens, right-click the icon for your connection and select Properties.
5. When the Properties dialog box appears, as shown in Figure 14.7, select Internet Protocol Version 4 (TCP/IPv4) and click the Properties button.
6. When the next Properties dialog box appears, as shown in Figure 14.8, select the Use the Following DNS Server Addresses option.
7. Enter the DNS service's preferred DNS server address into the Preferred DNS Server box.
8. Enter the DNS service's alternate DNS server address into the Alternate DNS Server box.
9. Click OK.

14

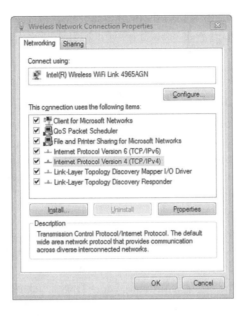

FIGURE 14.7
Editing Windows Vista's Internet Protocol settings.

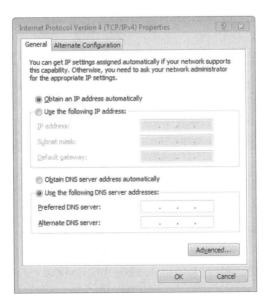

FIGURE 14.8
Entering new DNS server addresses.

With Windows thus reconfigured, you'll now access the third-party DNS server whenever you're web browsing—which should be slightly faster than what you're used to with your ISP's DNS server.

Increasing the Size of Your DNS Cache

Still on the subject of DNS lookup, Windows stores your most recently visited website addresses in a special DNS cache on your hard drive. Your web browser accesses this cache of known addresses before it goes out to the Internet to send a URL request to an external DNS server. If the web address you're looking for is in the cache, it gets used by your browser, saving valuable browsing time.

You can speed up your browsing by increasing the size of this DNS cache. A bigger DNS cache enables addresses for more websites to be stored locally, which means fewer external DNS lookups.

To increase the size of your computer's DNS cache, you have to edit the Windows Registry, which is the large database where all the configuration settings for your system are stored. You edit the Registry using the Registry Editor utility. Here's what you need to do:

Note

Learn more about tweaking the Registry in Chapter 7, "Cleaning Up the Windows Registry."

1. Open the Registry Editor.
2. Navigate to the HKEY_LOCAL_MACHINE\SYSTEM\CurrentControlSet\Services\Dnscache\Parameters key.
3. Select Edit, New, DWORD (32-bit) Value.
4. Name this new item **CacheHashTableBucketSize**.
5. Right-click this new item and select Modify.
6. In the Value Data dialog box, change the value to 1.
7. Select Edit, New, DWORD (32-bit) Value.
8. Name this new item **CacheHashTableSize**.
9. Right-click this new item and select Modify.
10. In the Value Data dialog box, change the value to 180.
11. Select Edit, New, DWORD (32-bit) Value.
12. Name this new item **MaxCacheEntryTtlLimit**.
13. Right-click this new item and select Modify.

14. In the Value Data dialog box, change the value to ff00.

15. Select Edit, New, DWORD (32-bit) Value.

16. Name this new item **MaxSOACacheEntryTtlLimit**.

17. Right-click this new item and select Modify.

18. In the Value Data dialog box, change the value to 12d.

> ### ⏱ Caution
>
> Take care when editing the Registry. All changes you make are immediately enabled; any mistakes you make can affect the running of your system.

For these changes to take effect, you need to close the Registry Editor and restart Windows. You should notice a slight speedup when next you browse the Web.

Enabling More Simultaneous Connections

We'll end this chapter with another little Registry tweak that can speed up web browsing for many users. This tweak has to do with how many files you can download at the same time from a web server.

By default, Internet Explorer is configured to enable just two simultaneous connections to a server. The problem comes when you visit a web page that contains lots of images and JavaScript content, all of which has to download to your browser. With just two simultaneous connections enabled, it can take awhile to download multiple images and such.

Here are the facts. Your browser has to make more than 40 requests to the server before it can assemble a typical web page. Requesting all those files 2 at a time is going to take longer than requesting 10 (or more) files at a time. If you can download more connections, you can significantly speed up the display of all web pages.

To enable more simultaneous connections from a single web server, you have to edit the Windows Registry, using the Registry Editor. Here's how to enable 10 simultaneous connections to a server:

1. Open the Registry Editor.

2. Navigate to the HKEY_CURRENT_USER\Software\Microsoft\Windows\CurrentVersion\Internet Settings key.

3. Select Edit, New, DWORD (32-bit) Value.

4. Name this new item **MaxConnectionsPer1_0Server**.

5. Right-click this new item and select Modify.

6. In the Value Data dialog box, change the value to 10.

7. Click OK.

8. Select Edit, New, DWORD (32-bit) Value.

9. Name this new item **MaxConnectionsPerServer**.

10. Right-click this new item and select Modify.

11. In the Value Data dialog box, change the value to 10.

12. Click OK.

13. Close the Registry Editor.

When you edit the Registry Editor, close Internet Explorer. When you restart your browser, the new value will be in effect—and your web browsing should be a little speedier!

The Bottom Line

If your web browsing is slower than everything else you do on your PC, you need to speed up your web browser. Here's the bottom line:

- One way to speed up browsing performance is to periodically clear out your browser's cache and cookies.

- Disabling various browser settings, such as image display and the Phishing Filter, can also speed up browser performance.

- You can use the Manage Add-Ons dialog box to disable unnecessary add-ons that can slow down browser performance. You should also remove any unnecessary toolbars from the browser.

- By configuring Windows to use an alternate DNS server, you can speed up the time required to look up website addresses.

- If you're comfortable editing the Registry, you can increase the size of your local DNS cache—and increase the number of simultaneous connections used to download web page elements.

Reconfiguring Your Internet Connection

I n the preceding chapter, we discussed ways to speed up your web browser. But sometimes sluggish web browsing is actually the result of a slow connection to the Internet. What can you do to speed up your Internet connection?

There are some obvious answers to that question and some not-so-obvious ones. We examine both in this chapter, as you learn how to speed up your computing experience by reconfiguring your Internet connection.

How Fast Is Your Internet Connection?

Before we talk about speeding up your Internet connection, let's examine just how fast your current Internet connection is. It may be faster than you think; sometimes even a fast connection feels slow when you're waiting for a fancy web page to load or a big file to download.

15

Dial-Up Versus Broadband Connections

First off, know that there are two primary types of Internet connections: dial-up and broadband. Dial-up is the older and much slower technology, while broadband connections are significantly faster.

Note

Modem stands for modulate/demodulate, which describes how the device translates the digital signals from your computer to analog signals that can be sent over standard phone lines.

It used to be that everyone had dial-up connections, because that was the only type of connection available. A dial-up connection works by connecting your PC to a normal phone line, using a piece of hardware called a *modem*. The modem, which physically connects between your PC and your phone line, dials into your Internet service provider (ISP) and logs in to your personal account. Your ISP plugs the signal from your computer into the Internet, so that your computer is now connected to the Internet, through your ISP. When you're done surfing the web, you disconnect from the ISP by essentially hanging up the phone line.

The problems with dial-up connections are twofold. First, you have to connect and disconnect manually; you don't have an always-on connection. Second, and most important, a dial-up connection is *sloooow*—transferring data at no more than 56.6 kilobits per second (Kbps).

In the late 1990s, slow dial-up connections began to be supplanted by faster broadband connections. Unlike an analog dial-up connection, a broadband connection is an end-to-end digital connection. When you don't have to modulate and demodulate the data from digital to analog (and back again), the all-digital data can travel much faster from your computer to other points on the Internet.

Broadband connections are typically available from either your telephone company (via what is called a DSL connection) or your cable company.

Broadband speeds are considerably faster than dial-up connections, 1.5Mbps (that's 1,500Kbps) or more for DSL and 6Mbps or more for cable Internet. At the lowest speeds, we're talking 60 times dial-up speed for DSL and 120 times dial-up speed for cable broadband—more than enough of a difference to notice!

Note

DSL stands for Digital Subscriber Line, and piggybacks on your existing telephone line. Similarly, cable Internet piggybacks on your digital cable signal.

Measuring Your Connection's Speed

The speed of your actual connection, however, may differ from these general data transfer speeds. That's because different Internet service providers offer different speed plans—and because your actual speed may not be the same as the promised speed. Your distance from the nearest network node affects actual speed, as do the number of other users connecting at the same time, as do numerous other factors. So just because your ISP promises blazing-fast 6Mbps rates doesn't mean that your connection will always be that fast.

Note

When a web page or file comes from a website to your computer, you're *downloading* that item. When a file moves from your computer to another site on the Web, you're *uploading* that item. Many ISPs provide different upload and download speeds to their customers; download speeds are typically faster. For example, Comcast's Performance plan offers 12Mbps download rates but only 2Mbps for uploads.

So how fast is your Internet connection? There are several sites on the Web designed to test the speed of your connection. All you have to do is access the site and click the appropriate buttons. The site will download and upload some small files to and from your PC, measure how fast it all takes, and display your current upload and download speeds.

Some of my favorite speed test sites include the following:

- Bandwidth Place Speed Test (http://bandwidthplace.com/)
- CNET Bandwidth Meter Speed Test (reviews.cnet.com/internet-speed-test/)
- DSL Reports Speed Test (www.dslreports.com/speedtest)
- MSN Internet Speed Test (tech.msn.com/speedtest.aspx)
- MySpeed (myspeed.visualware.com/)

Note that your connection speed may vary from day to day, or even at different hours of the same day. Test your connection a few times on different days of the week, calculate an average, and compare that to the speeds promised by your ISP.

What to Do If Your Speeds Are Low

Here's the dirty secret with all Internet connections, even broadband connections. The speeds you receive aren't always as high as those promised. In fact, many things can slow down a normally speedy connection, from bad cables

15

somewhere between your house and the main office to too many users accessing the network at the same time. (There's a fixed amount of bandwidth available; if you're the only user on the ISP's network, you'll connect faster than if everyone else in your neighborhood is connecting simultaneously.)

So here's the deal. Do your speed tests and if you find you're consistently connecting at less than the promised rate, contact your ISP's technical support. They should be able to check out the line, see what's wrong, and fix it. There's no reason for you to accept abnormally slow connection speeds!

Tip

It might not surprise you to know that the Internet itself (and the connection from your ISP) slows down when traffic is heavier. For that reason, you can speed up your surfing when Internet traffic is low—typically during weekday hours.

The Simple Speedup: Upgrading to a Faster Internet Connection

If you're still connecting via dial-up to AOL or some similar ISP, the solution to your speed problem is simple: Disconnect the dial-up and upgrade to a broadband connection! I know, I know, you have lots of reasons *not* to upgrade: Broadband costs more than dial-up (but not that much more these days), you don't want to lose your old email address (that's a small price to pay for faster speed), you've been with your ISP forever and you just don't want to change (sometimes change is good). But if you want a faster connection, moving to broadband is your only choice.

Besides, with broadband speeds going up and prices going down, there are no longer any good excuses for sticking with an antiquated dial-up connection—assuming that your telephone or cable company offers high-speed Internet, that is. If you live in a remote area, you might not have a broadband DSL or cable option; there are still areas in the United States where dial-up is the only game in town. But these areas are becoming fewer and farther between, so even if you didn't have the option of broadband a year or two ago, it may be available now.

Tip

If you can't get cable or DSL broadband, you can still get faster speeds by going with a satellite-based Internet connection. Satellite Internet connections reach speeds of 1.5Mbps (faster than dial-up but a little slower than most other forms of broadband) and are available from HughesNet (www. hughesnet.com) and WildBlue (www.wildblue.com).

15

Even if you already have a broadband connection, your ISP may offer faster speeds from so-called high-performance plans. For example, Comcast's standard cable broadband speed is 15Mbps, but it also offers a high-performance plan with a blazing 50Mbps connection speed. You'll pay more for a high-performance plan, of course, but if you do a lot of downloading or uploading of big files (such as movies or digital music), it may be worth the price.

Choosing Your Broadband Plan

If you have the choice, which should you go with, DSL or cable? It all depends on what's offered by your local telephone and cable companies, of course, so you'll have to do your own local comparisons. But just for the heck of it, I've put together a comparison of what's available in my neck of the woods, in the Twin Cities suburb of Burnsville, Minnesota. My cable company is Comcast; my phone company is Frontier, and Table 15.1 details the various plans they're currently offering (as of fall 2008).

Table 15.1   Broadband Plan Comparison (Burnsville, Minnesota)

Provider	Type of Service	Plan	Download Speed	Upload Speed	Monthly Price
Comcast	Cable	Performance	15Mbps	3Mbps	$42.95
Comcast	Cable	Blast	20Mbps	4Mbps	$52.95
Comcast	Cable	Ultra	30Mbps	5Mbps	$62.95
Comcast	Cable	Extreme 50	50Mbps	10Mbps	$142.95
Frontier	DSL	High-Speed Internet	3Mbps	768Kbps	$49.99

In my neck of the woods, I can get much faster service—and a lower price—from my cable provider (Comcast) than from the local DSL provider (Frontier). But that's just the way it is in my neighborhood. Check your local plans to see what's offered in your area.

Of course, looking at all these different plans raises the question of how fast is fast enough? This depends on your own personal needs. If all you do is browse the Web and send/receive email, the slowest broadband offerings are plenty fast enough. But if you download, upload, or email a lot of big files (spreadsheet and presentation files for work, or digital photos or movies for friends and family), a faster connection makes more sense. A faster connection is also nice if you watch a lot of online videos or if you download a lot of digital music or videos from iTunes or similar online music stores. It's also important if you play online games, where speed is of the essence.

15

The best advice is probably to sign up for the basic service first and see how it goes. If you find yourself wanting even more speed, you can upgrade to a faster broadband offering (if available) at a later date.

Making the Switch

Let's say you're convinced that it's time to ditch that old dial-up account. What's involved in switching from dial-up to broadband?

Let's start with the connection itself. Both DSL and cable broadband require the use of a special broadband modem. This modem connects like your dial-up modem, between your PC and the connection source. In the case of a DSL modem, it connects to any phone jack in your house. In the case of a cable modem, it connects to any cable jack. The modem typically connects to your PC via USB or Ethernet.

You'll probably have the choice of doing the installation yourself or having your ISP do the job for you. Professional installation is nice but not always necessary. In most instances you can opt to receive the modem via mail and make all the connections yourself. It's really just a matter of connecting the proper cables and running an installation disc. In a perfect world, the installation software configures the necessary network settings within Windows to recognize the new connection, and you're up and ready to surf—typically in less than a half hour.

Unless, that is, the connection doesn't go smoothly. In some cases you may need a technician to come out and tweak the line or do anything else necessary to get things up and running. Most installations go smoothly, but if yours doesn't, that's when you call the phone or cable company.

Once you're up and running, you'll probably have to deal with a new email account, unless you're using a web-based email service such as Hotmail or Gmail. For standard email, then, you'll need to reconfigure your email software to add this new account, and then notify all your friends, family, and colleagues of your new email address. It's a little bit of a bother, but no worse than changing telephone numbers.

 Tip

Some ISPs offer email transfer services that automatically notify everyone on your contact list of your new email address. If this type of service is offered, take advantage of it!

15

The Bottom Line

When all your Internet use—web browsing, email, and instant messaging—is sluggish, chances are the culprit is a slow Internet connection. Here's the bottom line:

- If you're using a dial-up connection, the fastest and easiest way to speed things up is to upgrade to a considerably faster broadband cable or DSL connection.

- In most areas, cable Internet is faster than DSL—although the exact performance differs from area to area and from provider to provider.

- You can check the actual speed of your connection using one of several speed test websites.

Speeding Up Your Home Network

If you have more than one computer in your house or office, chances are they're connected to each other over a local area network or LAN. A network can be either wired (via Ethernet cables) or wireless (using Wi-Fi technology), and is also used to let all your connected computers share a single Internet connection.

Because you use a network connection both to access the Internet and share data with other computers, any network sluggishness can affect your computing experience. If the network is slow, your Internet connection and file transfers are slow. It's not your PC; it can only work as fast as the network lets it.

With that in mind, let's look at how to speed up a typical home network. There are lots of things to look at, as you'll soon discover.

Troubleshooting a Slow Wireless Connection

Wireless networks are more prone to sluggishness than wired ones. That's because sending the network signal through the air, using radio frequency (RF) signals, is not as bulletproof as sending that same signal through a shielded cable. As you know from listening to AM and FM radio and watching television via rabbit ear antennae, lots of things can interfere with over-the-air signals.

 Note

If you already have a wireless network set up, I'm going to assume that you're familiar with all the components of the network: the router, which is the hub for all network connections, and the wireless adapters, one of which is connected to each computer on the network and enables the reception of wireless network signals.

A poor wireless connection most often manifests itself as a low signal, which provides slower data access than a faster signal. With that in mind, here are some things to look for when your wireless network starts slowing down.

Check Your Signal Strength

First things first: How strong is the wireless signal received by your computer? It's relatively easy to determine.

To view the strength of your current wireless signal, hover your cursor over the wireless connection icon in the Windows system tray. This displays a pop-up information window that describes the current network's signal strength. If the signal strength is less than 100%, your network connection is slower than it could be.

Move Closer to the Router

If your signal strength is low or your network connection seems sluggish, check to see how far away your computer is from the wireless router. It's a simple fact: The farther away your computer is from the router, the weaker the signal—and the slower the connection.

A simple solution, if you can do it, is to move your computer closer to the router. If that sounds like it's too easy, think again. The closer a remote computer is to the network router, the faster the wireless connection. If you don't believe me, position a notebook computer right next to the router and measure the wireless signal strength, then move it to the other side of the house and measure again. The wireless signal strength drops with distance, and less signal strength equals slower data transfer rates.

So if the wireless connection on your computer is feeling sluggish, try moving the computer a few feet closer to the router. Alternatively, you can move the router closer to the computer—whichever is easiest for you. But don't complain about slow network speeds if your computer is positioned at the extreme end of your router's range; move it closer to speed it up!

Don't Hide Your Adapter or Router

You can also increase signal strength—and speed up your connection—by not hiding your wireless adapter or router. If you use a USB wireless adapter, for example, it may be stuck down on the floor behind your PC, which is a perfect way to interfere with the Wi-Fi signal. Move the adapter out from behind the PC and raise it off the floor; you'll notice a marked increase in signal strength. The same thing goes with your wireless router; if it's hidden behind other equipment, you'll reduce its transmission range.

Along the same lines, you might be able to improve performance by moving or redirecting the antenna on your router or wireless adapter. Radio signals are directional; swiveling the antenna one direction or another can make a world of difference.

Move Devices That Might Cause Interference

You might not realize it, but placing a wireless router or adapter too close to other electronic equipment can reduce the effectiveness of the Wi-Fi signal. The other wireless signals effectively scramble the wireless network signal, reducing the resultant signal strength—and connection speed.

For example, I once ran into problems when I placed my wireless router between a cordless phone and my computer monitor—both devices that generate their own electronic signals or fields. Just moving the router to the other side of these devices dramatically increased its effective signal strength.

This last point reminds us that interference from other devices can affect the Wi-Fi signal. It's never a good idea to put your wireless router or adapter in close proximity to other cordless devices that use the 2.4GHz frequency band. In some instances, you may need to disconnect or turn off these other devices to get a clean Wi-Fi signal.

 Tip

If network interference is being caused by an older cordless telephone, consider upgrading to a newer 5.8GHz phone that doesn't operate in the same band as your Wi-Fi equipment.

This type of interference can sometimes be minimized by changing the wireless broadcast channel used by your router and adapter. Every router has the option of transmitting on any one of multiple channels, which use different portions of the available 2.4GHz band. If multiple devices (or multiple networks—such as yours and a neighbor's) use the same channel, interference can result.

To change the channel that your equipment uses, run your wireless router's configuration utility. Consult your router's manual for specific instructions.

Upgrading to a Faster Wireless Network

If your wireless network is consistently slow, consider upgrading to a faster router. Fortunately, the Wi-Fi standard is continually evolving.

Understanding Wi-Fi Protocols

Today's wireless networks use a type of RF transmission called *Wi-Fi* (short for *wireless fidelity*). This is the consumer-friendly name for the technology defined by the IEEE 802.11 wireless networking standard.

But here's the thing. There isn't a single Wi-Fi protocol. Instead, there are multiple 802.11 protocols, each designated by a single-letter suffix. Different versions of Wi-Fi offer different levels of performance. Which of these Wi-Fi standards you choose for your wireless network depends on your needs—and the equipment currently available for purchase.

 Note

The Wi-Fi standard was developed by an industry group called the Wi-Fi Alliance. Learn more at the Wi-Fi Alliance website (www.wi-fi.org).

Table 16.1 summarizes the specifications of the most popular 802.11 protocols for consumer use. Remember, the faster the data transfer rate, the speedier your network connection will be.

Table 16.1	Wi-Fi Protocols			
Wi-Fi Protocol	Release Date	Frequency Range	Data Transfer Rate (Max)	Transmission Range (Indoor)
802.11a	1999	5.0GHz	54Mbps	80 feet
802.11b	1999	2.4GHz	11Mbps	115 feet
802.11g	2003	2.4GHz	54Mbps	100 feet
802.11n (draft)	2009 (?)	2.4GHz	540Mbps (?)	325 feet (?)

What does all this alphabet soup mean? Here's the simple version. Older wireless equipment, sold from approximately 1999 to 2003, used the 802.11b protocol, which transfers data at 11Mbps. Equipment sold from 2003 to present use the 802.11g protocol, which transfers data close to five times as fast, at 54Mbps. Newer equipment is now available that use a draft version of the upcoming 802.11n protocol, which speeds things up by a factor of 10, transferring data at a potential 540Mbps. The newer the equipment, the faster the network.

Note

The stated data transfer rates for each Wi-Fi protocol are the theoretical maximum. Actual transfer rates typically average half the maximum. This is because wireless devices don't operate in a vacuum; walls, floors, and other obstructions and devices (as well as distance) negatively affect signal strength, and thus the transfer rate.

Fortunately, each newer Wi-Fi protocol is backward compatible with earlier versions. So if you buy a draft 802.11n router, you can still use it with older 802.11g adapters. This is another reason to buy the latest technology available—which, today, is the draft version of 802.11n, sometimes referred to as Pre-N.

A quick note is necessary about Wi-Fi transmission range, however. Radio signals don't suddenly stop when they get out of range; they weaken as you get farther away from the transmitter. So an 802.11g

Note

Some manufacturers today sell what they call Extreme G equipment. This equipment upgrades the standard 802.11g firmware to achieve data transfer rates of 108Mbps—twice the normal 802.11g rate. Note, however, that Extreme G equipment from one manufacturer may be incompatible with similar equipment from a different manufacturer, at least at the higher speeds.

network, for example, won't go completely dead when you get 100 feet distant. Instead, the data transfer rate decreases as the signal decreases. Get 100 or 110 feet away from an 802.11g transmitter, and you're likely to find your transfer rate decreasing from 54Mbps to something approaching 11Mbps.

With that in mind, what type of real-world performance can you expect from an 802.11n network? Actual data transfer rates should be at least 200Mbps and possibly up to 540Mbps. That's because 802.11n routers use "smart" multiple in, multiple out (MIMO) antennas that provide not only faster data transfer rates but also an extended transmission range. Whereas current 802.11b and 802.11g equipment have a usable range of about 100 feet between transmitter and receiver, 802.11n promises a range of at least 160 feet, and possibly double that, with less interference from other wireless household devices.

In other words, 802.11n is the way to go when purchasing new equipment.

Choosing a New Router

The key to creating a faster and farther-reaching network, therefore, is to upgrade your wireless router. If you have an older 802.11b or 802.11g router, upgrading to a 802.11n model, like the one in Figure 16.1, will increase both your network speed and range.

FIGURE 16.1

The Linksys WRT610n 802.11n wireless router.

Naturally, to gain full advantage of a faster router, you'll also need to upgrade all your wireless adapters to the matching standard. Move from an 802.11g to an 802.11n router, and you'll need 802.11n adapters to recognize the full speed improvement.

Note

An older 802.11g adapter will work with a newer 802.11n router, but at slower 802.11g speeds.

That said, sometimes upgrading your router will provide a signal strength improvement for existing adapters. As an example, I recently upgraded my network from an 802.11g router to an 802.11n model. I didn't upgrade all of my wireless adapters, but found that my most distant adapter now picked up a stronger signal from the new router. And, of course, a stronger signal is always desirable. The

Tip

Router manufacturers often make interim improvements to their routers that sometimes increase performance. These improvements are typically implemented via updates to the router's firmware—the built-in software that runs the router. To get the latest firmware updates for your router, visit the website for your router manufacturer.

stronger the signal, the more stable (fewer dropouts or dropped connections) and faster the connection—up to maximum protocol speeds, of course.

Installing a New Router

Upgrading your wireless modem is a deceptively simple task. After you purchase the new router, here are the basic steps you need to follow:

1. With your old router still connected, run the configuration software for the new router. (You need an existing connection to register and activate the installation software, as well as to download any necessary updates for the new router.)

2. When prompted, disconnect and remove the old router.

3. Place the new router in position and connect to it all existing cables.

4. Finish running the installation routine for the new router.

Naturally, if you change any network settings (such as the router's SSID or encryption passphrase), you'll need to reconfigure your other network devices for this new router. This might mean setting up a new network on each of your network computers, or simply changing configuration settings on all your wireless adapters.

 Note

SSID stands for service set identifier, which is the unique name assigned to a given wireless network.

Upgrading Your Wireless Adapter

When you upgrade your wireless router to a newer Wi-Fi protocol, you should also upgrade all your wireless adapters. So if you purchase an 802.11n router, you need to upgrade to 802.11n adapters for all your computers to gain full advantage of the new router's faster speed.

Upgrading to a new wireless adapter, like the one shown in Figure 16.2, is relatively easy. After you purchase a new adapter, follow these general steps:

1. Disconnect your current wireless adapter.

2. Uninstall any software used for the current adapter.

3. Run the setup routine for the new adapter.

4. When prompted, connect the new adapter to a USB port on your PC.

5. Configure the new adapter as necessary for your network.

16

FIGURE 16.2
D-Link's DWA-140 802.11n wireless adapter.

Naturally, you'll use your existing SSID, passphrase, and workgroup name to configure the new adapter. When installed, the adapter should use all the other existing network settings on the attached computer; all your network places, shared folders, and the like should remain the same.

Extending Wireless Network Range

You don't necessarily have to upgrade all your network equipment to get a faster network. Better performance can often be had by adding a piece of equipment or two to your network configuration.

Adding an External Antenna

Some wireless networks can be speeded up by replacing the router's built-in antenna with an external antenna. This type of antenna, bigger than the one built into the router, can provide greater range than the original—and greater range equals faster data transfer rates.

Most network equipment manufacturers sell external antennas for their routers. Some antennas, such as the one shown in Figure 16.3, are omnidirectional, and thus can service a large surrounding area.

Note

Most external Wi-Fi antennas are designed to be used with specific routers. Make sure the antenna you choose is compatible with your existing wireless router.

Others, like the one shown in Figure 16.4, are more directional antenna. (A directional antenna is best when your router is located on an outside wall and you want to focus your RF signals in a single direction—inward rather than beaming outside into your neighborhood.)

16

FIGURE 16.3

The Linksys HGA9N omnidirectional Wi-Fi antenna.

16

FIGURE 16.4

D-Link's ANT24-1800 directional antenna.

Adding a Wireless Extender

Another way to extend the range of your wireless network is with a wireless extender or repeater, like the one shown in Figure 16.5. An extender is a passive device that receives and then retransmits Wi-Fi signals, no network configuration necessary.

FIGURE 16.5

The Belkin Wireless G Universal Range Extender.

Installing a wireless extender is simplicity itself. In most cases, all you have to do is set it in place and plug it into a power outlet; no network setup is required. Position the extender at the farthest range of your current network, or halfway between your router and your farthermost computer. The device will extend your network from that point.

Switching from a Wireless to a Wired Connection

Even the fastest wireless network isn't as fast as a wired one. A new Gigabit Ethernet network transfers data at 1Gbps— one *gigabit* per second. That's equal to 1000Mbps, twice as fast as a new 802.11n wireless network or 20 times as fast as an older 802.11g network. You'll definitely notice that kind of speed increase.

For that reason, if you want really speedy network connections, you need to change from a wireless to a wired connection for the remote PC. To do this, you need a wireless router that also functions as a wired router. Fortunately, most current wireless routers also offer Ethernet functionality. Your remote PC must also have Ethernet functionality. Again, most desktop and notebook PCs sold in the past few years include Ethernet ports.

To switch a PC from wireless to Ethernet connection, follow these general steps:

1. Disconnect or deactivate the wireless adapter on the PC you want to switch.

 Tip

If you have a notebook PC that includes both a Wi-Fi adapter and an Ethernet connection, you can use both a wireless and a wired connection, depending on what you need at the time. When you're at a distance from your router, use the more convenient wireless connection. But when you're physically close to your router, just connect an Ethernet cable between the router and your notebook. When an Ethernet connection is made, it automatically overrides the wireless connection for faster speed. (On some notebooks, you might also need to turn off a wireless adapter switch.)

 Caution

If your PC doesn't have an Ethernet port built in, you'll need to install an internal network interface card (NIC) or external Ethernet adapter (typically to a USB port on the device).

 Tip

When shopping for a new router, look for one with Gigabit Ethernet capability. Some lower-priced routers come with the slower 10/100 Ethernet, which is capable of only (!) 100Mbps data transfer rates.

16

2. Uninstall the software for the wireless adapter.

3. Connect one end of an Ethernet cable to the Ethernet port on the PC.

4. Connect the other end of the Ethernet cable to a spare port on your network router.

Many computers and devices automatically detect the new network connection and perform any necessary configuration automatically. Other devices may need to be configured for the new Ethernet connection. Follow the instructions for your particular device.

Tweaking the Windows XP Registry for a Speedier Network

If you have a Windows XP computer, have you ever noticed that when you use the network to share data with other computers, it takes a long time for the files on that other computer to appear on your computer's screen? At times, it almost seems as if your computer is slowing down to a complete freeze before the folder window becomes active. Why is that?

The cause is due to the fact that before it displays shared folders, Windows XP looks for scheduled tasks on the remote computer. This can take some time on some computers and significantly slow down your network access, as your computer waits for a response from the remote computer.

And here's the thing: Unless you're an administrator on a big network, information about these scheduled tasks is totally useless. Your computer is waiting for something that is of no value to you.

Fortunately, you can disable this feature by editing the Windows registry using the Registry Editor utility. Here's how to do it:

1. Open the Registry Editor.

2. Navigate to the HKEY_LOCAL_MACHINE\Software\Microsoft\Windows\CurrentVersion\Explorer\RemoteComputer\NameSpace key and expand the folder.

3. Right click the folder labeled {D6277990-4C6A-11CF-8D87-00AA0060F5BF} and select Delete from the pop-up menu.

Note

This speedup is necessary only on computers running Windows XP. Windows Vista does not check for remote scheduled tasks the same way Windows XP does, and thus enables faster network browsing by default.

Note

Learn more about tweaking the Registry in Chapter 7, "Cleaning Up the Windows Registry."

After you have deleted this folder, close the Registry Editor and restart your PC for the changes to take effect.

The Bottom Line

Whether you're sharing files with another computer or accessing a shared Internet connection, the speed of your network connection affects what you're doing. Here's the bottom line:

- Wireless network speed is dependent on signal strength. Moving a remote computer closer to the network's wireless router will increase the signal strength and speed up the connection.

- You can vastly increase wireless network speed by upgrading to new 802.11n equipment.

- Other ways to boost performance of an existing wireless network include adding an external antenna to your router and using a wireless extender.

- For even faster network performance, switch from a wireless to a Gigabit Ethernet wired connection.

- If you're running Windows XP, you can speed up access to network folders by tweaking the Windows Registry.

16

PART

VI

The Ultimate Speedup: Buying a Faster PC

When Do You Need a New PC?

So far in this book, we've discussed things you can do to speed up the performance of your existing computer system. Some of these speedups involve reconfiguring system settings, some involve tweaking the Windows Registry, and a few even require upgrading specific components in your system. But they're all designed to help you get more speed out of your current system.

Unfortunately, not all speed problems can be corrected by updating your current PC. There are some PCs that, no matter how much you tweak them, can't shrug off their sluggish performance. And, perhaps more common, many new applications simply don't run well on older machines—and scream for you to purchase a new PC for optimum performance.

Fortunately, the prices of both desktop and notebook computers have taken a nosedive in recent years, so purchasing a new PC may be an affordable option for you. Read on to learn when to consider ditching your old computer for a new one—and then turn to Chapter 18, "How Fast a PC Do You Need?," for advice on what kind of new computer to purchase.

How Do You Know When Your Old PC Is Beyond Fixing?

Let's get right down to it. When is it time to drop back 10 and punt, PC-wise? When is your old PC too slow to continue using—no matter which speedups you attempt?

There are no hard and fast rules as to when to throw in the towel on your old computer system, but I'm willing to impart my advice and make a few recommendations. Remember, though, that the decision to purchase a new PC is purely a personal one; what might cause another user to pull the plug might not be enough of an argument for you. Use your own best judgment.

You've Tried Everything Else—and Nothing Seems to Work

Perhaps the most straightforward way to assess the need for a new PC comes from trying some of the speedup suggestions presented in this book. If you earnestly attempt to speed up your PC by removing unnecessary programs, adding more memory and disk storage, reconfiguring key system settings, tweaking the Windows Registry, and so on, yet still have sluggish performance, your only option may be to purchase a new computer. In other words, when all else fails, replace the old PC with a new one.

You're Not a Technical Wizard

You don't have to try *every* speedup in this book to conclude that a new PC is the way to go. After all, not every user is comfortable editing the Windows Registry or upgrading internal components. So if you've tried everything that's within your level of expertise and your system is still slow, you should consider buying a new system—rather than fumbling your way through technical upgrades to your old one.

Upgrades Are Too Expensive

Whereas it costs nothing to change a few configuration settings and wipe unnecessary programs off your hard disk (and out of system memory), other upgrades *do* cost money. Add up the cost of more memory, a bigger hard disk, a new graphics card, and the like, and you may soon be approaching the cost of a new low-end PC—which will probably outperform your old PC, even if

> **Tip**
>
> Time is money—especially your personal time. You can spend a lot of time trying to tweak your PC's performance, but that time might be better spent doing other things. So you should factor your time into the cost equation when contemplating a new PC. It's often a lot quicker to purchase and install a new PC than it is to try to speed up an old one.

upgraded. Add up the costs of potential upgrades (and the time involved to make them) and compare that to the cost of a new PC. It may be more cost-efficient—and time-efficient—to go the new PC route from the get go.

It's a Notebook PC—You Can't Upgrade It

Not all PCs can be upgraded. Specifically, there's a limited amount of upgrading you can do to notebook PCs. Yes, you can upgrade the memory and add an external hard drive; you can also reconfigure any number of system settings, of course. But if what you really need is a faster CPU or more powerful graphics card, you just can't do it like you can with a desktop model. For many users, buying a new notebook is the only way to achieve appreciable gains in performance.

It's Just Too Old

Remember that "three years and out" rule we discussed in Chapter 9, "Preparing for a Computer Upgrade"? The gist of it is that if your PC is more than three years old, it probably doesn't have the basic oomph necessary to accept upgraded components. As I said then, I might stretch that by a year or two, but if your PC is more than five years old (or running any version of Windows prior to Windows XP), I certainly can't recommend spending a lot of time or money in trying to speed it up. Yes, try the simple stuff, but if the system is still slow (and it likely will be), it's time to give it up and buy a new one. An old PC is only going to be so fast; nothing you can do will make it perform like a brand-new model.

What New Applications Might Demand a New PC?

Sometimes an old PC is plenty fast until you install a new application or two. If you find that your old PC runs your old programs just fine but chokes on that new one you just installed, that might justify purchasing a new PC to make that new program hum.

So what types of programs are the most demanding—that is, might require a new PC to run efficiently? Here's a short list.

Video-Editing Programs

If you take a lot of home movies that you want to edit on your PC, you probably don't want to do it on an older system. Video-editing programs, such as Adobe Premiere and Pinnacle Studio, are extremely demanding, especially when you get to the part where you "produce" (actually *encode*) the final video file.

Put simply, video encoding is one of the most demanding tasks that you can ask a PC to perform. It takes a powerful CPU to process the data quickly; processing a long movie can take an hour or more on a slow PC. In addition, the large file sizes tax both system memory and hard disk storage. If you're serious about video editing, tweaking an older PC probably won't get you to where you want to go. To get the job done, you'll probably need to upgrade to a much more powerful system.

Photo-Editing Programs

Although photo editing isn't near as CPU intensive as video editing, it still takes a bit of horsepower to handle and render the large files produced by today's multi-megapixel digital cameras. Just trying to display a screen full of thumbnails in Adobe Photoshop can max out an underpowered system; you need a decent CPU, a lot of memory, and tons of hard disk space if you want to accomplish your tasks in a reasonable amount of time.

Alas, most older PCs are just plain pokey when you put them to the task. It's not quite as bad if you're working with smaller files (fewer megapixels) and not adding a lot of special effects. But when you're displaying and processing the large files common with the latest digital cameras, a new system may be the only way to achieve the performance you need.

PC Games

You may think PC games are frivolous, but in reality they're the most taxing thing you can do on your computer. It's true; all those fancy graphics and gee-whiz sound effects definitely put your computer system through its paces.

In fact, to get the *best* game play possible, you need a truly state-of-the-art computer system. If your computer is an older one, it simply won't have the processing and graphics horsepower necessary to play the latest games quite as fast or as smoothly as you might have expected. In fact, it may not run some of the more demanding games at all.

The reality is that while you can upgrade an older system to run most of today's PC games, the cost of doing so may be prohibitive. After all, we're talking serious upgrades—CPUs and graphics cards and maybe even audio cards and monitors. That's a lot of upgrading; it might be simpler (and not much more expensive) to purchase a new system optimized for game play.

Upgrades to Existing Programs

You don't have to purchase new applications to obsolete your current PC. Sometimes just upgrading to a new version of an existing application will do the job. That's because software publishers often add a lot of new features when they upgrade their programs, and these new features may require more computing power. This is probably most apparent with already demanding applications, such as photo and video editing, but it can happen with other types of applications, as well. If you upgrade your favorite app and find that your PC either won't run it or runs it slowly, it may be time to consider upgrading to a new PC, as well.

Multitasking

Along the same lines, simply running more applications than you used to can also make your current PC too sluggish to bother with. We're talking *multitasking*—running multiple applications at the same time. To do this well, your system needs a powerful CPU and lots of RAM. Adding RAM is easy enough, but it might not be feasible to upgrade your system's CPU. So you may need to purchase a new PC if you start multitasking—or settle for really sluggish performance.

Windows Vista

Finally, if you want to upgrade from Windows XP to Windows Vista, your old PC may not be up to the task. Vista requires more processing power, more system memory, more hard disk space, and a much more powerful graphics card. You can't just tweak an old PC to make it Vista ready. For many users, the only way to upgrade to Vista is to buy a new PC built with Vista in mind (and with Vista already installed, of course).

A Few Other Reasons to Buy a New PC

Okay, so you may not have the technical wherewithal or the budget to perform the really big upgrades. Or your new applications may require newer hardware to run efficiently. Or you may have tried everything you can think of and your old PC still moans and wheezes its way through a computing day.

Those are all logical reasons why purchasing a new PC may be your best option. But these aren't the only reason you may want to buy a new PC—as you'll soon discover.

Your Old PC Is on Its Last Legs

Sluggish performance may be the least of your PC problems. What do you do if your PC is constantly freezing or crashing, or just stops working altogether?

Old PCs, just like people, sometimes slow down and die. If you think your PC is on its way to becoming a "late" PC, no amount of tweaking and upgrading will help the cause. It's time to start shopping for a new model—*now*.

You Want to Switch from a Desktop to a Notebook

Notebook PCs are all the rage. In fact, if you visit your local computer or consumer electronics store, you'll find a lot more notebook PCs than desktop models for sale.

There's good reason for that. Notebook PCs offer similar power in a smaller package than desktop PCs, and often for no price premium. Unlike desktop models, a notebook PC can be taken with you when you travel, or if you just want to check your email while sipping a latte at Starbucks. You can take your notebook from room to room in your home or office, or even use it in the family room or bedroom. It's versatile, truly personal computing—which is why they're the most popular models sold today.

So even though you might have a fully functional desktop PC, the desire for a portable notebook model might inspire you to dump your old machine for a new one before it become obsolete.

You Want a Smaller/Lighter/More Efficient Notebook

As noted previously, notebook PCs are not easily upgradable—especially when what you want to upgrade is the form factor. You may love your current notebook, but if you want one that's smaller or lighter or has a longer battery life, there's no way to upgrade it to make it so. If a different type or better performing notebook is what you want, you have to buy a new one—even if your old one is still running fine.

You Just Want a New One

Let's face it. Sometimes you just get tired of what you have and want something new. That happens with cars and TVs and houses, and it happens with personal computers, too. If you're tired of your old PC, that may be reason enough to buy a new one. That might sound wasteful to some, but if it's what you want, go for it.

Benchmarking PC Performance

There's one more way to determine whether your computer is best upgraded or replaced, and that's by benchmarking its performance. Benchmarking is a way of measuring a PC's performance, by clocking how fast it completes certain tasks or runs certain applications. You can then compare your computer's performance with that of other PCs, and with what you deem acceptable performance.

You can benchmark your PC's performance by manually using a stopwatch to clock how long it takes to do certain tasks, such as the startup and shutdown processes, but that can be quite time-consuming—especially if you're not a pro at it. A better approach for most users is to use an automated benchmarking utility to do the measuring for you. There are many of these utilities on the market, including the following:

- HDTach (www.simplisoftware.com)
- Maxon CineBench (www.maxon.net/pages/download/ cinebench_e.html)
- OpenSourceMark (sourceforge.net/projects/opensourcemark/)
- PassMark PerformanceTest (www.passmark.com)
- PCMark05 and PCMark Vantage (www.futuremark.com)
- SiSoftware Sandra (www.sisoftware.net)

You may want to try several of these benchmarking utilities, because they all tend to measure slightly different things. Most of these utilities are free or relatively low priced, so you don't have to spend a lot of money to see if your system is up to snuff.

17

The Bottom Line

Sometimes purchasing a new PC is a better approach than trying to upgrade or tweak a sluggish older computer. Here's the bottom line:

■ If you've tried all or most of the speedups suggested in this book and your computer is still sluggish, it may be time to buy a new PC.

■ If it costs more (or almost as much) to upgrade your computer as it does to purchase a new one, it may be time to buy a new PC.

■ If an upgrade is in order but you have a notebook computer, it may be time to buy a new PC.

■ If your computer is more than four or five years old or on its last legs, it may be time to buy a new PC.

■ If you're having trouble running a demanding new application, such as a video-editing program or graphics-intensive game, it may be time to buy a new PC.

■ If you want to upgrade from Windows XP to Windows Vista, it may be time to buy a new PC.

18

How Fast a PC Do You Need?

I f you read through the preceding chapter and determined that your sluggish old PC is beyond hope and you really do need a new PC, it's time to go shopping. The operative question, of course, is "how fast a PC do you need?" How much power determines what type of PC to buy—and how much money you have to spend.

If you're like most users, you end up buying a new PC every two to four years. If you haven't purchased a PC in awhile, the good news is that new PCs—even top-of-the-line models—are a lot less expensive than when you bought your last unit. With all this in mind, let's look at the different ways you might use a PC, and match new equipment with your own specific computing needs.

Understanding Key Components

We've discussed various computer components throughout this book, but now is the time for a quick summary of those pieces and parts that most affect system speed. The three most essential components, performance-wise, are the PC's CPU, memory, and hard disk—and, if you're doing video editing or gaming, the system's video card.

CPU

The CPU, or central processing unit, is the engine that drives your entire computer system. The more powerful the CPU, the faster your PC will run.

Two major companies, Intel and AMD, provide CPUs for most of the Windows-compatible computers sold today. While each company has its own adherents, the two types of chips are somewhat interchangeable; all of today's software applications will run on PCs powered by either type of CPU.

Today's CPUs utilize multiple microprocessors in a single chip, thus enabling more efficient and effective multiprocessing. Dual-core chips, such as Intel's Core 2 Duo and AMD's Athlon X2, include two microprocessors. Quad-core chips, such as Intel's Core 2 Quad and AMD's Phenom X4, include four microprocessors.

Most dual-core CPUs use 32-bit architecture, which can handle 32 bits of data at a time. Most quad-core CPU use 64-bit architecture, which can handle 64 bits of data at a time. As you might suspect, a 64-bit CPU is notably faster than a 32-bit model, at least when running applications written to take advantage of the technology.

The other gauge of CPU speed is its clock speed, measured in gigahertz. Obviously, a 2.4GHz CPU is going to be faster than one running at just 2GHz. That said, a quad-core CPU with a slower clock speed will probably be faster than a dual-core CPU with a faster clock speed. Remember, each core is a separate microprocessor, and more microprocessors are better.

Tip

If you're looking at a notebook PC, look for a CPU designed specifically for portable use, such as the Intel Pentium Dual-Core, Intel Mobile Core 2 Duo, or the AMD Turion X2. These CPUs draw less power than a typical desktop CPU, and therefore give you longer battery life.

Memory

The more random access memory your system has, the faster it will run. In the Windows Vista world, I view 2GB as the minimum amount of memory you want in a new PC. (Even though, to be fair, Microsoft says you can get by with 1GB; I find that little memory to be unacceptably sluggish.)

Note

If you have a 32-bit CPU running the 32-bit version of Windows Vista, you're pretty much limited to 4GB RAM maximum. You can use more RAM if you're running the 64-bit version of Vista.

You'll need more memory for more-demanding applications. For example, if you're using a heavy-duty photo-editing program like Adobe Photoshop CS, I recommend a minimum of 4GB RAM. If you're doing video editing or playing games, 6GB is recommended.

Hard Disk

Hard disk capacity is important, and fortunately for all of us, hard disk prices keep coming down. Even the lowest-priced computers today come with at least 160GB of hard disk storage, and some higher-end models are approaching storage at the terabyte level. The more and bigger files you'll be creating, the more hard disk space you'll need; this is especially important if you're editing and storing digital movies.

Video Card

Video movie editing is also demanding from a video card standpoint—as is PC gaming. For video editing, look for a 3D graphics card with at least 256MB of video RAM. For gaming, look for 512MB or more.

In the case of video editing, you also need a card with a full complement of video inputs and outputs, to connect all your video recording and playback equipment. Make sure the inputs/outputs on the card match those of your other equipment.

Windows Version

There's one last thing to consider when purchasing a new PC: Which version of Windows should you use? Every computer sold today comes with Windows Vista as the operating system, but Microsoft makes a half-dozen or so different versions of Vista, each with its own unique feature set. Which version should you look for in your new PC?

Table 18.1 details the versions of Windows you can come installed on a new PC.

Table 18.1   Windows Vista Versions

	Home Basic	Home Premium	Business	Enterprise	Ultimate
Target market	Home	Home	Small business	Corporate	Home and small business
Interface	Basic	Aero	Aero	Aero	Aero
Included applications	Internet Explorer, Windows Calendar, Windows Mail, Windows Media Player, Windows Meeting Space, Windows Movie Maker, Windows Photo Gallery	Internet Explorer, Windows Calendar, Windows DVD Maker, Windows Mail, Windows Media Center, Windows Media Player, Windows Meeting Space, Windows Movie Maker (HD), Windows Photo Gallery	Internet Explorer, Windows Calendar, Windows Fax and Scan, Windows Mail, Windows Media Player, Windows Meeting Space, Windows Photo Gallery	Internet Explorer, Windows Calendar, Windows Fax and Scan, Windows Mail, Windows Media Player, Windows Meeting Space, Windows Photo Gallery	Internet Explorer, Windows Calendar, Windows DVD Maker, Windows Fax and Scan, Windows Mail, Windows Media Center, Windows Media Player, Windows Meeting Space, Windows Movie Maker (HD), Windows Photo Gallery
Maintenance features	Manual file backup	Manual file backup, Scheduled File Backup	Manual File Backup, Scheduled File Backup, System Image-Based Backup and Recovery	Manual File Backup, Scheduled File Backup, System Image-Based Backup and Recovery	Manual File Backup, Scheduled File Backup, System Image-Based Backup and Recovery

Let's try to make sense out of all these different versions. If you're buying a low-priced PC, it's likely you'll get the Home Basic edition of Vista—which is a good reason to step up to a slightly more expensive model. That's because, for most users, the Home Premium edition (which has the better-looking Aero interface and a lot more useful applications) is the one you want. Of course, if you're in a small business or corporation, you might find the Business or Enterprise editions more useful. And if you want the version that has everything (essentially a superset of the other versions), you want Windows Vista Ultimate.

Tip

Whichever version of Windows Vista you have installed on your PC, you can easily upgrade to another version by using the built-in Windows Anytime Upgrade feature, available from the Windows Control Panel. All you have to do is select the version you want, make sure you're connected to the Internet, and then give Microsoft your credit card number. The upgrade process is automatic, using files already installed on your PC's hard drive.

That said, for most purposes Vista Home Premium is the way to go—although if you get Vista Ultimate offered, take it.

Choosing a Form Factor: Desktop Versus Notebook

When you're shopping for a new PC, you eventually have to decide whether you want a desktop or a notebook model. These days you'll probably see more notebooks at your favorite electronics or computer store, but that doesn't necessarily mean that a notebook is the best way to go for your particular needs—although it might be.

Notebook PCs: Pros and Cons

Let's face it. A notebook PC does everything a desktop does, but in a smaller, more portable form factor—and with the monitor built in. You can take your entire computing life with you—programs, data, you name it. You're no longer tethered to your office desktop, or even to a power outlet. Anywhere you can go, your notebook PC can go with you.

That means that you can both work and play outside the house and outside the office. You can work on a PowerPoint presentation at Starbucks, check email while eating lunch, or even make hotel reservations while you're stopped at a truck stop or resting in an airport lounge. You're always connected, and you're always ready to go.

A notebook PC also offers freedom of movement within your home. Many people buy notebook PCs and never take them out of the house. Instead, they use the notebook in the living room, in the kitchen, in the den, and in the bedroom. Just pick it up and take it to whatever room you want; there's no need to worry about power cords, Ethernet cables, and so on. You can work on a report while sitting on the living room couch, or write email messages from bed.

That doesn't mean, however, that a notebook is the perfect computer for your particular needs. Perhaps the biggest argument against a notebook PC is that it's probably a little more expensive than a similarly equipped desktop model. That's because all the normal components used in a desktop PC have to be shrunk down to the more compact size of a laptop model. A $500 desktop PC might translate into a $600 or $700 notebook, which is a lot if you're on a budget.

In addition, some people don't like working on a notebook's smaller keyboard and display. Other people don't like the notebook's touchpad pointing device,

18

preferring a traditional mouse instead. Then there's the issue of number crunching. Most notebooks don't have a separate numeric keypad, which makes entering numbers a pain. If you're an accountant by trade, you probably don't like the notebook PC form factor.

There are also a few technical limitations. Unlike a desktop PC, a notebook PC isn't very expandable. Want to upgrade the video card on your notebook? Tough luck. The configuration you buy is the configuration you have to stick with—save for the memory, which is just about the only thing in a notebook that you can upgrade.

And the configuration you get typically isn't as state of the art as on a comparable desktop PC. In particular, few notebooks come with top-line graphics capabilities, which can be limiting.

Bottom line? In general, a notebook is fine for home/office computing and digital music and movies, but less than ideal for video editing and game playing. (If you're doing photo editing, it's a bit of a toss-up; serious photographers will go the desktop route, due to the larger monitors, whereas more casual photographers can get by just fine with a decent notebook.)

Different Types of Notebook PCs

Although all notebook PCs have similar components, they're not all created alike. As you can see in Figure 18.1, some notebooks are smaller and lighter than others, whereas some models are more suited for multimedia use—for watching movies and listening to music while you're on the go.

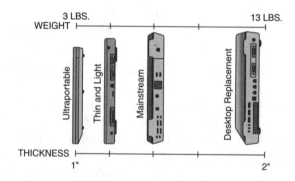

FIGURE 18.1

Different types of notebooks.

The smallest and most portable type of notebook PC is called an *ultraportable* or *netbook*. These models typically have a smallish screen (12-inch or so) with a traditional aspect ratio and weigh less than 4 pounds. Ultraportables are small and light enough to fit in a business briefcase and are perfect when all you need to do is check your email and do a little work when you're on the road. Because the screen is small and the PC horsepower is low, they get great battery life. On the downside, the screen is small and the horsepower is low, which means you can't do high-performance work; in addition, some users find the keyboards a bit too compact.

In the middle of the pack is the appropriately named *midsize* or traditional notebook. These notebooks are a little bigger and a little heavier than ultraportables but also offer bigger screens (14-inch to 15.4-inch) and more comfortable keyboards. These notebooks have enough horsepower to do traditional home/office computing tasks and typically have battery life in the two to three hour range.

If, on the other hand, you want a notebook that will do everything a desktop PC does and you won't be using it on batteries much, consider a *desktop replacement* model. These notebooks are big and heavy and have relatively poor battery life, so you won't be carrying them around much. They have big 17-inch screens and lots of computing horsepower, so they can perform the most demanding tasks—including high-octane game playing and video editing. As the name implies, you can totally replace your desktop PC with one of these notebooks.

Which type of notebook is best for you? If you travel a lot but don't use your PC much, consider a lightweight ultraportable. (These are also good for watching DVDs in the car or on an airplane.) If you use your notebook a lot and need to take your work with you, a midsize model is a good compromise. And if you want to totally replace your desktop with a notebook and know you won't be using it on battery power much, go with a more expensive desktop replacement model.

What Kind of Computing Do You Do?

Of course, what type of PC you buy depends on how you want to use it. Using your computer to check email and surf the Web doesn't require near the horsepower than if you're editing home videos or playing the latest graphics-intensive games. You need to match your system requirements to the applications you plan to run.

I find that most computer use falls into one (or perhaps more) of the following categories:

- **Home/office computing:** This describes the broadcast category of computer use, and recognizes that home and business users use their computers for pretty much the same tasks. These tasks include surfing the Web, sending/receiving email, and key office tasks—word processing, spreadsheets, and presentations. These users don't need a lot of computing power. Today's basic desktop and notebook PCs should be more than powerful enough.

- **Digital music and movies:** Many home/office users also use their PCs to manage their iPod music libraries and listen to music in the home or office. Some are even using their PCs to watch TV shows and movies via streaming Internet video, DVDs, and legally questionable BitTorrent downloads. These users need a basic PC with a big hard disk, to store all those digital media files. (And, in the case of a desktop PC, a good set of external speakers.)

- **Digital photography:** Most people today own digital cameras, and likely have a large collection of digital photographs. They use a program like Adobe Photoshop CS or Photoshop Elements to edit those photographs. The more sophisticated the editing program, the greater these users' PC needs. Serious digital photographers need a PC with midrange CPU, a fair amount of memory, and a large hard drive for photo storage.

- **Video movie editing:** A smaller number of people own camcorders and use their PCs to edit their home movies. But this is a very demanding task, and requires a PC with a very fast CPU, vast amounts of system memory, a powerful graphics card, and one or more large hard disk drives.

- **Gaming:** Today's graphics-intensive games are the most demanding applications for a PC. Serious gamers need the fastest CPU available, as much memory as they can afford, a state-of-the-art graphics card, a similar state-of-the-art audio card (and matching speakers, typically in surround-sound configuration), and a large hard disk drive—in other words, a top-end system.

Choosing the Right Features for Your Needs

Identifying your computing needs is just the first step in shopping for a new computer system. To make a final choice, you have to match PC features with your particular needs.

Although you could do a lot of online and in-store research, I've saved you the trouble. Table 18.2 describes the type of system that best fits the most common computing activities. Find your activities in the table and discover the basic specs to look for in a new PC.

Tip

Hardcore gamers should check out the ultra-high end machines available from specialty manufacturers such as Alienware (www.alienware.com), Falcon Northwest (www.falcon-nw.com), and Voodoo PC (www.voodoopc. com). These companies offer machines with incredible raw performance and truly unique styling, but at a price. Expect to pay anywhere from $2,000 or more for one of these custom-built screamers.

Table 18.2   System Requirements for Different Activities

	Home/Office Computing	Digital Music and Movies	Digital Photography	Video Movie Editing	Gaming
Processor (Minimum)	1.8GHz Intel Core Duo, Pentium Dual-Core, or AMD Athlon X2	1.8GHz Intel Core Duo, Pentium Dual-Core, or AMD Athlon X2	2GHz Intel Core Duo or AMD Athlon X2	2.4GHz Intel Core 2 Quad or AMD Phenom X4	2.6GHz Intel Core 2 Quad or AMD Phenom X4
Memory (Minimum)	2GB	2GB	3GB	4GB	4GB
Hard drive (Minimum)	160GB	250GB	500GB	750GB	750GB
Video card	Generic	Generic	Generic (256MB video memory recommended for serious users)	3D graphics with 256MB video memory, advanced video inputs/outputs	3D graphics with 512MB video memory
Notebook or desktop?	Either	Either	Either (desktop recommended for serious users)	Desktop	Desktop
Windows version	Vista Home Premium	Vista Home Premium	Vista Home Premium	Vista Home Premium	Vista Home Premium

18

I'm going to assume that each of these systems include at least one CD/DVD read/write drive and an appropriate monitor. If you have a desktop system, that means at least a 17-inch LCD monitor (19-inch or larger if you're doing video editing or game playing). For notebooks, choose a screen size that fits your portable needs. The 15.4-inch size is a good compromise between home and on-the-road use, whereas a 17-inch screen is great if you don't have to haul it around much.

Now let's look at some typical systems for each type of computer use. For the following examples, I chose systems that were readily available from Best Buy in November of 2008; you should be able to find similar (or better) systems when you decide to go shopping.

The Home/Office Computing PC

For typical home/office computing, you can get by with a relatively low-cost PC. You don't need a huge hard disk, but even low-end PCs today have 160GB or larger drives, which should be more than large enough for your needs. A dual-core CPU operating at 1.8GHz should deliver speedy performance, and 2GB of RAM should keep your applications popping along.

Tip

You can enhance any of these systems for your particular needs; these are just the *minimum* specs. If you want a bigger hard disk or more memory, go for it. The more you spend, the faster your new system will be.

Tip

When it's time to go PC shopping, do yourself a favor and do a little homework. Hit the Web for information direct from the manufacturers and to price shop the online retailers. I recommend checking the professional equipment reviews at CNET (www.cnet.com) and the user reviews at Epinions.com (www.epinions.com). It's also worth your while to read some of the monthly computer magazines, either in print or online; if nothing else, browsing through the ads will give you an idea of what's available, and for how much.

For our example system, I've chosen a notebook model, because most users today appreciate the advantages of portable computing. The notebook, shown in Figure 18.2, is the Sony VAIO model VGN-NR430, priced at $549. It has the following specs:

FIGURE 18.2

A perfect home/office notebook PC from Sony.

- **CPU:** 1.86GHz Intel Pentium Dual-Core mobile processor T2390
- **Memory:** 2GB DDR2 RAM
- **Hard disk:** 160GB SATA 5400 RPM drive
- **Graphics:** Intel Graphics Media Accelerator
- **Screen:** 15.4-inch LCD
- **Windows version:** Vista Home Premium

As you can see, this notebook meets all the specs detailed in Table 18.2 for home/office computing. It will do everything you need to do, and do so with more than acceptable performance.

The Digital Music and Movies PC

If you want to store your digital music library and watch movies and TV shows online, you need a home/office PC with a bigger hard disk. If you're sticking with the notebook form factor, which is fine, you may also want to go with a slightly larger screen, all the better for watching widescreen movies.

To that end, my recommendation for a digital music and movies PC is the Toshiba Satellite model L355D-S7825, shown in Figure 18.3. This model, priced at $699, offers the following specs:

FIGURE 18.3

A large-screen digital music and movies notebook from Toshiba.

- **CPU:** 2.0GHz AMD Turion X2 Mobile Technology TL-60
- **Memory:** 3GB DDR2 RAM
- **Hard disk:** 250GB SATA 5400 RPM drive
- **Graphics:** ATI Radeon X1250
- **Screen:** 17-inch LCD
- **Windows version:** Vista Home Premium

The CPU in this model is slightly faster than the one in the Sony home/office notebook, and you get an extra gigabyte of memory, as well. The hard drive is more than roomy enough to hold your digital media libraries, and that big screen is easy on the eyes. It's a good match for your digital music and movie needs—at a price that doesn't break the bank.

The Digital Photography PC

Although you can use a notebook PC for digital photography, serious photographers prefer a desktop model. A desktop PC lets you use a larger monitor than you get from even the biggest notebook, and typically provides a little better bang for your buck, power-wise.

Our example system is the Dell Inspiron model I530-115B, shown in Figure 18.4. The $599 price includes only the system unit; you'll need to spend another $200 or so for monitor and speakers. The specs are as follows:

FIGURE 18.4

A desktop for digital photography from Dell.

- **CPU:** 2.66GHz Intel Core 2 Duo E7300
- **Memory:** 4GB DDR2 RAM
- **Hard disk:** 640GB SATA 5400 RPM drive
- **Graphics:** Intel Graphics Media Accelerator
- **Windows version:** Vista Home Premium

What you get here is a very powerful desktop PC. The dual-core CPU runs at a speedy 2.66GHz, you get more than enough memory to run Adobe Photoshop CS or a similar program, and the 640GB hard drive will hold tons of digital photos. Pair this with a 19-inch or 21-inch widescreen LCD monitor, and you have the perfect digital photography workstation.

The Video Movie Editing PC

When you move up to video editing, you need a much more powerful PC. We're talking a desktop unit, of course, with a quad-core CPU and high-end 3D graphics card.

Dell's Studio MT model SMT-116B, shown in Figure 18.5, is an excellent example of such a high-end PC. For $799, you get the kind of performance you need for efficient movie editing and video rendering, as witnessed by the following specs:

FIGURE 18.5

A video-editing workstation from Dell.

- **CPU:** 2.33GHz Intel Core 2 Quad Q8200
- **Memory:** 6GB DDR2 RAM
- **Hard disk:** 750GB SATA 7200 RPM drive
- **Graphics:** ATI Radeon 3450 3D graphics with 256MB video RAM and HDMI output
- **Windows version:** Vista Home Premium

The quad-core CPU and 6GB of RAM provide the power, while the fast (7200 RPM) 750GB hard drive provides plenty of storage space for big movie files. The video card comes with sufficient video RAM and an HDMI output for connecting to a flat-screen HDTV. Naturally, you'd want to pair this PC with a large (21-inch or bigger) LCD monitor and a surround-sound speaker system. All things said and done, this is a system with a lot of "oomph"—and that still doesn't break the bank.

The Gaming PC

Breaking the bank may be an issue when you want to build the ultimate gaming PC. In fact, you probably can't find the PC you want at store like Best Buy or Circuit City. Most of these babies have to be ordered direct from the manufacturer or custom built from scratch.

Case in point is the Alienware Area-51, shown in Figure 18.6. This blazing-fast system can be special ordered (and customized to your liking) from the Alienware website (www.alienware.com). Our configuration runs $2,899 and features the following specs:

FIGURE 18.6
A high-end gaming PC from Alienware.

- **CPU:** 3.0GHz Intel Core 2 Quad Q9650
- **Memory:** 4GB DDR3 RAM
- **Hard disk:** 750GB SATA 7200 RPM drive
- **Graphics:** NVIDIA GeForce GTX 280 3D graphics with 1GB video RAM
- **Windows version:** Vista Home Premium

Like I said, a pricey system but one with lots of power. Also note the cool-looking case, which you can have in your choice of colors. This unit also comes with a beefed-up power supply and cooling system, the better to keep things running well during hot-and-heavy gaming sessions. Make sure to add a big monitor, surround-sound speaker system, and your favorite game controllers.

18

Getting Rid of Your Old PC

After you've purchased a new, speedier PC, you're faced with another problem: What do you do with your old computer?

If your old PC is still in decent operating condition (in spite of its sluggish performance), you might not want to get rid of it. There's no reason not to convert an old PC into a dedicated Internet machine, or give it to your children to use for homework. And if you go this route, it's easy to connect all your PCs together in a simple home network.

If your old PC *isn't* working well, or if you just don't have the space or need for it, you have a disposal issue. In most localities, you can't just throw the thing in the trash; computers, like most electronic equipment these days, have to be specially recycled.

How, then, to dispose of your old PC? First, check with your county's recycling center or your local waste-collection firm; they may have special programs for recycling computers and other electronics. In addition, the Environmental Protection Agency (www.epa.gov/osw/conserve/materials/ecycling/donate.htm) and E-cycling Central (www.eiae.org) both provide lists of local and national recycling programs. Finally, many retailers—including Office Depot and Staples—offer in-store drop-off for old computers, often accompanied by a store credit for your old equipment.

But whatever you do, just don't put your PC in the trash—that is *not* environmentally friendly!

 Caution

Before you give away your old PC, you should reformat the hard disk to make inaccessible all your old data and personal information.

The Bottom Line

When your old PC can't be speeded up any further, it's time to purchase a new computer system. Here's the bottom line:

- If you use your PC for typical home/office computing, consider a basic notebook PC with dual-core CPU, 2GB RAM, and 160GB hard drive.

- If you use your PC to manage and play digital music or movies, consider a notebook PC with a larger screen, dual-core CPU, 2GB RAM, and 250GB hard drive.

- If you use your PC for serious digital photo editing, consider a desktop PC with a large LCD monitor, dual-core CPU, 3GB RAM, and 500GB hard drive.

- If you use your PC for video editing, consider a desktop PC with a large LCD monitor, quad-core CPU, 4GB RAM, 750GB hard drive, and 3D graphics card with 256MB video RAM.

- If you use your PC for gaming, consider a desktop PC with a large LCD monitor, quad-core CPU, 4GB RAM, 750GB hard drive, and 3D graphics card with 512MB video RAM.

18

PC Performance Resources

Throughout this book I've presented dozens of tools—software utilities and websites—you can use to speed up your computer system. Well, there are lots more of these tools available. For your convenience and edification, then, I list some of the most popular and effective speedup tools here—use them to improve various aspects of your PC's performance.

General Performance Suites

These applications contain multiple utilities you can use to fine-tune various parts of your system.

- Advanced SystemCare (www.iobit.com/advancedwindowscareper.html), free
- Fix-It Utilities Professional (www.avanquest.com), $49.95
- Glary Utilities (www.glarysoft.com), free
- My Faster PC (www.myfasterpc.com), $39.95
- Norton SystemWorks (www.symantec.com/norton/), $49.99
- PC Booster (www.inklineglobal.com/products/pcb/), $59.95
- System Mechanic (www.iolo.com/system-mechanic/standard/), $49.95/year
- TuneUp Utilities (www.tune-up.com), $49.95
- WinSettings Pro (www.filestream.com/winpro/), $69.95
- WinUtilities (www.xp-tools.com/winutilities/), $49.99

Benchmarking

How fast is your PC, really? Use these benchmarking utilities to measure your system's performance—and find out what needs speeding up.

- HDTach (www.simplisoftware.com), free
- Maxon CineBench (www.maxon.net/pages/download/cinebench_e.html), free
- OpenSourceMark (sourceforge.net/projects/opensourcemark/), free
- PassMark PerformanceTest (www.passmark.com), $24.00
- PCMark05 (www.futuremark.com), $19.95
- PCMark Vantage (www.futuremark.com), $6.95
- SiSoftware Sandra Pro Home (www.sisoftware.net), $49.99

Startup Optimization

Use these utilities to manage those programs and utilities that start automatically when your Windows launches—and to delete unwanted "bundleware" from new computers.

- Autoruns (technet.microsoft.com/en-us/sysinternals/bb963902.aspx), free
- PC Decrapifier (www.pcdecrapifier.com), free
- Security Task Manager (www.neuber.com/taskmanager/), $29
- WinPatrol (www.winpatrol.com), free

File Cleaning

Need to clean up all those unused and duplicate files on your computer's hard disk? These file cleaning tools are for you—they'll find the files you don't use and get rid of them.

- CCleaner (www.ccleaner.com), free
- Duplicate File Cleaner (www.duplicatefilecleaner.com), free
- Easy Duplicate File Finder (www.easyduplicatefinder.com), free

Specific Program Removal Tools

Ever tried to delete a Norton or McAfee product—and found remnants of that program still clogging your PC? These products are notoriously hard to delete, hence the introduction of program-specific removal tools by the companies themselves.

- McAfee Consumer Products Removal Tool (download.mcafee.com/products/licensed/cust_support_patches/MCPR.exe), free
- Norton Removal Tool (ftp://ftp.symantec.com/public/english_us_canada/removal_tools/Norton_Removal_Tool.exe), free

Registry Cleaners

When a cluttered Windows Registry is slowing you down, use these utilities to clean up duplicate and unused entries.

- Auslogics Registry Defrag (www.auslogics.com/registry-defrag/), free
- CCleaner (www.ccleaner.com), free
- EasyCleaner (personal.inet.fi/business/toniarts/ecleane.htm), free
- Registry First Aid (www.rosecitysoftware.com/reg1aid/), $27.95
- Registry Healer (www.zoneutils.com/regheal/), $19.95
- Registry Mechanic (www.pctools.com/registry-mechanic/), $29.95
- RegSeeker (www.hoverdesk.net/freeware.htm), free
- Uniblue RegistryBooster (www.liutilities.com/products/registrybooster/), $29.95
- WinCleaner (www.wincleaner.com), $29.95
- Wise Registry Cleaner (www.wisecleaner.com), free

Hard Disk Optimization

Want to make your hard disk go faster? Then consider these hard disk optimization tools, which defragment, find errors, and fix problems with any hard drive.

- Diskeeper (www.diskeeper.com), $29.95
- PC Tools Disk Suite (www.pctools.com/disk-suite/), $39.95
- PerfectDisk (www.raxco.com), $39.99

Disk Imaging

These programs create a mirror image of your hard disk—perfect for backups, or for transferring data and programs from an old hard disk to a new one.

- Acronis True Image (www.acronis.com), $49.99
- BootIt Next Generation (www.terrabyteunlimited.com), $34.95
- Drive Copy (www.paragon-software.com/home/dc-personal/), $29.95
- Norton Ghost (www.symantec.com/norton/ghost), $69.99

Internet Speedup and Browser Optimization

Need to speed up a pokey Internet connection or make your web browser run faster? These tools are for you!

- Download Accelerator Plus (www.speedbit.com), free
- Expired Cookies Cleaner (www.astatix.com/tools/expired-cookies-cleaner.php), free
- FlashGet (www.flashget.com), free
- HackCleaner (hackcleaner.en.softonic.com), free
- IE7 Pro (www.ie7pro.com), free

Startup Program Databases

Want to know which startup programs are legit and which aren't? Then check out these free websites that list all the various programs and processes you're likely to find.

- AnswersThatWork Task List Programs (www.answersthatwork.com/Tasklist_pages/tasklist.htm)
- Application Database (www.greatis.com/appdata/)
- Bleepingcomputer.com Startup List (www.bleepingcomputer.com/startups/)
- Sysinfo.org Startup Applications List (www.sysinfo.org/startuplist.php)
- TechSpot Startup List (www.techspot.com/startup/)

Internet Speed Tests

When you want to know the actual speed of your Internet connection, check out these speed test sites, all free for the using.

- Bandwidth Place Speed Test (www.bandwidthplace.com/)
- CNET Bandwidth Meter Speed Test (reviews.cnet.com/internet-speed-test/)
- DSL Reports Speed Test (www.dslreports.com/speedtest)
- MSN Internet Speed Test (tech.msn.com/speedtest.aspx)
- MySpeed (myspeed.visualware.com/)

Free DNS Services

Use these free services to speed up URL lookup in your web browser.

- BrowseSafe (www.browsesafe.com)
- DNS Advantage (www.dnsadvantage.com)
- OpenDNS (www.opendns.com)

Index

Numerics

A

U

V

REGISTER

THIS PRODUCT

informit.com/register

Register the Addison-Wesley, Exam Cram, Prentice Hall, Que, and Sams products you own to unlock great benefits.

To begin the registration process, simply go to **informit.com/register** to sign in or create an account. You will then be prompted to enter the 10- or 13-digit ISBN that appears on the back cover of your product.

Registering your products can unlock the following benefits:

- Access to supplemental content, including bonus chapters, source code, or project files.
- A coupon to be used on your next purchase.

Registration benefits vary by product. Benefits will be listed on your Account page under Registered Products.

About InformIT — THE TRUSTED TECHNOLOGY LEARNING SOURCE

INFORMIT IS HOME TO THE LEADING TECHNOLOGY PUBLISHING IMPRINTS Addison-Wesley Professional, Cisco Press, Exam Cram, IBM Press, Prentice Hall Professional, Que, and Sams. Here you will gain access to quality and trusted content and resources from the authors, creators, innovators, and leaders of technology. Whether you're looking for a book on a new technology, a helpful article, timely newsletters, or access to the Safari Books Online digital library, InformIT has a solution for you.

informIT.com

THE TRUSTED TECHNOLOGY LEARNING SOURCE

Addison-Wesley | Cisco Press | Exam Cram
IBM Press | Que | Prentice Hall | Sams

SAFARI BOOKS ONLINE

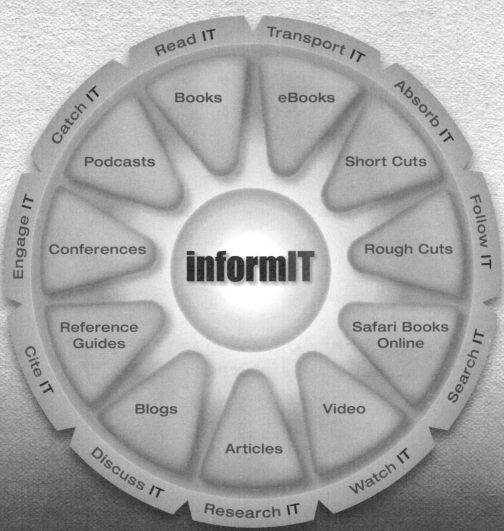

FREE Online Edition

Your purchase of **Speed It Up!** includes access to a free online edition for 45 days through the Safari Books Online subscription service. Nearly every Que book is available online through Safari Books Online, along with more than 5,000 other technical books and videos from publishers such as Cisco Press, Exam Cram, IBM Press, O'Reilly, Prentice Hall, Addison-Wesley Professional, and Sams.

SAFARI BOOKS ONLINE allows you to search for a specific answer, cut and paste code, download chapters, and stay current with emerging technologies.

Activate your FREE Online Edition at www.informit.com/safarifree

> **STEP 1:** Enter the coupon code: GIFVIVH.

> **STEP 2:** New Safari users, complete the brief registration form.
> Safari subscribers, just log in.

If you have difficulty registering on Safari or accessing the online edition, please e-mail customer-service@safaribooksonline.com